Suffrage and Power

The Women's Movement

LAW, CHERYL

SUFFRAGE + POWER   305.4

14.95

SOCIAL AND CULTURAL HISTORY TODAY

Published and forthcoming:

Suffrage and Power

The Women's Movement
1918-1928

Cheryl Law

I.B. TAURIS PUBLISHERS

London • New York

Paperback edition published in 2000 by I.B.Tauris & Co Ltd
Victoria House, Bloomsbury Square, London WC1B 4DZ
175 Fifth Avenue, New York NY 10010
website: http://www.ibtauris.com

First published in 1997 by I.B.Tauris & Co Ltd

ISBN 1 86064 478 3

A full CIP record for this book is available from the British Library

Designed and typeset by Dexter Haven, London

Printed by SRM Production Services Sdn Bhd, Malaysia

Contents

To my parents, Irene Harris and David Law,
with love and gratitude for the
gift of education

In loving memory of my Mam-Gu,
Rebecca Evans,
a fighter all the way!

Acknowledgements

This book began life as a PhD thesis so there are two sets of people involved to whom I owe thanks. Eva Gamarnikow, Monika Reinfelder, Sidika Talukdàr and Gareth Williams in the Department of Policy Studies at the Institute of Education deserve praise for their care and enthusiasm. Of the libraries, my thanks go to David Doughan at the Fawcett, the librarians at the TUC where, sadly, there is no longer a library, and the staff in Room 132 at the New Bodleian. I also had the privilige of interviewing a number of wonderful women kind enough to share their stories with me. Finally, Pat Thane took the trouble to encourage me to believe that the thesis should be published.

The transformation process was assisted by understanding colleagues at Birkbeck. Chief among these, my thanks go to Verity Barnett who took the pressure off for a term to enable me to have more time to write and Laurel Brake who read some chapters and gave valuable advice and reassurance.

Chapter 1
Introduction

Feminism's impulse is often, not surprisingly, to make a celebratory identification with a rush of Women onto the historical stage. But such 'emergences' have particular passages into life; they are the tips of an iceberg. The more engaging questions for feminism is then what lies beneath.[1]

The intention of this book is to contribute further to the unmasking of the work of the women's movement during the 1920s as a means of reinterpreting a period which has suffered at the hands of many historians' 'celebratory identification' of the pre-war militant campaign. The activism of the 1920s has had to struggle to the surface to prove its existence in contention with several fictions. These have been that all suffrage agitation ceased at the outbreak of war; that women's partial enfranchisement in 1918 was automatically conferred; that (incomplete) fulfilment of the suffrage goal was sufficient to satisfy the political aspirations of the majority of the movement; and that, in consequence, only a rump of campaigners limped into the post-war period.

Much of the historiographical depiction of the Edwardian phase of activism has served to reduce it to an isolated political pantomime characterised by eccentric middle class women, unrepresentative of their sex, propelling their cause with a flash onto the

1

historical stage before disappearing into satisfied anonymity. The implication of this portrayal has been that the pre-war suffragette campaign was an hysterical and isolated historical moment, a dynamic, yet brief, political intervention. Such a judgement impugns women's ability to sustain serious, long-term political participation, thus undermining the comprehension of women's political struggle for emancipation as a continuous process which can be traced from the beginning of the nineteenth century to the 1920s and beyond.

Using the militant phase as a yardstick for all subsequent political activity has undermined a sincere portrayal of women's participation. This focus has created an unrealistic template with which to review women's political achievements which has served to depict women's prior and ensuing activism as ineffectual. Such an interpretation serves both androcentric history and politics by consigning women to another 50 years of obscurity until they re-emerge in the so-called 'second phase' of the women's movement. The implications of challenging these fictions provides the starting point for this account.

This is an attempt to provide a flavour of the breadth of the women's movement's agenda during the 1920s, as its network evolved to tackle the political, economic and social emancipation of all women against the background of the 1918 partial franchise success. The ambitious scale of the movement's campaigning makes the task of giving an adequate account of the period a demanding one. I have tried to indicate the scope of the issues and organisations, and this in turn serves to establish the complexity and breadth of the network's interaction. It is the plotting of a map which outlines those salient features of the movement's development in terms of ideology and working practices. Because of the scale of the subject and the amount of extant primary material, the focus has been limited to fundamental aspects of the movement's work, such as the pursuit of political and economic power. Inevitably, the treatment of other fields, such as the occupation with welfare concerns, will suffer.

The distinguishing features are provided by: the continuity of the women's movement on its passage through the First World War into the 1920s, and the organisational network through which women campaigned to address existing inequalities; how they struggled to retain wartime advances; and the ways in which they extended their participation in all spheres of society. The questions posed relate to the ideological nature of those organisations; the issues and campaigns they dealt with; and the way in which the movement resisted containment by the Government and parliament while pursuing its goals. The account demonstrates how women in the movement utilised their new political power in their transition from outsiders to participators in the political process.

For the purposes of charting this network the organisations fall broadly within four categories: political, both party and non-party; employment, whether industrial or professional; welfare; peace and internationalist. Organisations, in whatever category, can be further codified by role: the role of co-ordinating agent, originating and disseminating policy and directing mass action; representing and fighting for the particular rights of its membership; or as a single-issue pressure group. However, the work of the single-issue organisations was far from being confined to their predominant subject of concern. As part of the larger support network, their interest also embraced the unifying issues of the movement: franchise extension and equal pay.

Both the concept of a movement and the feminism which moulds and informs it are liable to extensive interpretation, with definitions shifting with time. The definition used here to describe the participants follows Olive Banks's representation of the term as 'Any groups that have tried to change the position of women, or the ideas about women',[2] change which has made a positive contribution to the development of women's lives, in line with emancipation and liberation. She also maintains that 'At its simplest level it (feminism) represents a criticism of the position of women in relation to men and a desire to change that position'.[3] I would also want to consider Alberti's findings in her study of this period, that:

> The definition of feminist has been that their activities were informed by an understanding of the role and position of women in society which saw them as oppressed.[4]

Banks delineates three 'intellectual traditions' which gave rise to feminist activity: that of Evangelical Christianity which led to philanthropic and social welfare concern emanating from the notion of the moral superiority of women; secondly, the Liberal or Enlightenment school whose ideas resulted in the equalitarian mode of feminism; and finally, the Owenite or communitarian socialist mode.[5] These distinct origins are particularly helpful in consideration of the ideological disputes in the movement during this period. Such separate interpretations of feminism can all be accommodated within the framework of a movement; this is, after all, what distinguishes a movement from a sect.

But the existence of these three traditions can lead to a perceptual disparity in identifying what constitutes feminism, and the process of the self-designation of feminists. What might be construed by those outside the movement as the most visible construction or practice of 'feminism' may be denied as being such by women inside the movement. For instance, in 1926, the trade union organiser, Gertrude Tuckwell, asked by a journalist whether she was a feminist, replied:

> No, I am not a Feminist in the sense of believing that all legislation for both sexes can at this moment be identical. I am, however, deeply interested in helping forward everything that makes for the improvement of women's industrial and social conditions.[6]

Tuckwell, within the context of the protective/restrictive legislation debate of that time, was refusing to place herself within the equalitarian feminist camp. However, her work for women and political allegiance might be considered by others to identify her with the communitarian socialist mode of feminism.

The full import of Banks' definition is applied here and does not exclude the work of women either because they would not have designated themselves feminist, or because they did not subscribe to all the issues within the widest feminist agenda. As the three traditions demonstrate, it would be difficult to determine what a 'purist' feminist line might be. A unifying thread might be located in Kaplan's contention that 'consciousness among women that they constitute a community often appears when they share outrage'.[7] In pursuit of the defining features of a movement Riley asks, 'How is it that women ever come to rank themselves together? What are the conditions for any joint consciousness of women, which is more than the mutual amity or commiseration of friends or relations?'[8] The concept of a women's movement employed here duplicates that found in the literature of the 1920s women's organisations, a catholic term which embraced a wide variety of activity. It was an inclusive term encompassing the work of party and non-party groups engaged in improving women's lives. The particular aspects of women's lives which these activists chose to improve as their

4

primary campaigning goal was to a significant extent dictated by their personal social and economic circumstances.

The feminist vocabulary of the period has been reproduced from the primary sources consulted. The terms used will express the values and ideas current during the period, not those of contemporary usage which represent different meaning for women today than they did 70 years ago. The use of the term 'chairman' is a case in point and does not denote an oversight in using the contemporary gender-free form of 'chairwoman', 'chairperson' or 'chair', but is a reproduction of the use of the word during the period. Similarly women's names have been duplicated as found in the source material, the convention of using women's married or single title has been retained. This is helpful in tracing autobiographical information to determine whether a woman has left the movement or simply married, thus changing her surname. It also indicates the formality with which people addressed one another.

The status of feminist and female pioneer is also differentiated as women pioneers at this time were not necessarily feminists, although many women were both. Such pioneers have only been referenced when they also contributed directly to the movement's campaigns as did Mrs Elliott-Lynn, the pioneer aviator. She was an active member of the National Union of Societies for Equal Citizenship (NUSEC), the Women's Engineering Society (WES) and the National Union of Women Teachers (NUWT). However, there were many women who were passionate innovators in a 'man's world' who would, nevertheless, not identify themselves as feminists. Yet as *The Vote* often maintained when reporting such trailblazers, women who had achieved prominence in any sphere previously confined to men were assisting in the emancipation process by virtue of the visibility of their success.

The issues and campaigns are examined through the organisations as a way of determining their scale of importance to the movement. This can be assessed by the extent to which the issues were taken up, and by noting the allocation of time and resources given to individual issues. It is also possible to chart the extent of the opposition to women's emancipation by calculating the length of time that a particular issue was on the agenda. The responsiveness of the movement to new developments is a sound indicator of their operational progress and ability to set new priorities as they arose.

Tracing the links between organisations and the resulting network can be established in a number of ways. There were the official affiliations between organisations which were set up after the 1918 Representation of the People Act as a way of reaching more women. Other connections can be evidenced through personnel who held multiple memberships of societies. Accounts of joint demonstrations, public meetings, deputations and marches all provide corroboration of where patterns of co-operation emerged. Lists of subscribers and those who gave donations, together with details of speakers and lecturers at monthly meetings indicate a duplication of membership and a common pool of speakers. A growing number of women's clubs, restaurants and other favoured locations made up a circuit of venues which came to be regularly used by feminist groups for meetings, press conferences and celebrations. All such sources, when cross-referenced and compared, demonstrate the interweaving nature and extent of the support mechanism which criss-crossed the movement to promote the cause of women's emancipation.

There was also the cross-fertilisation of ideas through women who held numerous offices in organisations which supposedly represented different or competing strands of feminism and sectional interests. One such confluence of influences gave rise to professional organisations like the WES, started in 1921 to sustain employment for women in engineering, which in turn generated the Electrical Association for Women (EAW) in 1924, whose aim was to 'collect and distribute information on the use of electricity, more particularly as affecting the interests of women'.[9]

This attempt to involve women in the growth of an industry from its inception translated itself into a multiplicity of activity: enabling housewives to contribute to and receive information on labour-saving electrical devices; promoting the representation of women on public bodies, such as the new Electricity Boards; and taking advantage of possible new educational and employment opportunities for girls. The range of interests was demonstrated by the membership of the EAW's council, and its affiliations with, among others, the NUWT, the Women's Local Government Society (WLGS), and the Women's Co-operative Guild (WCG). Caroline Haslett, ex-Women's Social and Political Union (WSPU) member and secretary to the WES, who was also on the Executive Committee of the Six Point Group (SPG), was the EAW's founder. By 1927, the EAW's President was the first woman MP Nancy Astor, and one of its Vice-Principals was the Labour MP and ex-National Union of Women's Suffrage Societies (NUWSS) organiser, Ellen Wilkinson. It comes as no surprise, therefore, to find the

Electrical Association for Women taking part in many of the major franchise demonstrations of the late 1920s.

In reviewing this extended network, a tendency to dismiss, misinterpret or undervalue the work of some of the groups involved may result from adopting preconceptions about some of the organisations based on their contemporary profile. One such example might be the Young Women's Christian Association (YWCA), hardly considered today as having a feminist image. However, it made its contribution to the welfare of working women based on its belief that 'The YWCA holds that women should be given every opportunity by State and employer to earn a livelihood'.[10] It established hostels to provide badly-needed accommodation and leisure facilities for working girls. More significantly, its Industrial Law Bureau investigated complaints regarding working conditions, assisted with compensation claims, provided information on industrial law and ran its own health insurance scheme. Ishbel Macdonald, who worked for the National Council of Women (NCW) and became a member of the London County Council (LCC) in 1928, and was daughter of the Labour leader Ramsay Macdonald, ran the YWCA Youth Section, one of the under-thirties groups involved in the franchise extension campaign of the 1920s. Other redoubtable women fighters such as Nancy Astor, Margaret Wintringham, the second woman MP and a Women's Freedom League (WFL) member, and Margaret Bondfield, the trade unionist and Labour leader, were all members of the YWCA's 1924 fund-raising committee. The trade unionist Gertrude Tuckwell was a Vice-Chairman of the YWCA's law bureau and the overall President was Edith Picton-Turbervill.

Edith Picton-Turbervill is also a sound illustration of the diverse nature of women's participation in the women's movement network of the 1920s. She was a social worker and writer, a leading advocate of ordination for women and a suffrage worker. She first stood as a Labour Party candidate in the 1922 General Election, was a member of the NUSEC executive, the League of the Church Militant's (LCM) Vice-President in 1923. In the previous year she had been nominated as President of the Women's Sanitary Inspectors' and Health Visitors' Association (WSIHVA), who were franchise supporters, and was a member of the Consultative Committee of Women's Organisations'(CCWO) drafting committee. She was also a member of the WFL and the National Council of Women (NCW). On the international front she worked for the International Woman Suffrage Association (IWSA) and like her close friend and colleague Maude Royden, who was President of the LCM, she was one of the first women to preach in an Anglican Church in Geneva in 1920 at the IWSA's Congress.

Her record of work was a typical example of the fluid inter-meshing of a range of interest and involvement within the movement. It demonstrates such women's determination after the war to use the power of the vote to review and improve all aspects of women's lives, no part of which was understood to exist in iso-lation. The women who have been referenced in this account have been used as markers, mentioned only in terms of their activities within specific organisations, offices held, and participation in campaigns, rather than in biographical terms.[11]

In such an extensive account as this, the tendency to focus in greater detail on the larger organisations and place the emphasis on activity within London risks producing an unbalanced version of events. The apparent domination of the campaigning scene by the NUWSS and its successor, the NUSEC, for example, needs to be understood in the context of its place as an umbrella organisation which represented a heterogeneous regional web of societies and associations stretching as far north as the Isle of Skye.[12]

An attempt has been made to draw attention to major events in other cities and regions throughout Britain, as well referring to the regional organisations of Scotland, Ireland and Wales. Apart from Liddington and Norris's study[13], the neglect of regional develop-ments in the women's movement in previous secondary sources has led to an undervaluing of the contribution made by women all over the country. This may also, in part, have led to an underacknow-ledgement of the extent of regional participation by women in the movement. The briefest consultation of annual reports will testify to the continuation of a large regional network of women's organ-isations existing in this period. Further research into establishing the nature of this involvement would add greatly to recreating the flavour of the movement with something approaching veracity.

From the nineteenth century origins of the women's movement there were numerous men in public positions who supported the women's claims and assisted them in gaining access to power. The contribution of such men is part of the women's emancipation story. However, in this account, although male suffrage societies and individual male supporters, largely in the form of MPs, are included where their participation contributes to the description of events, reference to such participation is minimal. This is in no way because their co-operation and participation is being deliberately denied or minimised, but because this study strictly concerns the women's movement and the feminist network, rather than the contribution of men to the women's movement. The essence of this investigation concerns how people, both individuals and groups, exercise power and influence. The perspective adopted is positive, in that it attempts to examine what women achieved or tried to achieve, looking at how they instituted and sought to exercise their rights, as well as how they resisted the attempts to prevent them claiming those rights. Contrary to the way in which it has often been portrayed as a less than exciting period, the period seems most exciting, in that it was a time when women were engaged in the transformative stage from wielding influence to exercising power.

The size and complexity of the movement together with the breadth of issues under review makes the task of doing justice to this subject problematic. One inherent danger lies in failing to take diversity into account, treating women as a single category, not appreciating that it was a movement which consisted of many types of women with reflected allegiances of class and religious belief. However, despite the extent of Britain's Empire, and membership of the International Alliance of Women for Suffrage and Equal Citizenship (IAWSEC) by countries such as Jamaica, Puerto Rica, South Africa, Uruguay, and China, considerations of race were limited. Most often when these countries were mentioned it was in relation to the rights of white women living there, not the indigenous population. Although there was plenty of rhetoric concerning 'women worldwide', the 'concept of human solidarity as superior to racial, or national solidarity'[14] usually only embraced white women; establishing the participation of non-white women in the British movement is difficult. A notable exception concerned the position of Indian women and there is evidence, for instance, of Indian women participating in the 1926 franchise extension demonstration.[15]

This diversity brings inevitable contradictions arising from the presence of people who nevertheless qualify as members of the same movement, underpinning the belief that history is 'an inquiry... a process advancing through contradiction'.[16] Such contradictions in no way undermine the validity of those people's work, but illuminate a reality in all lives. Phillips's analysis of such difficulties is also helpful:

The nature of women's oppression does not point to a neat and easy solution, and the choices faced through the centuries have rarely been between 'right' and 'wrong' ideas.[17]

Designating such pitfalls is a bid to avoid them, while Harrison's assessment of such historiographical complications, that 'The task is impossible, but well worth attempting'[18], offers a measure of reassurance.

The underlying motivation for this research was, to borrow Trevelyan's words, an 'imaginative sympathy with the actual passions of the past'[19] and a desire to make a connection from the past with today's politics; to reclaim more of our political heritage as a tool for completing the work these 1920s women were engaged in; and to understand why so many of their demands remain unfulfilled at the end of the twentieth century.

In the months leading to the 1997 general election the echoes from the 1920s replicated in today's media are apposite to this study:

We want to encourage women to think for themselves. It is up to women to take control of their own political destiny, but at this point we still do not know where the political parties stand on many of these important issues.[20]

A comparison of this statement with those in chapters 6 and 7 is proof enough of how crucial it is to keep holding up the mirror to our past.

Notes on Chapter 1

1   Riley, Denise, *Am I That Name? Feminism in the Category of 'Women' in History* (London, 1988, Macmillan Press), p 8

2   Banks, Olive, *Faces of Feminism* (Oxford, 1981, Martin Roberston), p 3

3   Banks, Olive, *The Biographical Dictionary of British Feminists Volume 1 1800-1930* (Brighton, 1985, Wheatsheaf Books), p vii

4   Alberti, Johanna, *Beyond Suffrage: Feminists in War and Peace 1914-28* (London, 1989, Macmillan), p 6

5   Banks, Olive, *The Biographical Dictionary of British Feminists Volume 1 1800-1930* (Brighton, 1985, Wheatsheaf Books), pp 7 & 8

6   Low, Florence B., *An Englishwoman Looks at the World*, D/4, Gertrude Tuckwell Collection

7   Kaplan, Temma, 'Female Consciousness and Collective Action: The Case of Barcelona, 1910-1918' in N.O. Keohane, M.Z. Rosaldo & B.C. Gelpi (eds), *Feminist Theory: A Critique of Ideology* (London, 1982, Harvester Press), p 61

8   Riley: *Am I That Name?*, p 10

9   EAW, Draft Rules, 1924, Lady Astor Collection, p 1

10   Gates, G. E. (ed.), *The Woman's Year Book 1923-24* (London, 1924, Women Publishers Ltd for the NUSEC), p 544

11   See Alberti, Johanna, *Beyond Suffrage: Feminists in War and Peace 1914-28* (London, 1989, Macmillan) and Harrison, Brian, *Prudent Revolutionaries: Portraits of British Feminists Between the Wars* (Oxford, 1987, Clarendon Press) for biographical accounts of leading activists in this period.

12   See NUSEC, Annual Report, pp 36-37 for an indication of the geographical range of its affiliates.

13   Liddington, Jill & Norris, Jill: *One Hand Tied Behind Us: The Rise of the Women's Suffrage Movement* (London, 1984, Virago)

14   *International Women's Suffrage News*, October 1922, p 11

15   *The Daily Herald*, Monday 5 July 1926, p 5 contains a photograph of the 'Indian Contingent of the British Commonwealth League'. Mrs N.C. Sen and Mrs Sarojini Naidu were involved in the Britain and Indian Association and worked with the other organisations in the women's movement. Eleanor Rathbone campaigned on child-marriage, Indian widowhood and unskilled midwifery practices in India. The movement was also interested in child slavery (mui tsai) in Hong Kong which it fought for many years. It also tackled the issue of 'native' prostitutes in tolerated brothels in the British colonies of Malaya and Kenya. Winifred Holtby also concerned herself with the position of black women under South Africa's repressive laws.

16   Williams, Gwyn A., *The Dragon Has two Tongues* (Cardiff, 1985, Gwynedd Archive Service), introductory cover

17 Phillips, Anne, *Divided Loyalties: Dilemmas of Sex and Class* (London, 1987, Virago), p 12

18 Harrison, Brian, *Separate Spheres: The Opposition to Women's Suffrage in Britain* (London, 1978, Croom Helm), p 15

19 Trevelyan, G.M., 'Bias in History' in *History*, XXXII/115 (1947), pp 1-15, p 11

20 Liz Bavidge, co-chair of the Women's National Commission, reported in 'Parties told women hold the key to election result: agenda to give women equality' in *The Guardian*, Wednesday 18 September 1996, p 10

Chapter 2

Setting the Scene: The Movement's Response to the First World War

━━━━►●◄━━━━

Is the work of eight long years to be scrapped on account of this war?[1]

The belief that the women's movement abandoned its entire campaign for the enfranchisement of women and other women's rights at the outbreak of the First World War belies the complexity of wartime events and the composition of the movement. It underestimates the movement's ability to respond to altered political circumstances and adapt to wartime conditions its strategies for the promotion of women's rights. To propose that the decision taken by the leaders of the Women's Social and Political Union (WSPU) to support the Government's prosecution of the war was echoed by all factions of the women's movement is to misrepresent the nature of the movement, its membership and its work.

Wartime Phases of Development and the Movement's Response

There were several factors which influenced the type of activity which the different factions of the women's movement engaged in during the war, and those differing priorities reflected the hetero-geneity of the movement. Such priorities, however, shifted in response to the different home front phases dictated by the war and were sometimes in contention.

For a large part of the movement, its over-riding commitment to women's suffrage held firm. After 50 years it would have been difficult to betray such a commitment; even a temporary respite would have felt like betrayal to many women. The movement realised that its capacity to defend and protect women's rights would be needed as much as, and perhaps more than, in peacetime, particularly where working class women and children were con-cerned. The National Union of Women's Suffrage Societies (NUWSS) and other women's organisations acknowledged that although war causes disruption and additional problems, the original issues affecting women remained and many would be compounded by the war. Members understood how much damage an indefinite period of inactivity might cause, and that keeping the franchise in view was essential[2] because 'It is organised opinion that counts. Those who are keeping our societies together and our machinery well-oiled, are rendering inestimable service to the Cause.'[3]

A broad categorisation of the movement's wartime activities reveals a fluid tripartite separation: those who worked for peace; those who 'kept the suffrage flag flying'; and those who supported the war effort through welfare and industrial work. However, the apparent clarity of those divisions was complicated by a reality in which women claimed multiple involvement and seemingly contra-dictory behaviour resulted. Avowed pacifists went abroad and joined the war effort, nursing British or allied soldiers, while those who supported the war were also involved in peace groups. Women who had supposedly suspended all vestiges of political work for the war's duration plunged back into the struggle as soon as the suffrage issue resurfaced, and were in bitter contention with the Government and employers over numerous women's rights issues. These patterns of participation may be viewed not as contradictory but as an inevitable outcome of wartime develop-ments and their effect on women's lives. For women activists to ignore such issues would have been politically unacceptable.

From the outbreak of war to the spring of 1915, working class women were badly hit by unemployment caused by the immediate halt in non-essential production and the international disruption of trade, which particularly affected 'women's' trades such as the textile industry. This was an eventuality the Government had neglected to plan for and were slow to respond to. The second phase of the war, spring and summer of 1915, brought a massive enlistment of female labour into munitions work and heavy industry, with the attendant need for the protection of women's employment rights. Towards the end of 1915 and in the following year, as casualties increased and conscription was introduced, the substitution of male labour by female in all sections of industry, commerce and the service industries marked out the third phase of the war's effect on the home front and on women. At the beginning of 1916, government initiatives to redraft the franchise register introduced a fourth phase, restoring the suffrage struggle to centre stage with demands for women's inclusion in the new bill.

The three most prominent campaigns of the war years tackled by the women's movement concerned the equal moral standard, equal pay, and the adoption of a franchise bill to include women on the same terms as men. Any idea that all political agitation for women's rights went into abeyance for the duration of the war has to be re-examined in the light of these events.

The Peace Women

The involvement of the women's movement in the development of a peace campaign has already been well documented.[4] The links between feminism, suffrage, peace and internationalism had long informed women's networks, and in wartime there was a heightened recognition of the divisiveness of an ideology which sought to embody the power of the state in force and militarism. The Irish Women's Franchise League (IWFL) declared such a credo to be 'the negation of the feminist Movement'.[5]

The debate for suffrage women at the outbreak of war centred on the combination of tactics which would best serve to sustain the Cause during the war. For many, the peace issue was of greatest significance, not to the exclusion of the suffrage Cause, but in order to throw the suffrage question into sharper relief. Peace groups regarded it as essential to triumph over the revival of the anti-suffragist argument arising from force. This argument attested that the power of the state lay in its capacity for physical force. It also defined citizenship as including only those individuals strong enough to bear arms in defence of the state. Women's supposed incapacity for such a role in turn meant that they had no right to the franchise[6]. It was this policy, which cut across international sisterhood and endorsed the absoluteness of 'might', which the peace women recognised had to be resisted if the issue of women's equality were to stand any chance of success. The urgency for women to be enfranchised in order to have the power to prevent such conflicts kept women's peace organisations involved in the wartime suffrage campaign. As the Women's Freedom League (WFL) contested:

> One share of the arguments brought against the enfranchisement of women is to the effect that since women have no share in war they should not be given a voice in decisions of peace and war. After the sack of Louvain... can it be said any longer that women have no share in the horrors of war?[7]

Socialist feminists, committed to international solidarity and the class struggle, had a double motivation to resist the tide of war. Estrangements in the movement inevitably resulted when support for the war effort given by some suffrage societies could not be tolerated by those members whose pacifism was an integral part of their socialist and feminist beliefs. Helena Swanwick, for example, resigned her position on the NUWSS executive in 1915 because of the Union's wartime policy. Inspired by the ideal of international sisterhood, Swanwick remembered how Labour Party and Independent Labour Party women's groups had 'stood their ground as pacifists far better than the men's'.[8] The combination of effort on all fronts by the Women's Labour League (WLL) was reported to its members in its annual report for 1917 when it spoke of its 'pioneer work' for 'a people's peace'.[9] Labour women also sustained international links with women abroad during the war through the Women's International Council of Socialist and Labour Organisations.[10] These were links which the movement had always treasured as providing the basis for its work for the international emancipation of women, and they were the loyalties felt to be under threat from women who were sustaining the war through their support.

Keeping the Suffrage Flag Flying

A further section of the women's movement comprised those suffrage societies which judged that their major priority, despite the demands of the war, was to sustain their suffrage propaganda work. Difficult to quantify, there was a hardcore of societies that was continuously active throughout the war. This core consisted largely of groups with militant tendencies or a section of the membership with a history of militant activity. Their one concession to the war, however, as with the WFL, was to suspend militant tactics. The three largest active organisations were the WFL, the East London Federation of the Suffragettes (ELFS) and the United Suffragists (US). Originated by breakaway members of the WSPU in 1907, the WFL worked under the presidency of Charlotte Despard who, as a socialist, was an example of the women in the movement who were active on all three fronts of suffrage, peace and relief work.[11] Sylvia Pankhurst's East London Federation of the Suffragettes (ELFS) predominantly championed the rights and relief of working class women, and the United Suffragists drew its membership from many different suffrage groups, with a female and male membership.[12] The ex-Women's Social and Political Union (WSPU) activist, Evelyn Sharp, was on its executive committee and the US aimed to function as an umbrella organisation to unite the movement during wartime.

At a special meeting on 10 August 1914, the WFL 're-affirmed the urgency of keeping the suffrage flag flying' and the need 'to organise a Woman's Suffrage National Aid Corps whose chief object would be to render help to the women and children of the nation'.[13] Working closely with the WFL, the ELFS reflected the passionate socialism of its founder, Sylvia Pankhurst, which had caused her expulsion from the Pankhursts' WSPU in the early months of 1914. The ELFS's membership refused to compromise or sacrifice the needs of working class women whose overburdened lives would inevitably become harder as a result of the war. As war was declared, *The Woman's Dreadnought*, the ELFS's paper, made its position clear: 'to bring pressure to bear on the Government... to secure justice for the working women of the country'.[14] One of the promptest ways of achieving this goal was framed in the fifth of the Federation's demands, which was to grant women the franchise immediately. Anticipating the nature of wartime problems, the ELFS also argued for government control of food supplies, the provision of work for men and women with equal rates of pay and reserved places for working women on government committees dealing with food, prices, employment and relief.

Emmeline and Frederick Pethick-Lawrence, former WSPU leaders and current members of the WFL, had made a valuable contribution to the wartime franchise Cause by giving their newspaper, *Votes for Women*, to the US in August 1914. Under new ownership, the US made its stand clear, echoing the Government's slogans of 'Business as usual' and 'Flying the flag', its policy being:

> ... to serve the Cause of women, peace, and progress all over the world, to express the women's point of view, and to bring about her ultimate enfranchisement by every means in our power.[15]

It also pledged to help with relief work through the Women's Emergency Corps (WEC).[16] The WEC was a volunteer force begun by Lena Ashwell, who was a member of the US and the Actresses' Franchise League (AFL). The AFL was one of the smaller groups involved in the continuing franchise struggle. In the early weeks of the war there was still a great deal of interest in the franchise issue, with the AFL's regular Hyde Park meetings and its stall at White City still being well patronised. On the basis of this continued public sympathy, the AFL seized the opportunity to keep such interest alive by carrying on with its propaganda work.[17]

The Forward Cymric Suffrage Union (FCSU), with its network of branches in Welsh and English counties as well as 28 branches in London, had placed a notice in papers in England and Wales at the outbreak of war 'pointing out the need of the voice of women in the government of the nations'.[18]

Under the Presidency of Edith Mansell Moulin, who had been a member of the WSPU and the Church League for Women's Suffrage (CLWS), the FCSU worked a good deal with the ELFS and also intended to combine relief work for the women and children of Wales with its franchise work. Two Irish societies which continued their involvement were the Belfast Women's Suffrage Society (BWSS) and the militant IWFL. The BWSS was also concerned to combine its political and welfare work, and the IWFL's determination to continue the struggle arose from its outrage at the suffering that women would be caused in a conflict not of their making. It believed that suffragists ought to be neutral with regard to the war, and concentrate their efforts on pressing for women's suffrage in order to secure a tool which would enable women to prevent such future conflicts. The IWFL's analysis differentiated between the response of women as individuals and as adherents to a cause, and highlighted the possible conflict of interest which it considered should be suppressed for the good of the suffrage campaign.[19]

In addition to these and many other established groups which continued the franchise struggle, four new organisations emerged. These were the Women's International League for Peace and Freedom (WILPF), which originated at the Women's International Peace Conference in the Hague in April 1915; the Suffragettes of the Women's Social and Political Union (SWSPU), which held its initial meeting in October 1915; the Independent Women's Social and Political Union (IWSPU) which was formed in March 1916; and the Standing Joint Committee of Industrial Women's Organisations (SJCIWO), founded in February 1916.

The British branch of the WILPF was founded in September 1915 as a result of the disillusion and discontent of a number of suffrage women at the failure of several peace initiatives. The links between pacifism and feminism were reflected in its aims to 'establish the principles of right rather than might... and the emancipation of women and the protection of their interests...'[20] True to its objectives, in addition to its peace work, the WILPF also supported the work of the hard core of suffrage societies in their wartime campaigns.

The SWSPU's and the IWSPU's following were originally members of the Pankhursts' Women's Social and Political Union. In August 1914 Mrs Pankhurst circularised the membership to the effect that the union's activities were to be temporarily suspended.[21] She enjoined her followers to take advantage of the respite provided by the war 'to recuperate' after their struggles, and assured them that at the first possible opportunity they would press the Government to pass the necessary legislation. Emmeline and Christabel Pankhurst and a handful of 'loyal' WSPU women subsequently proceeded to work with Lloyd George in a fervour of jingoistic propagandising. A year later, other WSPU members began to voice their displeasure at the Pankhurst's activities. Although many women, regarding Emmeline Pankhurst's advice to take a rest as unpatriotic, had already left the WSPU to support the war effort, both members and ex-members from all over the country attended a meeting in Westminster in October 1915. There was also a sizeable volume of supportive letters and telegrams sent to the meeting to decry the leadership's policy of 'voicing a male philosophy and receiving the applause of men'.[22] Chaired by Mrs Rose Lamartine Yates, the meeting resolved to condemn the present work of the WSPU 'officials' and their abandonment of suffrage work. While reaffirming its own belief in the women's movement, the meeting also called for the production of WSPU audited accounts, as no annual report had been produced for several years.

A second meeting on 25 November, chaired by Elinor Penn Gaskell, accused Mrs Pankhurst of participating in political activities which were outside the union's remit and of using WSPU assets and staff in the process. The membership was aggrieved that the union's resources, rather than being utilised to assist in safeguarding the wartime interests of women and children, had been funding promotion work for Lloyd George.[23] Christabel responded to this challenge in her characteristically autocratic tone, telling a reporter that 'I cannot take the matter very seriously... My mother and I are at the head of this movement and we intend to remain there'. Similarly, Mrs Pankhurst was apparently 'treating the (new) movement with the contempt it deserves'.[24] Sylvia, now totally estranged from both her mother and sister, had no comment to make; others were less reticent. Charlotte Despard and Nina Boyle of the WFL viewed it as the inevitable result of the WSPU's undemocratic rule, and Dora Montefiore, also an ex-WSPU member, was more scathing in her belief that the Pankhursts' private ambitions for power and status had at last been exposed.[25] What was left of the WSPU membership then formed two new groups, the IWSPU and the SWSPU, and the Pankhursts were left with what Helena Swanwick described as 'a very small body of extremists'.[26] The SWSPU stated its case as being that of 'a body of members of the old WSPU who differ from their former leaders in thinking it right to continue suffrage propaganda during the war'.[27]

The last new organisation of this period, the SJCIWO, was formed at a meeting called by the Women's Trade Union League (WTUL) on 11 February 1916. The call for closer co-operation among the women's groups representing female industrial workers originally came from the WLL. Initially, therefore, the SJCIWO comprised the WLL, the Women's Co-operative Guild (WCG), the Railway Women's Guild (RWG), the National Federation of Women Workers (NFWW) and the WTUL. Its three aims were to draw up a register of women willing to become representatives on government committees to protect women's interests; to devise a policy for Labour women on these committees to assist them in their work; and to initiate joint propaganda campaigns with the rest of the women's movement on subjects of concern to industrial women.[28] At the outbreak of war, *The Labour Woman* contained many articles by Labour activists condemning the horrors of war and emphasising the need for international socialism in the face of this capitalist conflict. But rhetoric soon yielded to pragmatism as first unemployment and then exploitation at work engulfed women industrial workers. The SJCIWO's objectives enabled it to dovetail its work with the active suffrage societies' campaigns whenever their interests coincided. Working links and joint memberships facilitated an exchange of ideas and resources which strengthened combined ventures. One only has to look at the list of women who were on the British Organising Committee for the Women's Peace Conference at the Hague in April 1915 to trace the collaborative network represented by such women.[29] All these societies were pledged to remaining active in the defence of women's rights on a broad front. Indeed, the WFL specified that it had adopted the role of 'watchdog' for women's affairs during this period of special need.[30]

Supporting the War Effort

When Britain declared war on Germany on 4 August 1914, both politicians and the military expressed the conviction that the war would be over by the end of the year. Churchill's enjoinder to the civilian population 'Business as usual' reinforced this false expectation. Britain's revulsion at Germany's invasion of Belgium, a small neutral country, was reinforced by distaste for the Prussian army's arrogance and German expansionism. This combination of factors bred an almost hysterical British patriotic fervour.

To Victorian and Edwardian women, especially those of the middle class raised on the concept of 'duty', an immediate response was required. The duty of the membership of the largest constitutionalist suffrage organisation, the NUWSS, was spelt out by its leader, Millicent Fawcett as being one of 'resolute effort and self-sacrifice on the part of every one of us to help our country'.[31] Many other suffrage societies could see where their 'duty' lay and also directed their resources to the war effort. Such a response might have been thought predictable for the law-abiding and cautious constitutionalists, nevertheless the interpretation of 'doing one's duty' and to whom this duty was accorded changed with time as the progress of the war and developments on the home front unfolded. That everyone expected the war to be at an end by Christmas 1914 might be considered to have influenced the NUWSS's membership (consulted by post in August), who agreed to the suspension of political activity. Certainly the efficiency and speed with which the NUWSS and other suffrage groups threw themselves into relief work indicated a desire to dispatch the whole business as swiftly as possible and get back to their real work. Even those societies that had pledged all their support to the war effort and a cessation of political activity, at no time relinquished the franchise philosophy on which their organisations were founded. The NUWSS's 1915 annual report made it very clear that 'the Societies have in no sense departed from their devotion to the cause for which they exist, or from their determination to obtain it'.[32]

Patriotic duty may have been a prime mover, but women were shrewd enough to realise that such duty could serve not only their country, but also the women's movement and its suffrage goal. As relief work progressed through the weeks and months of the war, it presented many opportunities to demonstrate what a major contribution women could make to society in the public sphere. After its first year of war work, the NUWSS reported that 'The work of the National Union this year includes little direct Suffrage propaganda, but suffragists have done work of first-rate importance to the interests of women and to the furtherance of the cause of their enfranchisement'.[33] These women knew their own worth and wanted a wider audience to recognise that their ability to make this public contribution was a direct result of experience gained through their suffrage activities.[34] They were also serving the Cause by serving women. One of their wider functions within the movement had always been to support and encourage women by the very act of association in societies. They were not only continuing to do this by recognising and encouraging the welfare and relief work which women were doing during the war, but also by implementing initiatives which were helping the war effort, but which would be of use to women in the future. The training centres which the London Society for Women's Suffrage (LSWS)[35] set up, for instance, taught women new skills which could improve and expand their future employment prospects. Education and lecture programmes designed to inform women about the war and related issues provided education which was permanently enriching.[36]

As the war progressed there were developments which confounded these societies' declarations to suspend political activity and support the Government. Ironically, they found themselves in contention with the Government as they fought for women's representation on wartime committees in a bid for the power to protect women's interests. In defending women's wages and conditions in the factories undertaking wartime production, they were frequently in dispute with the Government, employers and trade unions.[37] This was not inconsistent behaviour for women pledged to support their country: it was, in fact, what they had always intended. As Millicent Fawcett claimed, 'The alleviation of distress among women caused by the dislocation of employment due to the war was our first object'.[38]

Protecting Women's Welfare and Employment Rights

Minority groups learn to develop survival strategies and manipulate situations to advantage. It seems that this was exactly what the women's movement did during the war to sustain its agenda for women's emancipation. At this time, a wider range of expertise was needed to deal with new situations, especially industrial relations, and co-operation was the way to locate and foster such specialisation. This meant that new links were forged which were intended to extend the network. NUWSS branches such as the Manchester and District Federation, for instance, created new alliances with groups working on women's industrial issues in order to survey and collate information regarding the position of women working in wartime production. Old allegiances were strengthened as suffrage societies and women's industrial groups worked together on committees such as the NUWSS's Women's Interests Committee. The Manchester Federation subsequently set up its own Women's War Interests Committee with representatives from the NUWSS, other women's organisations and trade unions.[39] The movement was courageous in its pursuit of accountability from the Government, employers and male trade unionists at a time when such activity was likely to lead to accusations of unpatriotic behaviour. The movement's handling of industrial circumstances to enhance its public standing and win concessions for women by refusing to concede to the status quo was yet another instance of political opportunism.

The increased poverty and hardship for working class women and children, which the movement had feared inevitable in the event of war, was not long in making itself felt. The immediate patriotic surge of enlistments meant the loss of the sole breadwinner for many families, or a considerable cut in the family income. Added to this, at the start of the war, was the loss of women's wages because of the disruption and eventual cessation of women's traditional employment. The cost of living rose steadily and high prices for basic commodities compounded the problem. The suffrage papers carried columns of examples of women and their families who were suffering such destitution. Anticipating the increase of hardship to those already living in woeful poverty, many suffrage and Labour women were anxious to warn middle and upper class women that to rush into offering their services in a voluntary capacity for war work would be at the expense of paid employment for their poorer sisters.[40] The Central Committee on Women's Employment, the first ever all-woman government committee, dealt with schemes which provided work for women and girls. The presence of women such as Mary Macarthur (WTUL) and Margaret Llewelyn Davies (WCG) on this committee forced its wealthier members, 'sewing ladies' as Mrs Simm (WLL) termed them, to face up to some grim wartime realities on the home front.[41]

As well as giving a voice to the plight of such women and lobbying the Government about the deficiencies in its planning, many women's societies took direct action to alleviate this poverty by establishing their own small workshops to provide employment opportunities and training. The NUWSS provided work for 2000 women in 40 workshops, while the ELFS started a toy-making factory. Allied with this provision, the WFL and the ELFS set up restaurants providing cheap meals, and the ELFS also established baby clinics and milk centres. The movement's web of activity tried to provide for the immediate basic needs of working class women and their families. Fuelling this work was the belief that women would not have been in such a vulnerable position if they had had the vote and political power to enable them to assert their opposition to the war.

The protection of women workers' pay and conditions had been of concern to the ELFS since war began. The equal pay debate had been on the women's movement agenda since the latter part of the nineteenth century, and no appeal to patriotism would induce the movement to yield this principle. This was especially the case as soon as the principle of dilution[42] was introduced in 1915. This meant that conditions of employment for women workers needed to be high on the movement's priority list because appeals to the national interest by the Government and employers provided a justifiable opportunity for exploitation.

In March 1915, the Board of Trade appealed to all women who were 'willing and able', to sign a national register at the local employment exchanges and enter the wartime employment market.

This 'ill-considered' action, as the NFWW considered it, was a cause for concern. The NFWW feared that women volunteers would rush to respond to this patriotic appeal with no thought of their own employment rights. Accepting employment, no matter what the working conditions and pay, could not only undercut the rights of the regular workforce, but store up problems for restoring post-war employment conditions. As a result of this concern, Walter Runciman, President of the Board of Trade, received a deputation in April from women's organisations whose fears he hoped to allay with the Government's policy of 'a fair minimum wage for time work and... for piece work the same rates as were paid to men'.[43] The female representatives rejected this assurance as totally insufficient to protect the majority of unskilled women from exploitation, as its only guaranteed application was to a minority of skilled women.[44]

In an attempt to prevent such problems of exploitation arising from the Board of Trade's appeal for women recruits, the Workers' War Emergency Committee held a National Conference on War Service for Women in April 1915. The committee was chaired by Arthur Henderson, secretary of the Labour Party and member of the War Cabinet, with male representatives from all the socialist parties and the trade union movement. There were also four Labour women representatives on the executive committee: Mary Macarthur (WTUL), Margaret Bondfield (WCG), Marion Phillips (WLL) and Susan Lawrence (Labour Party). There were, in addition, women delegates from 16 suffrage societies, including the NUWSS, the LSWS, the Catholic Women's Suffrage Society (CWSS) and the United Suffragists (US); from the women's trade unions of the WTUL, the NFWW and the Association of Women Clerks and Secretaries (AWCS); also from eight other groups such as the WCG, the Women's Industrial Committee (WIC) and the Fabian Society Women's Group (FSWG).

Included in the first resolution was that 'the principle of equal pay for equal work should be rigidly maintained',[45] while in line with the long-established practice of linking economic and political freedoms, the third resolution dealt with votes for women. This was only the first in a long line of meetings during 1915 to protect the position of women workers. In the wake of the July Munitions Act, which introduced increased control over munition workers, there were a number of equal pay demonstrations. The Government's compulsory national register, to be taken of all women between the ages of 15 and 65, prompted another large protest meeting on the day known as Registration Sunday.[46] The meeting was supported by the Labour movement and suffrage societies such as the Suffragette Crusaders (SC), the Women Writers' Suffrage League (WWSL) and the FCSU. The compulsory nature of the register was seen to offer a further opportunity to widen the exploitation of women who were already subject to industrial conscription. Such women represented a class with no power to resist government compulsion because of its disenfranchised status. The movement urged women to write a message of protest on their completed registration forms and to 'demand a man's wage for women who do a man's work'.[47] Such continuing demonstrations were vital for propaganda purposes, as well as for disseminating information to the public and women workers.

Despite the WCG and ELFS's demand for a £1 a week minimum wage for unskilled work, women were still being employed in munitions work at only 10s to 15s a week.[48] The Manchester and District Women's War Interests Committee's research had shown that this was the average wage for shell-making.[49] On skilled work, such as oxy-acetylene welding (for which the NUWSS had started a Women's Welding School), women were only receiving 18s to £1, when the men's rate was over double that at £2 2s a week. Employers were still ignoring the Government's directive on equal pay for piece work, which Lloyd George later falsely represented as having been 'sedulously enforced by the Ministry throughout the duration of the War'.[50] Press reports of 'the millionaire working girls' who were 'having the time of their lives'[51] added insult to injury when women were suffering from sweated wage levels which were often as low as 9s per week. An additional barrier to achieving wage equality, and further witness to government coercion was that under the Munitions Act, an employer's permission was required before an employee was allowed to seek alternative employment. This made moving jobs to improve wages virtually impossible.

The Annual Trades Union Congress in Bristol in September 1915 provided an extended platform and focus for suffrage societies and women's industrial groups to push for supportive resolutions on the equal pay issue. The same month saw the War Emergency Committee publishing 'An Appeal to Women Workers' in *The Labour Woman* to persuade salaried and wage-earning women to strengthen the struggle and increase the movement by joining the appropriate union to work for equal pay and equal working conditions. This appeal was signed by an impressive list of women, representative of the Labour, co-operative and trade union worlds, with many women who also carried joint membership of suffrage societies.[52] By January 1916, this same committee reported that women in armaments work were being paid, on average, only 15s for a 53 hour week, whereas the male rate was three times as much at 45s a week for the same number of hours. Increasingly, the debate was widened to anticipate the post-war position of women, and to emphasise the fundamental nature of the equal pay issue as being a pivotal one in the fight for women's industrial and political equality. The NUWSS and the LSWS, despite the self-imposed 'political ban', had been taking part in demonstrations to improve women's employment rights; and in November 1916, the LSWS passed a resolution to uphold the principle of equal pay, and an insistence on the need for training for industrial and professional women.[53] This tendency to place equal pay within the wider context of political equality saw the equal pay issue becoming absorbed into the latest stage of the campaign for women's enfranchisement.

The Equal Moral Standard

Women's organisations did not have long to wait after the outbreak of war before their campaigning skills were needed. A triple attack was launched by the Government against the perennial target of women's morality. This consisted of subjecting women's behaviour, in private and public, to observation and control by both army officials and the police. As ever, the women who suffered most were working class, although the regulations which were imposed did not preclude women of other classes also being affected. The issue of an equal moral standard had been on the agenda and fought by sections of the women's movement since Josephine Butler first took on the challenge of the Contagious Diseases Acts in 1870. Active suffrage societies and other groups in the women's movement were now outraged at fresh attacks on women's morality with their implications for women's freedom.

Wives and dependents of soldiers were entitled to separation allowances for themselves and their children. Initially, there was a lengthy verification process involved to ensure that allowances were not paid until the claimant's status was confirmed. However, in October 1914, a War Office order was issued through the Home Office which resulted in the Secretary of State instructing the police authorities to provide assistance in the detection of 'serious misconduct' by female claimants. 'Serious misconduct' could be construed as immorality, criminal charges, gross neglect of children or habitual drinking. The local police were to liaise with the relief agencies to pass on the results of their surveillance of army wives. Where 'unworthiness' was detected, the woman was warned, and if the offence persisted, her allowance was withdrawn.

Linked to this control of separation allowances was the Army Council's order of November 1914 stating that women were not to be served in public houses after 6pm. There were also 'unofficial' agreements, such as that in the London Metropolitan District where women were also to be refused drinks before 11.30am.[54] Such restrictions were particularly stringent in districts where there was a large military presence. It was in such military zones that the third step impugning women's behaviour was also to be enforced. This concerned the virtual reintroduction of the Contagious Diseases Act, which was authorised under the Defence of the Realm Act (DORA). The Army Council, under the aegis of DORA, issued orders for a curfew whereby women 'of a certain class' found on the streets in districts frequented by military personnel between the hours of 7pm and 8am were to be arrested. In the autumn of 1914, the WFL discovered that the Plymouth Watch Committee had suggested to its town council that the Contagious Diseases Acts should be revived. The WFL instigated an immediate opposition campaign. Joined by the US, the British Dominions Woman Suffrage Union (BDWSU), the ELFS and other local suffrage groups, they succeeded in defeating this move in Plymouth. A curfew order was actually in operation in Cardiff; three women had already been arrested and sentenced to over 60 days' imprisonment. Rapidly mobilising its local network, women's groups achieved yet another success to secure the women's release and quash the curfew.[55]

Never satisfied with mounting rearguard actions alone as a response to attacks upon women's rights, the movement sought to be more creative by instituting measures which would offer some protection to women in public places. The WFL organised a Women Police Volunteer Corps at the end of August 1914, with Nina Boyle as its chief. It provided uniformed women on duty in parks, gardens and commons during the summer, and in those cases where women were arrested, women police volunteers were present at every Metropolitan Police Court to oversee their interests in what could often be a hostile environment.

Pursuing the equal moral standard campaign, a demonstration was held in Trafalgar Square in January 1915 organised jointly by the WFL, the US, the ELFS and the Northern Men's Federation of Women's Suffrage (NMFWS). The large crowd passed a resolution protesting at legislation where 'restrictions are enforced against women only, and vice is regulated in a way that protects men only. That this meeting demands the enfranchisement of women without further delay.'[56] In the weeks that followed, similar meetings were held around the country by the US, while the ELFS demanded that women should be treated and punished by the civil law on equal terms with men. However, no progress had been achieved two years later in 1917 when the Home Secretary introduced a Criminal Law Amendment Bill which contained clauses authorising the detention of 'common prostitutes' for medical examination. According to the Association for Moral and Social Hygiene (AMSH), 'A demand for proper definitions must inevitably raise the whole question of why promiscuity is a crime in a woman and not in a man'.[57] Again, there were mass protests, lobbying and packed public meetings. The NUWSS passed a resolution at its 1917 annual conference condemning compulsory examination and the inequity of the legislation, and at a protest meeting that year 12 societies combined to launch a campaign to oust the bill. Maude Royden (NUWSS/LCM) declared an unexpected triumph for the campaign at this meeting when she announced that the Government had abandoned its plans for compulsory examinations. But the societies were not content to haggle over further amendments and demanded the complete withdrawal of the bill. The WFL did manage to secure an assurance from the Home Secretary that the bill would be delayed until he had met a women's deputation. Although that assurance was still in place by February 1918, the fight continued, fuelled by government declarations of 'punishments for infected women', the opening of 'tolerated brothels' in France for the use of British soldiers, where conditions of total degradation for the women involved and the issuing of prophylactic kits to soldiers were reported. Maud Arncliffe-Sennett (NUWSS/AFL/WFL), President of the NMFWS, noted with irony parliament's hypocrisy, considering that 'This shameful crime was... perpetrated on the race of women parliament had just "freed"'.[58]

The campaign continued to gather momentum, as in the early months of 1918 there was still no expectation of an end to the war. An AMSH protest meeting in June at the House of Commons was attended by representatives of 56 organisations that had an estimated membership of up to 2 million. In the wake of this demonstration, a further 50 protest meetings were held all over the country. But despite the popular support mobilised by the movement there was no victory in sight, and the pursuit of an equal moral standard continued into the post-war period.

The Representation of the People Act

The scale and variety of valuable work achieved in the promotion and defence of women's rights by the women's movement during the war can be appreciated by reading the annual reports; but nothing was more important to realising its future goals than the attainment of the franchise. Many accounts of the achievement of a limited franchise for women over 30 in February 1918 tend to present it as the unreserved accolade of a grateful Government and country, 'awarded' spontaneously in 1918 in recognition of women's war service. On closer examination, the penultimate chapter of this 50-year struggle was not quite as straight-forward as has been suggested. As Millicent Fawcett observed, 'Our future course at the time was not all quite such plain sailing as it may appear now to those who only look back upon it'.[59] Tracing the series of events that resulted in the partial enfranchisement of women in the 1918 Representation of the People Act illuminates the truth of Fawcett's words. Even as some societies were actively 'keeping the suffrage flag flying', by November 1915 a new protest heralded a further phase in the suffrage struggle which was to draw in the rest of the movement.

Lloyd George in his *War Memoirs* outlined parliamentary discontent with the electoral system as it stood and how the advent of the war had further complicated the situation. Plural voting, reform of registration and franchise qualifications, redistribution issues and, of course, votes for women were all on the agenda.[60] The existing parliament was due for dissolution in January 1916; however, to highlight electoral inequities during wartime, when the need for national unity was paramount, was felt to be far from advisable. Attempting to contain such disquiet, the elections and Registration Act of July 1915 delayed the municipal elections of that year and waived the compilation of a new electoral register, stating that in the Coalition Government's opinion elections should wait until after the war. This holding operation resulted in a further difficulty: if political circumstances arose which forced an election, no up-to-date electoral register would be available for use. This, in turn, meant that because of their enforced absence from their permanent place of residence, members of the forces and some munition workers would be disenfranchised by virtue of the residential qualification. A political catastrophe for a government could ensue when men who were risking their lives for their country discovered that, as a consequence of this sacrifice, they had been disenfranchised. There was also the sensitive issue of those men in the services who were defending their country and who still did not have the franchise.

In the autumn session of 1915, Lord Willoughby de Broke was ready to introduce a Service Vote Bill enfranchising every serviceman over 21. He was persuaded to withdraw it by Lord Lansdowne, who assured him that the Government was to introduce a new register for the electorate by the end of the war.[61] Consequently, rumours were rife that during parliament's 1915 autumn session, some kind of franchise reform was inevitable for the near future, but it would probably be restricted to a manhood suffrage measure. This came as no surprise to the women's movement which had been forewarned in June of that year of continued resistance to its franchise claims. Despite his declaration in 1913 that at the very next opportunity for franchise legislation, women would be included, by June 1915 Prime Minister Asquith had seemingly forgotten his previous promise. When replying to a question in the House asking him if it were likely that Britain would soon follow Denmark's example and give British women the vote, Asquith replied that this was 'a highly controversial question which could not be dealt with at the present time'.[62] Although the women's movement had operated a low-key holding operation for the past 18 months, the likelihood of new legislation omitting women necessitated moving the campaign up a gear.

A preparatory event sending the signal for renewed campaigning came in November 1915. The Qui Vive Corps, a body which existed to unite suffrage workers for specific events, staged a march from Edinburgh to London to protest against the exclusion of women from future franchise bills. Later, in December 1915, the suffrage societies galvanised themselves to pursue the women's claim by sending a letter to Asquith on behalf of 11 societies insisting that women be included in any new Registration Bill. *The Woman's Dreadnought* of 4 December announced that a joint delegation of societies would be held in December to discuss mounting a suffrage campaign in the New Year.

The movement was really back in business when in 1916 the NUWSS, true to its pledge to re-enter the fray when events demanded, wrote to Asquith reminding him of his 1913 promise and, most significantly, that this promise had never been redeemed. The letter ended by assuring Asquith that the union 'has not abandoned its principles nor the right to take action should the necessity arise. Alterations of the franchise involving the continual exclusion of women would be the case for such action.'[63] War or no war, the women were not going to allow yet another opportunity for franchise reform to escape them. It was this imperative for action which prompted Mrs Lamartine Yates to urge the formation of the Independent Women's Social and Political Union.[64] Mrs Arncliffe-Sennett assured the press in February 1916 that:

> ... there is not a single suffrage society from the National Union of Women's Suffrage Societies... to the smallest organisation in the land that has not remained and is not keenly alive now to the great issue of Women's Emancipation, as on the day when Britain joined issue with Germany...[65]

Labour women were now mobilising, as was their party. During the Labour Party Conference in Bristol at the end of January 1916, a week-long suffrage campaign culminated in a call for the inclusion of women in any franchise extension at a meeting where Charlotte Despard, Catherine Marshall (NUWSS) and Sylvia Pankhurst spoke. Robert Smillie, the Miners' Federation President gave his 'heart and soul' support, which was in stark contrast to the 1912 Labour Party Conference where he had cast his vote, and that of his 600,000 members, against the women's suffrage resolution.[66]

Bearing in mind the 3 million disenfranchised men, the issue of adult suffrage as opposed to women's suffrage was in contention, especially in Labour circles. The US in its February council meeting examined its operation and objectives in the light of new government action; some members were also in favour of supporting adult suffrage, but many believed that this would simply result in manhood suffrage. Many subscribed to Mrs Pethick-Lawrence's opinion that 'equality was not really secured by giving women the vote on equal terms with men, because the household qualification ruled out so many wives of working men'.[67] In March 1916 the ELFS, reflecting its increasingly socialist stance, changed its name to the Workers' Suffrage Federation (WSF) and amended its constitution to secure 'human suffrage'. This change increased its appeal in the Labour camp, and a letter sent by the WSF to Asquith and every member of parliament in July 1916, was signed by, among others, Margaret Bondfield, Isabella Ford, Susan Lawrence and Marion Phillips, all prominent Labour and trade union women. Nevertheless, the WSF was still appealing for the women's franchise where this was appropriate, circulating a petition, for example, to factories where dilution was in operation. They had a good response, 80 organisations having passed the resolution which began 'We, the undersigned workers, realising that if a woman can cast a shell she can cast a vote...'[68]

By May 1916 the women's movement attempted to take direct action by requesting that the Prime Minister and other Coalition leaders receive a deputation in a letter signed by many prominent individual suffrage supporters, 18 suffrage societies and several trade unions.[69] In August two bills were introduced, one to prolong the life of parliament for another eight months and the second, the Special Register Bill, to initiate a new register for May 1917. The first was passed, but many members felt that the terms of the Special Register Bill in relation to extending men's suffrage was inadequate. This inevitably raised the issue of the total absence of women's suffrage in the proposed legislation. A Speaker's Conference was subsequently instituted, with an all-male committee, to discuss the many aspects of electoral and franchise reform. The WFL, not unreasonably, had expected that suffrage societies' representatives would be invited to sit on this committee in relation to the women's claim. They were forced to content themselves with a consultative committee of women's suffrage societies representing 15 societies, maintaining contact with the Speaker's committee.

By January 1917 the Speaker's committee had managed to agree, unanimously, on all but three of the 37 controversial agenda items. But despite the praise accorded to the 'heroines' of the nation for their war effort, the conference could not agree on the women's franchise. It had agreed, by a majority, on some kind of suffrage for women, and recommended the qualification that:

Any woman on the Local Government Register who has attained a specified age, and the wife of any man who is on the register if she has attained that age, shall be entitled to register and vote as a parliamentary elector. Various ages were discussed, of which 30 and 35 received most favour.[70]

The Independent Suffragette was moved to speculate that:

> Behind the 'numerical' argument we find entrenched our old friend the 'physical force' argument... We may be sure, however, that we have not heard the last of that terrible bogie 'petticoat government'... Will they never realise that what we want is neither the one nor the other, but co-operation between men and women?[71]

The result of the Speaker's report left the movement in a difficult position. It was a mixed blessing: as well as omitting those women under the age limit, it effectively excluded the majority of working class women. Although there had been a debate within the movement about resisting an age differential, there were those, such as the SWSPU, who were prepared to accept whatever was awarded, in order to get the sex barrier removed. In Millicent Fawcett's mind '... we preferred an imperfect Bill which could pass to the most perfect measure in the world which could not'.[72]

The Woman's Dreadnought published the responses of many societies who, while welcoming the establishment of the principle of women's suffrage, were still most critical of the restrictions. The WFL, in a letter to the Government published by the WSF, did not hesitate to correct the historical amnesia of the Speaker's committee:

> The 'approval' of the Speaker's Conference by a majority vote on the principle of Woman Suffrage is at least a generation behind the times. The House of Commons 'approved' this principle in 1870 by a majority of 33 and six times since that date it has passed the second reading of a Bill for Woman Suffrage. Before the War more than 180 Councils in this country 'approved' the principle by a majority vote.[73]

After 50 years of struggle, parliamentary duplicity and disappointment, the movement knew that it was not safe to relax now. In February 1917, there was a London suffrage meeting with Margaret Ashton, chairman of the Manchester Suffrage Society, a Labour Party member and a founder member of the WILPF, trade union leader Mary Macarthur, Mrs Barton (WCG) and Millicent Fawcett as principal speakers, anxious to extend the terms for working class women. The NUWSS staged a massive Women Workers' Demonstration in February which was supported by the societies of the consultative committee, representatives of 70 occupations, as well as other women's organisations. Millicent Fawcett, Ray Strachey (LSWS) and Mrs Creighton (NCW) made it clear that the terms of the Speaker's Report did not deliver the full equality for which they had fought. However, as 6 million women would be enfranchised, they considered that it was a measure worth putting into effect immediately.[74] Although a compromise, it nevertheless established the right of women to vote. The women knew that after such a major electoral reform, which gave the vote to the majority of men, parliament was unlikely to enter into such legislative reform again for some time. The end of the war was also still uncertain. Their claims had been dashed so many times in the past, they dare not risk holding out for more and gaining less. Anti-suffrage organisations had re-emerged and there were at least 100 die-hard Tories who declared irrevocable opposition to women's enfranchisement. Such a limited measure gave them the acceptance of a principle, access to power which would, they thought, enable them to extend their sphere of effective influence.

Nevertheless, demonstrations all over the country attempted to force an extension of the recommended franchise. In March 1917, a 90-strong women's suffrage deputation was received by the new Prime Minister, Lloyd George. Millicent Fawcett again emphasised that although the recommendations did not go far enough, the women were, in the final analysis, willing to accept them.[75] Keeping up the pressure at a mass meeting in April that year, Charlotte Despard, Eva Gore-Booth (NUWSS), Evelyn Sharp (US), Helena Swanwick (NUWSS) and others urged the franchise extension for women.[76]

On 15 May 1917, the Representation of the People Bill was introduced and passed without a division. Both Asquith and Lloyd George underwent last-minute 'conversions' to the women's side; although later Lloyd George professed that he reminded the House that he had always supported votes for women! Having passed its second reading with a majority, on 19 June clause IV of the bill concerning women's suffrage was discussed in committee, and after two attempted amendments seeking to omit the measure, it was carried. It was thought by some of the press that the House of Lords would not dare to reverse the House of Commons decision, especially that of an all-party vote. But there was still a formidable body of anti-suffragists in the Lords, and two last-minute attempts to hijack the Bill sent it seesawing between the two chambers. By the beginning of February 1918 the press were speculating that the bill was dead, but a compromise solution was eventually achieved.[77] The act was only to give women over 30 the vote, subject to a property qualification and a sizeable number of other restrictions which became the subject of the movement's continued suffrage struggle throughout the post-war decade.

In June 1917, when the bill had passed the committee stage, *The Nation* reinforced the point that women would never have won the vote even now 'without years of arduous and determined work'.[78] One wonders how much longer women might have had to wait for enfranchisement without the suffrage societies' incessant wartime campaigning and their swift utilisation of the procedural opportunity presented to them by the electoral register. The lavish, but essentially empty, praise of the women's war effort seems not to have played as large a part in the suffrage victory as politicians claimed, especially when it turned so rapidly to blame when demobilisation began.[79]

Conclusion

At the outbreak of the war there were difficult decisions to be made at a time of shock and confusion. Mixed loyalties could not feasibly facilitate the maintenance of a purist ideological stance by individuals, especially at a time when there was so much work to be done by and for women. The differentiation between the path to be followed as adherents of an ideology and a movement, and as individuals, highlighted one of the complications for many in the women's movement. Emmeline Pethick-Lawrence later pointed up this contradiction:

> ... the woman suffrage movement (at least many sections of it) was split by the war. In our own and many countries the idea of the solidarity of women had taken a deep hold upon many of us; so deep that it could not be shaken even by the fact that the men of many nations were at war.[80]

The duty of supporting the nation while sustaining loyalty to relations and friends directly involved in the fighting was not an easy one to dispute and vied with suffrage women's loyalty to personal political agendas. But whatever accommodations were adopted, and whatever permutations of allegiance and action resulted, the continuity of ·the women's movement was never threatened, nor the suffrage struggle abandoned, because as the militant WFL had warned, 'it behoves Suffragists to be watchful'.[81]

Notes on Chapter 2

1   *Votes for Women*, 21 August 1914, p 705

2   The emphasis which all the societies placed on keeping their newspapers and literature distributed during the war indicates their awareness of this factor. See *Votes for Women*, 31 December 1915, p 109

3   NUWSS, Annual Report of the Oxon, Berks and Bucks federation, 1915-16, p 5

4   See Wiltsher, Anne, *Most Dangerous Women: Feminist Peace Campaigners of the Great War* (London, 1985, Pandora Press) and Liddington, Jill, *The Long Road to Greenham: Feminism and Anti-Militarism in Britain since 1820* (London, 1989, Virago)

5   *Jus Suffragii*, 1 April 1915, p 274

6   *The Argument from Physical Force*, NUWSS pamphlet, 1909, p 1

7   *Votes for Women*, 11 September 1914, front page

8   Swanwick, Helena, *I Have Been Young* (London, 1935, Victor Gollancz), p 284

9   Women's Labour League, Executive Report, 1917, p 1

10   *Jus Suffragii*, 1 November 1914, p 190

11   See Liddington, Jill, *The Long Road to Greenham: Feminism and Anti-Militarism in Britain since 1820* (London, 1989, Virago)

12   A distinguishing feature of the influential men on the United Suffragists Committee was that a number of them were writers and journalists, such as Henry W. Nevinson, the 'distinguished' journalist, husband of the suffrage worker, Margaret Wynne Nevinson; Gerald Gould, academic, journalist and author, whose wife, Barbara Ayrton Gould was also on the committee; Albert Dawson, who was the London Correspondent for American papers; as well as John Scurr, a Labour Party activist, later MP for Stepney;

George Lansbury, editor of the Daily Herald and Labour MP, was also a great women's suffrage supporter who chaired many of the US public meetings.

13 Gerard, Mrs, *Hats off to the Past, Coats off to the Future* (London, undated, WFL), p 4

14 *The Woman's Dreadnought*, 15 August 1914, front page

15 *Votes for Women*, 11 September 1914, front page

16 *Votes for Women*, 21 August 1914, p 705

17 *Votes for Women*, 11 September 1914, p 731

18 *The Woman's Dreadnought*, 29 August 1914, p 92

19 *Jus Suffragii*, 1 April 1915, p 274

20 WILPF pamphlet, Catherine Marshall, (London, 1916, WILPF), p 379

21 Pankhurst, Emmeline, WSPU circular from the headquarters to the membership, 12 August 1914

22 *Jus Suffragii*, 1 November 1915, p 24

23 Arncliffe-Sennett Collection, Vol 26, 6 February 1914-December 1915 p 26

24 *Weekly Dispatch*, 28 November 1915, p 1

25 Ibid.

26 Swanwick, Helena, *I Have Been Young* (London, 1935, Victor Gollancz), p 284

27 *The Suffragette News Sheet*, May 1916, p 1

28 *History of the SJCIWO*, SJCIWO, undated, p 1

29 See Wiltsher, Anne, *Most Dangerous Women: Feminist Peace Campaigners of the Great War* (London, 1985, Pandora Press), pp 82-83

30 *Jus Suffragii*, 1 April 1915, p 274

31 *Women's Service*, London Society for Women's Service pamphlet, August-September 1914, p 1

32 NUWSS, Annual Report, 1915, p 10

33 NUWSS, Annual Report, 1915, p 10

34 *Suffragists and the War*, LSWS, FCLWS, CLWS, WFS joint leaflet, 1914

35 The LSWS was one of 603 societies comprising the NUWSS; it carried out the NUWSS's work in London and the suburbs, with a membership in November 1914 of 5000 in 63 groups, with additional 'organised but non-subscribing supporters', totally over 23,000. See 'The woman suffrage movement and the war: some of its leaders and their ideas', *The Ladies' Field Supplement*, 21 November 1914, p 18

36 LSWS, Annual Report, 1916, pp 15-16

37 LSWS, Annual Report, 1916, pp 13-14

38 Fawcett, Millicent Garrett, *The Women's Victory and After: Personal Reminiscences, 1911-18* (London, 1920, Sidgwick & Jackson), p 89

39 NUWSS, Fifth Annual Report of the Manchester and District Federation, 1915, p 12

40 *Votes for Women*, 21 August 1914, p 703; *The Labour Woman*, September 1914, p 243; Women's Labour League Annual Report, 1914, p 21

41 *The Labour Woman*, October 1914, p 250

42 Dilution was the term given to the industrial practice of substituting women workers and men rejected as medically unfit for the army for those men who could be recruited for military service. It was a practice which was unpopular with the trades unions as it undermined the safeguards for skilled work which they had fought for.

43 Lloyd George, David, *War Memoirs of David Lloyd George Volume I* (London, 1938, Odhams Press), p 175

44 While industrial and suffrage women's organisations were working to protect women workers, Emmeline and Christabel Pankhurst, together with their close friends and colleagues, Mrs Flora Drummond and Annie Kenney of the WSPU, led a Women's War Pageant in July 1915 to welcome the national register and urge women to help their country.

45 *War Emergency*, Workers' National Committee pamphlet, National Conference on War Service for Women, 16 April 1915, p 3

46 Registration Sunday was on 15 August 1915

47 *Votes for Women*, 13 August 1915, p 376

48 £1 consisted of 20 shillings; 1 shilling was equivalent to 5p in decimal currency.

49 *Women in the Labour Market During the War*, Manchester, Salford and District Women's War Interests Committee pamphlet, undated, p 19

50 Lloyd George, David, *War Memoirs of David Lloyd George Volume I* (London, 1938, Odhams Press), p 175

51 *Votes for Women*, 3 September 1915, p 401 and October 22 1915, p 27

52 *The Labour Woman*, September 1915, p 321. Some of the women who were signatories were Ethel Bentham (WLL), Margaret Llewelyn Davies (WCG), Charlotte Despard (WFL), Isabella O. Ford (WLL), Katherine Bruce (WLL),

Helena Swanwick (IWC), Gertrude Tuckwell (WTUL), Julia Varley (WU), Beatrice Webb (Labour Party).

53   LSWS, Annual Report, 1916, p 24
54   *Votes for Women*, 28 February 1915, p 183. Before the war there had been no restrictions on public house opening hours.
55   *The Vote*, 8 January 1915, p 454; *Jus Suffragii*, 1 April 1915, p 274; Arncliffe-Sennett Collection, Vol 26, 6 February-December 1915
56   Arncliffe-Sennett Collection, Vol 26, 6 February 1914-December 1915
57   *Votes for Women*, June 1917, p 267
58   Arncliffe-Sennett Collection, Vol 28, 1918-36
59   Fawcett, Millicent Garrett, *The Women's Victory and After: Personal Reminiscences, 1911-18* (London, 1920, Sidgwick & Jackson), p 134
60   Lloyd George, David, *War Memoirs of David Lloyd George Volume II* (London, 1938, Odhams Press), p 1164
61   Arncliffe-Sennett Collection, Vol 27, 1916
62   Parliamentary Debates, House of Commons, 3 June-2 July 1915, Vol LXXII, col 363
63   *Jus Suffragii*, 1 January 1916, p 50
64   Arncliffe-Sennett Collection, Vol 26, 6 February 1914-December 1915
65   Arncliffe-Sennett Collection, 1916, Vol 27
66   *Votes for Women*, 7 January 1916, front page; Arncliffe-Sennett Collection, Vol 27, 1916
67   Arncliffe-Sennett Collection, Vol 27, 1916
68   *Jus Suffragii*, 1 July 1916, p 147
69   *The Suffragette News Sheet*, June 1916, p 2. This letter demonstrates the range of the groups still active in the suffrage struggle: the BSS, CWSS, FCLWS, FLWS, IRL, ISF, SCLWS, SSS, SWSPU, US, WFL, WSISS, WTFU, WTRL, WWSL. There were also three men's groups: MMLWS, NMFWS, NLMPU.
70   *Jus Suffragii*, 1 March 1917, p 85
71   *The Independent Suffragette*, June 1917, front page
72   Fawcett, Millicent Garrett, *The Women's Victory and After: Personal Reminiscences, 1911-18* (London, 1920, Sidgwick & Jackson), p 146
73   The *Woman's Dreadnought*, 10 February 1917, p 669
74   NUWSS information folder containing the Women Workers

Demonstration programme and propaganda leaflets, 20 February 1917

75 NUWSS, Women's Suffrage Deputation, 29 March 1917, Arncliffe-Sennett Collection, Vol. 27, 1917

76 Arncliffe-Sennett Collection, Vol. 27, 1917

77 *Votes for Women*, February 1918, front page

78 NUWSS, Weekly Notes: the Passing of the Women's Suffrage Clause, 26 June 1917, p 3

79 See Braybon, Gail, *Women Workers in the First World War* (London, 1981, Croom Helm)

80 Pethick-Lawrence, Emmeline, *My Part in a Changing World* (London, 1938, Victor Gollancz), p 307

81 *Votes for Women*, 31 December 1915, p 109

Chapter 3
Survival and Progress

... there is no closed door we do not intend to force open; and there is no fruit in the garden of knowledge it is not our determination to eat.[1]

During the period from the autumn of 1917 until the armistice in November 1918, a new foundation for the 1920s work of the women's movement was being laid. Gaining the vote in February 1918 did not mark the end of a 50-year struggle, it signified the opening of a new chapter, as armed with 'the power of the vote' the movement sought to achieve the social, political and economic equality of women. Of primary concern was the setting of a new agenda to carry the struggle forward into the post-war period. The immediate aims were to ensure the rapid extension of the franchise to include all women over 21; to institute a policy of political education for women citizens to utilise their new power; to prepare for the exigencies of post-war reconstruction; and to sustain the equal pay and the equal moral standard campaigns which had gained prominence during wartime.

The Review Process

In spring 1918, Millicent Fawcett gave voice to the movement's elation at achieving the partial franchise when she spoke of the exhilaration for women in having the power of the vote behind all they did. She also believed that the last two years had been 'wonderful' for women because of the liberating effect of the war and of the freedom which women had gained in the industrial world.[2] In the light of this new franchise legislation, the women's societies scrutinised their aims, methods, organisational structures and even their names to reflect this political power shift. For many, such as the London Society for Women's Suffrage (LSWS), this process was already well under way.[3] An inevitable component of this review process was the reconsideration of the relationship between the sexes in order to accommodate the movement's new political position and to determine any changes in its working practices to secure full emancipation.

With entry into the political arena as citizens, the women's movement had to examine its strategy in preparation for participation in a system evolved by and for men, and still dominated by them. After all, if the conditions of membership had undergone some expansion, the institutions had not altered. Achieving the franchise signalled a momentous change in culture for women who for decades had been operating in women-centred organisations. Although they had always liaised with men and been supported and assisted by men in political parties and other walks of life, they were now moving from the position of women exerting influence outside exclusively male operations, power by proxy as it had been, to women operating power in their own right but inside institutions which were overwhelmingly dominated by men. This had distinct psychological repercussions, not only for their mode of operation, but also in the formulation of the philosophical precepts on which their future policy would be based. They had gained the powers associated with citizenship, but how would they accommodate this new political power with the power they held as the independent initiators of their own power base?

The National Union of Women's Suffrage Societies (NUWSS) anticipated the centrality of this issue to its future conduct and also which outcome of the gender debate would best deliver equality for women:

In determining the future of the Union it had to choose between two conceptions – women as women have a set of special interests, distinct from those of men, which the Union should work to further; or that women's interests and men's interests coincide when once men and women are on an equal footing in all spheres of life, and that consequently a feminist body such as the NUWSS must logically confine its work to the securing of equality of opportunity for women with men.[4]

A decision was taken to adopt the latter ethos, designated as equalitarianism. Apart from its prime aim of franchise extension, the NUWSS now expanded its objectives to 'all other such reforms, economic, legislative, and social, as are necessary to secure a real equality of liberties, status and opportunities between men and women'.[5]

In October 1918 a national conference on Women's Civic and Political Responsibilities was held in London at the instigation of the SJCIWO. It was attended by delegates from all the political parties, industrial women's groups, trade unions, professional and suffrage societies. An urgent resolution was passed concerning the protection of women workers during and after demobilisation, as well as other resolutions dealing with the franchise extension, equal civil rights, housing, health, food control and the withdrawal of Regulation 40D.[6] But the most significant debate dealt with the political organisation of women when Marion Phillips moved the resolution:

> That this conference recognises that the political power of the women's vote is dependent upon the extent of organisation amongst them, and urges them, in considering the methods of organisation to be adopted, to throw their strength into the development of a strong political organisation embracing both men and women, and not to follow the line of sex division.[7]

While Mrs Fawcett and the NUWSS delegates supported this stance, a claim for sustaining a measure of separatism was made in an amendment (which was lost) moved by Florence Underwood (WFL) 'affirming that separate organisations of women were necessary as a measure of expediency in removing the disabilities under which women still laboured'.[8] The debate concerning whether the pursuit of equality consisted of equality with men or the pursuit of issues of specific concern to women, and how far these two objectives dictated the political organisation of women remained unresolved. In fact, as the 1920s progressed it became more contentious.

Much of the suspicion of the idea that women should organise themselves on gender lines was strengthened by Emmeline and Christabel Pankhurst's latest political activity. The Women's Social and Political Union (WSPU) had responded to the climate for change and re-evaluation in rather a different way by launching the Women's Party (WP) in November 1917. But it was Sylvia Pankhurst who reassured the conference that 'too much importance should not be attached to the Women's Party, which was using the name 'Women's' in a way which none of us could accept'.[9] The Women's Party paper, *Britannia*, proclaimed its nationalist intention of ensuring that 'The Women's Party will use the vote to make Britain strong for defence against the outside foe, and to strengthen Britain from within...'[10] It was not only subverting the accepted concept of the rationale for women-only organisations, but as Susan Lawrence maintained 'there was an objection to a Party really political calling itself a non-party organisation'.[11]

Women in the Labour movement were also addressing the organisational divisions between women and men. The Women's Labour League (WLL) reported that, like the LSWS, 'As soon as it became clear that women would obtain the Parliamentary Franchise in the new Reform Bill, the Executive of the Women's Labour League decided that they must take special action with regard to the organisation of women'.[12] Consequently, a sub-committee was formed which produced a report for the Labour Party in 1917, prepared by the WLL's Organising Honorary Secretary, Dr Marion Phillips (SJCIWO), to institute a national system of regional women workers to expand current membership.[13] A joint committee of four women from the WLL and four Labour Party members was then established to implement developments in the organisation of Labour women. Its first suggestion was that four women should be appointed, two each for the WLL and the Labour Party.[14]

The suffrage societies' post-franchise resistance to abandoning their non-party status was highlighted by what was to happen to the WLL in 1918. Part of Arthur Henderson's plans for 'moulding the Labour Party for government'[15] necessitated a new constitution, drawn up by Beatrice and Sidney Webb, which introduced individual membership and separate sections for men and women. This, in turn, meant the dissolution of the WLL, with women members subsumed into Labour Party women's sections. Instead of defining their own role and operational practices and sustaining an independent voice within the party, Arthur Henderson outlined the role he envisaged for women within the party. He 'welcomed the help that women would be able to give, not only with their votes, and with work at election times, but in helping to form the policy of the party and in the way of political education'.[16] Socialist feminists were thus presented with a dilemma emphasising the division between class and sex loyalty, which was to dictate the development of Labour women's participation in the women's movement throughout the 1920s.

Many women were sceptical as to Henderson's promise of 'mutual advantage'. Mrs Lowe (NFWW/SJCIWO), the conference chairman, presented a cleverly couched response which more closely mirrored the understanding of women-only groups outside the Labour Party: 'I have no doubt that our burial, if such it is to be, is preliminary only to a speedy resurrection with much increased power and opportunity'. She then went on to acknowledge the need for innovative structures to mirror new opportunities and 'the need from time to time to discuss special women's problems and under circumstances that will give special opportunities for the self-expression of women'.[17] Mrs Lowe was signalling to the leadership that women needed and would have their own platform for their own issues; it was a refusal to be silenced. But claiming their own space was just what they would not be able to do under the new constitution, which laid out that:

> The right to hold a National Annual Conference would be impossible without giving a similar right to men's sections, and thereby instituting a sectionalism of a national kind throughout the party.[18]

In other words, party solidarity was to be preserved at the expense of Labour women's political independence. This was an ironic outcome of the franchise victory where Labour women's citizenship rights were being captured for the advantage of the Party while curtailing their rights within the Party.

During discussions on the women's sections at what was to be the last WLL conference, Marion Phillips attempted to calm the disquiet of some members concerning the new constitution. One member, Mrs Corrie from Coventry, feared that it would reduce Labour Party women to an auxiliary position not unlike the Primrose Dames of the Conservative Party. Her branch wanted to retain its independence 'to be at liberty to go with the progressives, not to find itself tied to what might be the retrograde party'.[19] The women did not want to have to ask permission for their every political move. Mrs Corrie also wanted to know if there would be an opportunity for amendments before the WLL was dismantled in June 1918.[20] A Mrs Robinson of the Manchester Central Branch thought that the conference ought to be discussing the underlying issue of whether this new system would produce progress for women's political organisation and what opportunity women would have 'for expressing the women's point of view in the counsels of the Labour Party'.[21] Such disquiet was well-founded: many of the implications of this takeover produced immediate, negative results and long-term disadvantage in terms of power-sharing, evident to the present day. Hannah Mitchell later prophetically recorded her response to the new Women's Sections: 'These I did not like. I believed in complete equality and was not prepared to be a camp follower, or a member of what seemed to me a permanent Social Committee, or Official cake-maker to the Labour Party.'[22]

The new inequality extended to a system of differentiated membership rates, 1s for men and 6d for women. Some women at the 1918 conference felt that if they were supposed to be equal to their male colleagues, as they had been reassured, they should pay the same rate.[23] Marion Phillips was eager to point out, as if in compensation, that there were to be four reserved places for women on the Labour Party executive committee. The WLL was not given any real option to continue; Phillips told the conference that branches had already had time to send in amendments, and that no new resolutions could now be taken. As Christine Collette has observed:

Branches had, of course, been presented with a fait accompli; the time for negotiation with the Party was past because its new constitution had been agreed; women's representation in the new structure was voted upon not by the League, but by the delegates (still overwhelmingly male) at the Labour Party conference.[24]

The WLL's fate had been decided for it.

There were many women within the Labour Party who believed in and had worked towards the equality of men and women within the party working together as comrades. These were women who had always seen the separation of women in the Labour and Union movements as a transitional stage towards this moment, with the priority being the fight for socialism. But there were other women who were concerned that women's issues would not be accorded a hearing within the Labour Party without women having the independence and power to ensure that such issues were placed on the agenda.

Although Labour women were promised occasional, 'special' conferences on women's subjects, regular women's conferences were disallowed and, as they were no longer an independent body, they could not be affiliated to any outside bodies. This excluded Labour women from participating as representatives in any other women's organisations, unless their local Labour Party affiliated to such societies on their behalf. This meant no affiliation to groups which Labour Party men believed to be in conflict with its policies or philosophies, which was an effective curtailment of the women's autonomy as contributors to the wider women's movement. The foundation for entrenching the divisions between party and non-party sections of the women's movement was thus laid. Ensuring Labour women's role as handmaids to the party and class politics was a shrewd way of undermining women's political solidarity which was to have repercussions for the women's movement in many of its future campaigns.

The Effects of War

There were many contradictory adjustments for women to make in a post-war world which had to accommodate their expectations of the achievements that might derive from their new-found citizenship status. The movement undoubtedly had a deep-seated appreciation of the returning soldiers' position, but there was also a desire to continue working:

> During the war a generation of middle class women acquired the habit of independence in a manless England. This sudden achievement of all that feminists had dreamed for a hundred years was more than society at large had bargained for. In 1918 women were expected to surrender

what they had gained, and to behave as if nothing had happened to themselves or to the world in the previous four years.[25]

Many working class women had also improved their lives. Girls from rural districts with little or no opportunity for employment had moved into towns, worked in munition factories and earned regular money. Now came the return to 'normality'. For society it meant coming to terms with the waste and horror of the war and the ensuing economic chaos; for those soldiers who returned, it meant a reintroduction to civilian life and the changed women they came home to; and for women, it meant an accommodation with what they had become as independent women and what society would allow them to be in the post-war world.

The apprehension about post-war reconstruction, which the women's movement had been articulating since 1915 and urging the Government to plan for, was now a reality. The Women's Freedom League's (WFL) editorial three days after Armistice Day signalled both optimism and fear:

> We must see, too, that the girls and women who responded so spontaneously to their country's call for work in munition factories... are treated with consideration when demobilisation takes place. They must not be thrown to the wolves, but have safeguards for future employment, equal facilities and equal terms with men in every branch of industry.[26]

Mindful of international sisterhood, the movement reinforced the message that such a process was not simply national, but international. The *International Woman Suffrage News* in December 1918 carried messages from leading suffrage women and organisations to their sisters worldwide who had suffered as a result of the war. Mrs Fawcett looked forward to a League of Nations to unite them, while Charlotte Despard wrote of women's need to 'hold and grasp the secret of power'.[27] Isabella Ford (NUWSS/WLL/ILP) put her faith in 'world reconstruction', while Helena Swanwick, Maude Royden, Margaret Ashton and Kathleen Courtney of the NUWSS, hailed the power of the modern woman who:

> ... enfranchised in mind and heart, will set their minds and hearts to the future; will lift up their hearts heavy with grief

and deeply troubled with wrong, with the mighty gesture of the free woman. They will cry: 'This is the day of the women!'[28]

The armistice combined the relief of peace with the realisation of the enormous cost of the war. At the cessation of hostilities Britain was left with 800,000 dead and 1.5 million disabled men. This was exactly what those 'dangerous' peace women had struggled to prevent; now there were men, and women, for whom the war would never be over. Vera Brittain recalled that 'When the sound of the victorious guns burst over London at 11am on 11 November 1918, the men and women who looked incredulously into each other's faces did not cry jubilantly: "We've won the War!" They only said: "The War is over"'.[29] Instability and disillusion beset Britain in the winter following the end of the war. During that winter the great influenza epidemic killed 200,000 in Britain and 27 million worldwide. In Britain there was a coal shortage which had severe effects on a country where coal was the main industrial and domestic fuel. The Government was calling for a 'united national effort', a demand that was to have special significance for women, and testified to Mowat's theory of the regressive nature of post-war politics.[30]

The State of the Post-War Movement

Despite the suffering which so many women and their families had endured, the wartime employment advances for women could not be denied. But the most fundamental change was in women's relation to the state now that they had the vote, although the women's movement was only too aware that its work was far from finished. The symbol of their emancipation now had to be given substance; they had to use their newly-acquired power to achieve the original goals which had prompted the formation of the movement's political, professional, welfare and industrial organisations.

The scale of the women's agenda required a broad base of expertise. Essential for success was a network of organisations whose constituent parts could concentrate on specialist issues, working out policy and campaigning tactics. But the amalgamated strength of the movement was also needed to mount mass actions on common goals, such as franchise extension and economic parity, at critical points during a campaign. In such a way, expertise common to all could be pooled when required, without impeding the progress of the movement's separate ventures. Ray Strachey recorded that:

> The actual division of responsibilities among the societies was complicated and variable... With the granting of the vote all the organisations of women became more or less feminist and political... The war, too, had left a legacy of co-operation among them. The volume of women's groups in existence after the war, which continued to grow during the 1920s, profiles the variety of reforms which constituted the movement's agenda for the decade.[31]

Many suffrage groups, like the United Suffragists (US), wound up their operations in February 1918 directly after the passing of the Representation of the People Act. The US felt that 'to widen our scope by undertaking other reforms would be but to add to the number of societies already in existence for such a purpose'.[32]

By 1919, suffrage societies were involved in a second phase of re-evaluation in response to the challenges of reconstruction. As the largest society, the NUWSS, under its new president Eleanor Rathbone, presented itself as 'the co-ordinating organ of all feminist activity throughout Great Britain'.[33] It revised its constitution to enable other women's organisations to affiliate to the union to counteract the 'danger that feminist activity may come to little if too widely diffused'.[34] Like the Women Citizens' Associations (WCAs), initiated by the National Council of Women (NCW) in the previous year, which were also affiliated to the National Union of Societies for Equal Citizenship (NUSEC), this affiliation system ensured an expansion of the movement, an opportunity to welcome more women into the organised struggle.

In its publication, *Women Citizens' Association Handbook*, the NUSEC outlined how to start such a group, and the lists of organisations, speakers and literature included in the pamphlet are good indicators of the catholic direction which the movement was taking. WCAs acted as a means of binding different interest groups together into a community of women. The lists cut across political and religious boundaries, indicating the path along which the movement was travelling. Such co-ordination was an essential element in fulfilling their ambition for equality.[35] By October 1919 there were already 182 WCAs, Equality Groups and Local Correspondent Groups covering England, Wales and Scotland.

The LSWS also realised the war's positive outcome for the movement in that:

> Thousands of women have for the first time realised the meaning of the Suffrage Movement from their personal experience of work during the war. Thousands have begun to understand that it is necessary to organise and to co-operate, and that they look to the London Society and to its Women's Service Bureau as to their natural protectors.[36]

To respond to this demand and facilitate growth, the LSWS had appointed an organiser in 1918 with sole responsibility for establishing WCAs in the London region. In February 1919 it responded to the 'altered character of the work to be carried out', revising its rules and constitution, changing its name to the LSWS and specifying its aim 'to stand for equal suffrage and equal opportunities for women, but resolve to concentrate its efforts for the present on obtaining economic equality for women,'[37] a shift in focus which did not go unopposed.[38]

As well as maximising the movement's potential, the NUSEC, as it was now called, sought to counteract possible diffusion by restricting its programme to six objectives at any one time. The NUSEC's new policy illuminated three important considerations: its awareness of the need for continued collective campaigning; the unifying foundation of the equality goal held in common by the movement; and the necessity for different groups to concentrate on specific issues. Whereas the NUSEC originated policy and campaigns, as well as acting as a co-ordinating body, the NCW of Great Britain and Ireland operated solely as a co-ordinating organisation on a local and national level. By 1918 it had 126 local branches all over Britain, with 142 affiliated women's organisations covering every aspect of women's activity. These included the whole gamut of women's concerns, including feminist groups, such as the Irish Women's Suffrage and Local Government Association (IWSLGA), the Association for Moral and Social Hygiene (AMSH), the NUSEC, the Fabian Society Women's Group (FSWG), the Church League for Women's Suffrage (CLWS), the National Federation of Women Teachers (NFWT) and the WFL. The business of the NCW was carried out through its 15 sectional committees, dealing with industrial, parliamentary, welfare and legislative matters. Its varied membership, which crossed party-political lines, made it a valuable vehicle to feed representative ideas into the movement's activities.[39]

This theme of the wartime 'common effort' was endorsed by the WFL's president, Charlotte Despard, in 1918: 'You will notice how Conferences, deputations, protests, demonstrations, have been carried through with marked success by women's societies working together. This augurs well for the future.'[40] Although a good deal smaller than the NUSEC, it had 50 or so branches, widely distributed throughout England, Scotland and Wales. Many of the organisations which were affiliated to the NUSEC and the NCW were also WFL subscribers, such as the Association of Women Clerks and Secretaries (AWCS), the Federation of Women Civil Servants (FWCS), the NFWT and the Women's Industrial League (WIL).

Many of the suffrage societies which had 'kept the flag flying' during the war were also still in existence and subscribed to the WFL, adding their weight to the movement's work. Among them were the Actresses Franchise League (AFL) and the Catholic Women's Suffrage Society (CWSS), together with the Independent Women's Suffrage and Local Government Association (IWSPU) and the Women Writers Suffrage League (WWSL). The British section of the WILPF's membership was largely drawn from the suffrage societies, so that it also supported campaigns other than that of peace throughout the 1920s. The Irish women's suffrage groups were also still operating: the Women's Political League in Belfast (formerly the BWSS) and the IWSLGA in Dublin, which had become the Irish Women Citizens' and Local Government Association (IWCLGA) in November 1918. Both groups sustained their strong links with the movement until after the Anglo-Irish Treaty in the summer of 1921, when the partition of Ireland meant that they became more involved with activities in Northern Ireland and Eire. There were also the smaller local and regional groups such as the Hendon Women's Election Committee, the Birmingham United Suffragists and various Women's Councils. Many such groups were affiliated or subscribed to the larger societies such as the NUSEC or the WFL and were contributing to the continued heterogeneity of the women's movement.

The process of demobilisation, with its effects on the labour market, ensured that women's groups concerned with the protection of women's employment were particularly active from 1918 to 1922. Three unions which represented professional women and worked in close harmony with the suffrage societies during this time had a particularly high profile: the FWCS, the AWCS, and the NUWT. The FWCS orginated in 1913 from an equal pay struggle, and comprised six constituent clerical associations.[41] Its policy was to achieve equality of opportunity for women in the civil service, as well as working 'to secure the removal of the civil and political disabilities of women'.[42] This awareness of the larger context in which its professional claims were set had made it an effective advocate of the woman's Cause, participating in pre-war suffrage processions and demonstrations.

The FWCS's close colleague was the AWCS which aimed to protect clerical workers and abolish sex differentiation within clerical work. It was most emphatic about the importance of co-operation with other organisations which were pursuing the same ends, and the need for women to defend their rights and take the responsibility for accomplishing their own personal objectives. This was a perennial realisation throughout the decade, that women's emancipation could not be left to others, but must be advanced by women themselves: 'We are all beginning to realise what a powerful weapon combination is... Those of us who are new to economic independence must realise that if we wish to retain it we must act collectively.'[43] The AWCS was flourishing, with 300 new members in the month of August 1918 alone.[44] The increasing organisational sophistication of these groups mirrored the personal confidence of the membership.

Another professional women's union was that of the NFWT, which began in 1904 as an Equal Pay League formed by women and men to pressurise the National Union of Teachers into improving women teachers' pay and position. The League's name was changed to the NFWT in 1906 and as a result of the fierce hostility they experienced from a majority of their male colleagues by 1908 the federation had taken up the suffrage issue and was firmly entrenched in the women's movement. The federation grew rapidly: by 1919 it had its own offices with a General Secretary and over a dozen full-time workers.[45]

Another section of the movement was represented by women's industrial organisations which, unlike the professional women's groups, were to experience decline during the early 1920s. The assimilation of the WLL into the Labour Party machine was to set the pattern for women's industrial groups – they were increasingly absorbed by male organisations after the war, a process which not only altered the focus of industrial women's power, but to many minds, denuded it. However, in 1919 this independent women's representation was still largely in place, with the major players being the Standing Joint Committee of Industrial Women's Organisations (SJCIWO), the National Federation of Women Workers (NFWW), and the Women's Trade Union League (WTUL).

The escalating numbers drawn into heavy industry during the war reflected the success of the women's unions which introduced women to the principles of co-operation and the protection of their rights. After the war, the NFWW saw its largest branches in industrial centres such as Newcastle-upon-Tyne, Barrow and Woolwich 'melt away', but what the female union officials and membership had learned during those years would not disappear. Although they were not as appreciable in size after the war, women joined branches set up in new employment areas. The movement was still significant enough for the NFWW to claim that:

> Having regard to the circumstances of the times, we believe the aggregate results are magnificent, and are eloquent testimony to the educational work of our branch officers... we are not unmindful of the great work done by those who have stood by the declining branches when everything seemed to be slipping away from them.[46]

In the summer of 1918, the NFWW began negotiations with the National Union of General Workers (NUGW) with a view to a merger in 1920, when the NFWW was to become the Women's Department of the NUGW. During the two year transitionary period, the NFWW continued to work for women's employment rights, including the operation of its legal advice bureau which had built a successful reputation by securing compensation for women from insurance companies, employers and government departments.[47]

At the beginning of 1919 there was an impressive network of organisations marshalled to promote and protect women's rights during the reconstruction period. However, almost without exception, the annual reports disclose the perilous financial position in which the movement found itself, stripped as it was of any reserve assets. The suffrage societies' wartime fundraising had been used to finance their welfare work and wartime disruption had made it difficult to collect sufficient subscriptions to keep the societies' accounts healthy. The decline in union membership, as women were forced to leave industrial employment, also meant a dramatic loss of revenue. However, the NFWW's accumulated funds had risen from £3,005 at the end of 1914 to £32,081 at the end of 1919, an indication of its wartime recruitment success.[48]

Even societies as large as the NUSEC and the LSWS had to decrease the numbers of paid staff to rationalise their operations. The precarious post-war economic position meant that donations decreased, costs increased and organisations had no surplus to fall back on.[49] The LSWS found that its work in 1919 was impeded by the shortage of office staff since there was no decrease in the amount of work to be done. Financial stress was an additional burden, although such financial constraints were a perennial problem for the movement, which it always faced with ingenuity. Because of women's financial position in society, having to rely largely on them for subscriptions, donations and participation in fund-raising, was bound to result in limited incomes for women's organisations. This was why the involvement of wealthy middle and upper class women had always been so vital to the continuation of the movement's activities. Nancy Astor's papers, for example, reveal a constant stream of donations to women's groups;[50] large donations from Eleanor Rathbone and Millicent Fawcett to the NUSEC were regular, and Maud Arncliffe-Sennett had used money from her business for the East London Federation of Suffragettes (ELFS) and to look after imprisoned suffragettes' children in the pre-war struggle. Although every organisation relied heavily on volunteer workers, when it came to paid staff the women's societies were insistent on the need to set an example and pay their staff well. It was a demonstration of valuing women's work and recompensing them accordingly. The LSWS saw little point in its involvement in demanding equal pay and higher standards for employment and training if it did not take a lead in setting fair wage levels and reflecting its principles in practice.

Organisational Growth

Despite such financial constraints, the years 1918 to 1922 saw the formation of organisations which dealt with specific post-war and reconstruction problems. The attack on women's right to work which resulted partly in a contraction of new opportunities for middle class women brought with it additional resistance from new groups such as the WIL, the Women's Engineering Society (WES) and the Council for Women Civil Servants (CWCS), all organised by middle class women. The WIL, founded in November 1918 with Margaret Haig, Lady Rhondda, as its President, was 'to organise public opinion and to keep the Government up to its promises'.[51] Although not intended as a trade union, it did seek to educate and encourage women about the benefits of combination. Equal pay for equal output was one of its main policies and its General Organising Secretary, Miss Key Jones, saw its aim as being 'to see women's status raised politically, industrially and professionally'.[52] The WIL sought to provide protection for women who were working in industry from the inevitable disruption that the end of the war would bring. It attempted to do this by keeping the relevant issues in the public arena, pressing for the employment of women in government initiatives, and bringing matters to the Government's attention by means of petitions, deputations and questionnaires. It issued reports on women in industry, held public meetings and arranged discussion groups, lectures and speakers' classes for working women. The organisers represented a cross-section of suffrage and industrial experience with Rhondda and Key Jones joined by Betty Archdale, a young lawyer, as Honorary Secretary and Julia Varley, an ex-WSPU and WLL member, who as an active trade unionist regularly addressed the league's meetings.[53]

The other industrially-based professional association was the Women's Engineering Society (WES), inaugurated in February 1919 by three women with traditional male skills and qualifications, who had considerable private means to finance the society. Lady Rachel Parsons, a qualified engineer, was its president. Laura Willson had started her working life at the age of ten as a half-timer in a textile factory and had worked in the trade union movement. She had taken sole charge of her husband's factory during the war, although her own trade was house-building. The third figure was Lady Moir, who had been in charge of the supervision of relief work at munition factories during the war. The Secretary of the WES, Caroline Haslett, former WSPU member, saw her job at the WES as 'one of consolidation so that the inroads into engineering women had made during the war years should not be whittled away'.[54] The WES aimed to overcome the barriers to women entering engineering by providing information, keeping them abreast of modern developments, arranging lectures and annual conferences, giving them support and encouragement in establishing new ventures, providing a communication channel via their own magazine, *The Woman Engineer*, and raising members' status through their affiliation in an accredited engineering society.[55] This last aim was an important development in the movement's history, as women discovered new ways of gaining access to power by creating their own institutions for networking. This was one of the barriers to women's professional progress, as Lady Rhondda had experienced: 'Though one is in the life, one is not, one cannot yet be, altogether of it. No person who is cut off from the gossip of their professions... can realise how immensely important that talk is.'[56]

Women who had been settled in a profession before the war now found their jobs under threat as the post-war situation tended to affect their conditions of service and opportunities for advancement. In February 1920 three women civil servants in Bristol wrote to the Chief Woman Organising Officer, Miss Sanday, at the Ministry of Labour in London and set in motion the machinery for setting up the CWCS.[57] Several reconstruction committee reports had resulted in injustices relating to equal pay, access to promotion and appointment procedures, and the women determined to redress these inequalities by acting through their new organisation. Their Chairwoman was the veteran pioneer, Adelaide Anderson, who had been the first woman factory inspector at the end of the nineteenth century, and had a wealth of expertise to place at their disposal.[58]

There was an enormous disruption of women's lives which the women's movement needed to deal with after the war, with psychological adjustments to be made as well as physical needs to be addressed. For women who were intent on sustaining their independence and had abandoned the idea of returning to the parental home, whose husbands or betrothed had been killed, or who had no intention of marrying, there was a desperate shortage of suitable housing. Groups such as Women's Pioneer Housing (WPH) were established to provide homes specifically designed to cater for the needs of professional women. Many women who were prominent in the women's movement were involved with the WPH, either on the management committee or as holders of shares in the loan stock and as supporters of the project.[59]

As the war had drawn to a close, the IWSN noted in November 1918 that 'All the world is holding conferences just now and passing feminist resolutions'.[60] The women's movement's legendary tenacity had endured and it had survived the war; it had helped both the country and itself and was optimistic and confident about the future. As individuals, women's optimism was tempered with exhaustion, disillusion and sorrow. Nevertheless, many women who had worked hard for peace were determined that women would be in a stronger position in the future to play their part in preventing any repetition of the horrors of such a war. The immediate post-war period saw the women's movement operating within a society experiencing the strains of social and economic transformation, and such a combination of tensions could not easily facilitate its struggle for equal social, economic and political power. But the movement demonstrated its ability to adapt and meet the new challenges of the post-war world, and it was this reorganised movement that was now ready to tackle what was to be the largest immediate obstacle to women's progress, demobilisation.

Notes on Chapter 3

1. Schreiner, Olive quoted in Holtby, Winifred, *Women and a Changing Civilisation* (London, 1936, John Lane, Bodley Head), p 71
2. *International Woman Suffrage News*, 1 April 1918, p 107
3. LSWS, Annual Report, 1917, p 16
4. *International Woman Suffrage News*, April 1918, p 107
5. Ibid.
6. *International Woman Suffrage News*, November 1918, pp 17-18
7. *The Labour Woman*, November 1918, p 76
8. Ibid.
9. *The Labour Woman*, November 1918, p 76
10. *Britannia*, 11 January 1918, front page
11. *The Labour Woman*, November 1918, p 76
12. WLL, Executive Committee Report, 1917, p 8
13. Ibid.
14. WLL, Executive Committee Report, 1917, p 9
15. Shinwell, Emmanuel, *The Labour Story* (London, 1963, Macdonald), p 97
16. WLL, Annual Conference Report, 21 & 22 January 1918, p 46
17. Ibid.
18. WLL, Report of the Executive Committee of the WLL on the Draft Constitution of the Labour Party and their Recommendations in Connection Therewith, 1917, p 3

19   WLL, Annual Conference Report, 21 & 22 January 1918,
      p 43
20   Ibid., pp 46-47
21   Ibid., p 46
22   Mitchell, Hannah (ed. Mitchell, G) *The Hard Way Up: the
      Autobiography of Hannah Mitchell, Suffragette and Rebel*
      (London, 1977, Virago), p 189. Mitchell was accurate in her
      prediction. I remember my first Labour Party meeting in
      Consett, County Durham when 'the ladies' were asked to
      make sandwiches for the AGM, and that was in 1980!
      Consett had previously had its own WLL branch.
23   WLL, Annual Conference Report, 21 & 22 January, p 47
24   Collette, Christine, *For Labour and For Women: The
      Women's Labour League 1906-18* (Manchester, 1989,
      MUP), p 176
25   Kornitzer, Margaret, *The Modern Woman and Herself*
      (London, 1932, Jonathon Cape), p 24
26   *The Vote*, 15 November 1918, p 460
27   *International Woman Suffrage News*, December 1918, pp
      26-27
28   Ibid.
29   Brittain, Vera, *Testament of Youth: An Autobiographical
      Study of the Years 1900-1925* (London, 1978, Fontana),
      p 460
30   Mowat, Charles Loch, *Britain Between the Wars 1918-1940*
      (London, 1955, Methuen), p 9
31   Strachey, Ray, *The Cause: A Short History of the Women's
      Movement in Great Britain* (London, 1978, Virago), p 374
32   *Votes for Women*, February 1918, p 332
33   *International Woman Suffrage News*, April 1919, p 90
34   Ibid. Immediate affiliates were the AMSH, the NFWT, the
      AWCS, the UJW, the WIC, the WIL, the IWSSLGA and the
      BDWCU.
35   *Women Citizens' Association Handbook*, NUSEC, 1918, pp
      20-21
36   LSWS, Annual Report, 1917-18, p 13
37   Ibi., p 21
38   Letter from Ray Strachey to her mother, Mary Costelloe, 25
      February 1919, Smith Papers, Oxford, in which she
      describes the opposition which resulted from some members
      thinking that equal suffrage and opportunities should not be
      sidelined for economic issues. This difficulty of prioritisation

of demands was to prove increasingly contentious as the decade progressed among those suffrage women who had a purist interpretation of the emancipation programme.

39   *Handbook and Report of the NCW of Great Britain and Northern Ireland*, NCW, 1918-19

40   WFL, Report of the Eleventh Annual Conference, 23 & 24 February, 1918, p 5

41   These were the Association of Post Office Women Clerks, the Association of Women Clerks in the Ministry of Labour, the National Health Insurance Women Clerks Association, the Association of Women Clerks in the Board of Education, the Association of Women Clerks in the Public Trustee's Office, the National Health Insurance Women Clerks Association (Scotland) in Association Notes, October-December 1918, p 266

42   Ibid.

43   AWCS, Newsletter, October 1918, p 1

44   AWCS, Association Notes, October-December 1918, p 266

45   Phipps, Emily, *History of the NUWT* (London, 1928, NUWT). For a recent history see Kean, Hilda, *Deeds not Words* (London, 1995, Pluto Press)

46   NFWW, Tenth Annual Report for the Two Years Ended 31 December 1919, p 5

47   Ibid., pp 18-19. NUGW, Women Workers' Section First Annual Report Ended 31 December 1921, pp 23-25

48   NFWW, Tenth Annual Report for the Two Years Ended 31 December 1919, p 4

49   WFL, Annual Report, May 1919-April 1922, p 5; NUSEC, Annual Report, 1920, pp 25-26

50   See Societies IV, Women's Associations, Lady Astor Collection, MS 1416/1/1 822-828

51   *The Common Cause*, March 1919, p 615

52   'Work of the Women's Industrial League', *The Globe*, 11 November 1919, Gertrude Tuckwell Collection, 702a/14

53   The WIL did experience some opposition from women trade unionists who seemed to suspect the interference in industrial protection by the likes of Lady Rhondda, who as a wealthy businesswoman, industrialist and non-party woman may have been viewed as 'the enemy'.

54   Messenger, Rosalind, *The Doors of Opportunity: A Biography of Dame Caroline Haslett* (London, 1967, Femina Books), p 33

55   *The Woman Engineer*, March 1921-June 1928

56   Rhondda, Viscountess, Margaret Haig, *This Was My World* (London, 1933, Macmillan), p 230

57   Letter from the Misses Deane, McCleverty and Sadler to Miss Sandy (Sanday), 28 February 1920, CWCS Archive

58   CWCS, Report of the Standing Joint Committee of Women in the Higher Grades of the Civil Service, 1920-23, CWCS Archive, p 4,

59   WPH, Minutes, 10 January 1921-December 1922, WPH Archive. The WPH was started in 1920 as a co-operative society by Etheldred Browning, and is still in existence. Elizabeth Macadam and Eleanor Rathbone, NUSEC; Lady Denman, NCW and the NFWI; Lady Shelley-Rolls, WES; Mrs Rollo Russell, WIL; Lady Rhondda, SPG, WIL; Ray Strachey and Lady Emmott, LSWS; Betty Archdale, WIL; Dorothy C.S. Peel, suffragist and writer on homelessness were some of the movement's activists involved with the WPH.

60   *International Woman Suffrage News*, November 1918, p 17

Chapter 4
Demobilisation: 1918-1922

> All women are not now in their right places. Many got out
> of them in the War and need readjusting; there is much work
> for women which women refuse to do, and there are women
> in posts where, from any point of view, men should be.[1]

It must have seemed to those in the women's movement that they
experienced no less opposition to their work during the post-war
reconstruction period than in the days before achieving the partial
franchise. The demobilisation process intensified the objections to
women's employment and their attempts to extend the franchise
continued to be contended, to say nothing of the resistance to other
reforms. All this was tackled against a background of economic
and social unrest which did nothing to smooth the women's path.
A brief economic boom in 1919 resulting in inflation, followed by
a two-year slump and an economic depression, meant that these
years were 'a journey through chaos. The rulers of England were
as unprepared for the problems of a sudden reversion to peace as
they had been for the problems of sudden war in 1914.'[2]

After the 1918 general election, the most demanding challenge
for the newly constituted women's movement was the demobilisation of women war workers. Enfranchised women were eager to
participate as citizens in the nation's reconstruction and to

complete their work of gaining full emancipation for all women. However, the chaos of demobilisation brought with it the realisation that recent gains were being lost and progress reversed. Instead of going forward from the war, the women's movement realised that it was going to have to battle to retain rights which it thought secure, otherwise, as *Votes for Women* had predicted in 1914, it would be a case of 'exploitation during the war and contemptuous neglect after it is over'.[3]

Other accounts[4] have investigated the demobilisation process: this study outlines the women's organisations' response to the problems of demobilisation for women. The significance of demobilisation and the subsequent women's unemployment lay not just in the short-term suffering which it caused for women and their dependents, but in the long-term implications for the struggle for women's economic power.

Almost as soon as women entered wartime employment early in 1915, women trade unionists, suffrage organisations and political groups were concerned about the need to face these reconstruction issues. Having largely been responsible for salvaging some kind of order from the disruption caused by the outbreak of war and the ensuing unemployment for women, they were adamant about the need to prevent a repetition of these events when peace came. They believed that forward planning and co-operation between the Government, trade unions and representative women's groups might achieve a smoother transition to the post-war world, one in which women could retain the advantages they had accrued during the war. Referring to the National Conference on War Service of April 1915, the National Federation of Women Workers (NFWW) recalled its plans to the Government to deal with the inevitable post-war unemployment situation for women, and the fact that this advice had been ignored.[5] By the spring of 1918 the need for a contingency plan was evident to Anna Munro of the Women's Freedom League (WFL); without it she predicted that 'mental and physical degeneration, particularly to women, will inevitably ensue'.[6]

There were 3.5 million men to be resettled into civilian life during the reconstruction process. There was widespread unrest throughout the country, with police strikes in August 1918 and 1919; in Glasgow, factory strikes, riotous behaviour and the raising of the red flag seemed to herald the possibility of a general strike in the New Year of 1919 as other sections of industrial workers also threatened industrial action.[7] The difficulty was that 'Like the wartime generals, Lloyd George and his ministers were confronted with problems beyond their capacity to master within the time at their disposal'.[8] Perhaps Lloyd George thought he had succeeded in defusing the 'woman problem'; that by 'giving' them the vote their co-operation was assured as they would now feel that they had to prove they were capable of appreciating the responsibility of citizenship.[9] Having conceded sufficient power to invalidate women's status as rebels, by denying women under 30 political freedom, he had retained a measure of control by restricting women's power. He had created a sub-group which might become apathetic to the political system, and thereby apolitical. He had also prevented women from becoming the electoral majority; but as so many men feared that such a situation would be a political catastrophe, this must have given women a psychological advantage. However, the limitation of their enfranchisement was a signal reminder of who still retained political control.

Although this partial attainment of the vote had increased women's political effectiveness, as male MPs had to acknowledge the political existence of women, in some ways such limited power worked against women. It meant that opposition now took on a more devious flavour which was harder to combat and resulted in what the National Union of Societies for Equal Citizenship (NUSEC) experienced as a 'Parliament, friendly to such an extent in name only'.[10] There was also the invidious position in which women were placed by their attempts to resist government policy intended to return women to their 1914 employment position, and in many cases to an even worse one. But complex as it was for individual organisations to prioritise the catalogue of demands, there was a general consensus that life could not return to its pre-war state, and many women totally rejected the conditions which had previously controlled their lives. Eleanor Rathbone, speaking at the opening conference of the Liverpool Council of Women Citizens in October 1918, declared that 'Women would never go back to the leper-compound of unskilled trades they had occupied before the war'.[11] In this way, the issues of reconstruction reinforced the continuing concerns of the movement; they were not separate or an interruption, but a continuance of the fight for equality.

In the latter part of 1916, the Standing Joint Committee of Industrial Women's Organisations (SJCIWO) had issued a report on the position of women which was presented to the Joint Committee on Labour Problems After the War. Its conclusion was the forerunner to many similar assessments of women's industrial position, and suffrage societies incorporated similar views in their new policy statements in 1918. The SJCIWO maintained that:

> ... the war has changed the whole outlook as regards women's work, and has removed some of the disabilities, We, therefore, urge that every advantage should be taken to secure a far higher standard of life for women, and a position of general industrial equality with men.[12]

Having sustained the equal pay struggle during the war and increased women's union membership, the movement now wanted to build on this industrial strength using the new-found personal confidence of its members. Simultaneously it realised that it was essential to take steps so that 'the regrettable antagonism between men and women workers must be averted after the war'.[13]

The Pattern of Demobilisation

The demobilisation process, as far as women workers and the women's movement's response was concerned, was dictated by government policy and economic conditions. The first phase, at the end of 1918, related to immediate fears of mass unemployment for women resulting from the unplanned demobilisation of women who had no interim insurance benefits, no training programmes and no suitable alternative employment on offer. The movement's immediate concern was to pressurise the Government into making all three provisions available.[14] The introduction of the Pre-War Trade Practices Act in the early summer of 1919 marked the second stage, which not only outlawed women from existing pre-war trades, but also from new war-time employment developments and subsequent work which was now on offer. It was essential for the women's organisations to challenge this legislation in order to prevent the enshrinement in law of this type of prejudice.[15] Thirdly, the end of 1919 saw attempts by the Government to transform temporary, wartime expedients for stabilising the country into standard practice applying to government employees.[16] This third phase particularly affected women civil servants, but the women's movement was concerned to demonstrate that 'Our fight is the fight of all women workers'.[17] As unemployment escalated in 1920 due to the demobilisation programme and the worsening economic situation, women's economic plight became acute, and the consequent pressure on the authorities to introduce ameliorative measures increased.

The final development came in 1921, when married women were singled out for specially punitive treatment and the implementation of a marriage bar began to be used by local councils to reduce their female workforce. This final attack saw the women's organisations escalate their campaign to redress a situation at crisis point which threatened effectively to destroy all the economic progress which they had made prior to and during the war.

The Immediate Post-War Situation

Whilst working class women had always had little choice about their participation in the workforce, the position for middle class women had been very different, and the war had enabled them to grasp new freedoms:

> It was pathetic to see how many able-bodied women one house could contain, all 'housekeepers'... the war changed all that. The war called them out of their homes: taught them their value to the State; taught them also what greater value would have been theirs had they been able to offer the State not merely devoted service but trained service;... taught them that they too had a market value. It seems impossible that they should ever return to the old life of dependence and restriction and aimless days.[18]

But for all women, of whatever class, loss of employment brought the loss of economic power, status, self-esteem, access to possible training, personal development, contact with the world outside the domestic domain and the right to make a contribution to society.

It was not a question of refusing to surrender a new-found freedom as if it were an exciting novelty: what women were refusing to surrender was a key ingredient in the struggle that was 'establishing themselves "fairly and squarely" as citizens and workers'.[19] Women's groups constantly reiterated the fact that they had never had any intention of taking work away from the returning soldiers or of working in opposition to men. In line with their new post-war ethos they wanted to co-operate with men for the general good because 'The interests of men and women are the same. We say this until we are tired of saying it because we believe it, and because it is true.'[20] Rather it was men whom women might well have been justified in accusing of the instigation of a 'sex war', as Mrs Schofield Coates (WFL) did: 'The so-called sex war is waged by men in their efforts to keep back women who are endeavouring to render service and justify their existence'.[21] There were also the immediate practical difficulties created by disabled men, unable to work and provide for their wives and families; and the existence of widows and other female dependents of the dead with no alternative but that of earning a living to support their families. It also became evident to the women's movement, as these different phases of the demobilisation process unfolded, that what they were witnessing was the establishment of an employment agenda which was intended to set future employment patterns. It was, therefore, absolutely essential to 'strain our powers of resistance to the utmost to hold our own against the forces of reaction, for it is now a moment when ground once lost may take years to recover'.[22]

Assurances about the existence of employment for women after the war by press and politicians omitted to discuss what kind of work it would be or how the transition would be made from universal employment.[23] Nor, indeed, did they mention how large the problem would be with 4.5 million women in industry, 1.5 million of them in 'men's' jobs. The severity of the situation made itself clear at an early stage with 50,000 women unemployed by June 1918 and 113,000 women discharged only two weeks after the cessation of war.[24] By April 1919 the unemployment figure had risen to approximately 600,000 but the real figure was probably much higher, as not all women would have registered as unemployed.[25] The figure carried on escalating until the demobilisation process was almost complete in June 1922. Unlike the provision made for demobilised soldiers where every non-commissioned ex-serviceman was provided with a free unemployment insurance policy,[26] there was, initially, no such help available for the 'heroic' women war workers.

Women's expressions of reluctance and resistance to return to the 'narrow and hopeless conditions of a working woman's life'[27] were to result in public hostility. At the start of 1919 this was mingled with a backlash against the war and a curious psychological antipathy to anyone who had participated in it. Vera Brittain on her return to Oxford University after her war work as a Volunteer Aid Detachment (VAD) nurse realised that 'Obviously it wasn't a popular thing to have been close to the War; patriots, especially of the female variety, were as much discredited in 1919 as in 1914 they had been honoured'.[28] What began as an aversion gathered momentum and developed into vitriolic attacks on women who continued to work or fight for employment rights. The London Society for Women's Suffrage (LSWS) was astonished to discover that women were actually being 'punished' for their participation in the war: 'That women should be refused the chance of other work simply because they have served their country during the war seems almost incredible, but it has been proved again and again by concrete instances that employers are refusing to consider the applications of women with war service behind them'.[29] Perhaps employers feared the independence and emancipated views of women who had previously taken over men's work with such successful results.

Such hostility could be contrasted with the lavish praise which had been showered on the 'heroines' of the war, as women helped to sustain the home front and manufacture supplies for battle.[30] Although initially, women had also experienced a degree of opposition when they took over men's jobs, which manifested itself in male workers refusing to talk to them, train them, or work with them; hiding their tools, being abusive and calling them names.[31] Now, after the war, they were viewed as opportunists who had ridden to economic freedom at the expense of the fighting man. Margaret Wynne Nevinson also divined that this anger at newly enfranchised women manifested itself in a darker way through an increase in violent domestic crimes against women,[32] although such violence against women was not unknown during the war.[33] Opposition to women taking their place in the employment market was supported after the war, particularly by the middle class. Those who could afford it still insisted that unmarried women should remain at home, on call, even where there were servants, as 'heaven-sent conveniences upon whom "duty" laid the combined functions of nurse, companion, secretary and maid-of-all-work'.[34]

With no women MPs, as yet, in the House of Commons to speak in defence of women's employment position, the women's movement had to ensure that it challenged the regressive effects of the Government's demobilisation policy. From 1915 on, the movement had been pressing for the equal representation of women on all reconstruction committees as a method of protecting women's post-war interests. This had set a precedent which the movement wished to continue, although there was still an evident reluctance to include women on government committees in anything like representative numbers. In 1918 women's groups were complaining that there were only three women on the advisory committee of the Ministry of Reconstruction, out of a total of 37 members.[35] It was Margaret Bondfield, trade unionist and Labour Party activist, who had sounded the alarm for industrial women in 1916, when she warned them that 'Women workers will be wise, however, not to depend too much on "paper patriots"; they must learn to take care of themselves, to fight their own battles'.[36]

The National Conference on War Service for Women in April 1915 had recognised the right of returning soldiers to take precedence over women who had taken the soldiers' place; however it also passed a resolution which sought to ensure that 'Women who are displaced in this way shall be guaranteed employment'.[37] But no such arrangements had been honoured by the Government. Mary Macarthur of the NFWW had been on that conference committee, and in November 1918, when the Woolwich munition workers were sacked, the NFWW responded with a spontaneous protest march through Whitehall. Mary Macarthur marched with the 6,000 women who came from Woolwich, one of the union's largest branches, and from other districts in London, the grounds for the march being that discharged women were only receiving 7s a week unemployment benefit. Others, such as the dock workers, had been dismissed with no notice or wages: regarded as casual workers, they were to receive no unemployment payment.[38] The women demanded action on the promised 20s unemployment donation which had still not been implemented. They made five other demands, the most important being that any unemployment donation should be backdated for all demobilised women workers. The Government responded by making 25 November the date for implementing its 20s donation.[39] The women's movement celebrated this victory with the NFWW; whilst viewing it as a 'triumph', they realised that it had only been a partial success, because their real demand was for 'work not doles'.[40] Although they wanted the interim award of unemployment benefit for women, what they really needed to establish for women's long-term prosperity and success was the principle that women were entitled to work as of right.

The NFWW followed this November success with a mass meeting in February 1919 at the Albert Hall on the Unemployment of Women. Charlotte Despard (WFL) and Susan Lawrence, the Labour Party member of the London County Council and Women's Trade Union League (WTUL) worker, addressed the meeting. The WFL, recognising the necessity for mass organisation, were keenly promoting a membership drive for women to join their trade unions, with the reminder that they must ensure that they were admitted on equal terms. The resolutions passed by the meeting concerned the right to work, the right to live and the right to leisure. The right to work was interpreted as the provision of suitable work; the right to live as an adequate living wage; and the right to leisure concerned the regulation of working hours.[41] However, the Government's interpretation of 'suitable' work for women at this time was a return to traditional female trades, and pre-eminent amongst these was domestic service. A large number of women had left domestic service to take up war work, and they were now expected to return to it. However, such work was also being offered to women who had no such previous experience and were in possession of completely different skills. Even worse was the offering of domestic posts by employment exchanges at pre-war wages and conditions, the final insult being that often women were expected to provide their own uniforms.[42]

The attempt to force women into such work was reinforced by the economic position in which they found themselves. Unemployment benefit for women was lower than that for men, and was further reduced in the spring of 1919 until it was barely sufficient to live on. But when it was discovered that women were refusing domestic work, a new rule was introduced which made such women ineligible for benefit. The only further recourse for such women was an appeal to the Court of Referees which operated on stringent, not to say punitive, grounds and was often taken to task for its treatment of female claimants in the pages of *The Labour Woman*.[43] The final insult was that if a woman succumbed to all this pressure and entered domestic service, she became ineligible for any future unemployment donation, as domestic service was one of only two categories not covered by insurance legislation. By instituting such regulations to serve its social policy, the Government was refusing to acknowledge exactly what the women's movement sought, the recognition of women's right to economic self-determination. Where women desired to continue a process which had begun before the war, and turn the temporary expedient operated during the war into accepted practice, the Government wanted women back in the home, their own or someone else's, depending upon their marital status and class position. What the movement had to do was to gain freedom of choice for women in employment opportunities. They attempted to achieve this by pressing for equal benefit entitlement, fair rates of pay, good working conditions and training schemes. By working for equal pay or improved wages, they wanted women to be in a position to support adequately themselves, and their dependents, if necessary. In such a way, they would be shedding the image of dependency and asserting their right to employment.[44]

A sub-committee of the women's advisory committee of the Ministry of Reconstruction, which was chaired by Susan Lawrence, had also written a report on the necessity for vocational training for women, at the end of 1918. They were particularly concerned about the lack of provision for widows, of which in the first six months of 1919 they estimated there to be approximately 190,000. On this matter the sub-committee followed the government line, stressing that this training should be extremely practical in order to fit the type of work where there were vacancies available.[45]

In contrast, one of the continuing demands of the movement was that training and education programmes should be provided for women on the same scale as it had for servicemen. The bone of contention was not so much the nature of the courses, but that insufficient funds had been made available to cater for the number of women who wished to take advantage of this re-training.[46] Making that level of funding available for women's training would have been an acknowledgement of women's right to access to state funding on a par with men, and provision of the kind of work which required training for every woman who wanted to work. The Government was not prepared to make either of those acknowledgments, and it had the excuse of an economic crisis to legitimate its refusal.

There was some dissension within the movement concerning support for the establishment of training programmes for domestic work, which brought together state funding and the residue of money from the wartime Queen's Work for Women Fund. These monies financed the Central Committee for Women's Training and Employment programmes which were all directed towards some form of 'housecraft' training. However, the position was a complex one, especially with the Government's insistence that the only abundant employment available for women was domestic work, and the desperate nature of women's unemployment. It was the necessity for pragmatism in hard times that brought about the acceptance of this expedient.[47] Organisations such as the NFWW, the WTUL,[48] the Fabian Society Women's Group (FSWG) and the LSWS were all concerned to raise the status of domestic work.

They maintained that domestic work was a highly skilled occupation which needed a range of expertise women ought to be trained for. This was a way of elevating what had always been regarded as unskilled labour into a skilled occupation. In turn, this meant that work which was broken down into separate skill levels became better paid and therefore more highly regarded. It was an ingenious attempt to combine a pragmatic stance of capitalising on available employment opportunities with elevating its status.

Three women from the FSWG, Marian Berry, Margaret McKillop and Lilian Dawson tried to take this one step further when they envisioned transforming domestic work into a profession by making it a public service which would be on offer to all classes. This level of training would raise its status and destigmatise it; as a 'profession' it would be better organised, and organisation would bring protection for its workers.[49] The NFWW's annual report at the end of 1919 gave details of a domestic workers' section which had been set up. Women who had previously been in the union as members of their local munition factory branch now transferred to this section and brought to it their union experience 'demanding a much greater amount of freedom and better wages and conditions than before'.[50] By the end of 1921 the domestic workers' section had continued to expand, and members were receiving job training, although frequently the poor working conditions which they still encountered acted as a reminder of the need for union organisation.[51]

For the women's movement to have refused to deal with the domestic service issue would have meant abandoning women who had no choice but to take such employment. These women were often living on as little as 7s a week under employers who were constantly attempting to raise their number of working hours. It was the stated role of women's organisations to improve women's lives by supporting women caught in that domestic service trap, as well as pressing the Government to introduce alternative measures. By the spring of 1919 the number of women's protests was rapidly increasing as official policy took effect. In March 1919 the SJCIWO sent a strong protest to the Government dealing with a number of items: its failure to provide alternative employment; the reduction of the benefit rate; the treatment of women through the Court of Referees; and the enforcement of inadequately paid work.[52] On 20 March, the Women's Industrial League (WIL) held a public meeting which demanded free access for women to all trades and professions, equal pay and representation on public committees. The speeches which were made on 'the economic liberty of women' were reported to have been received with great enthusiasm.[53] The protests went on, with the NFWW and the Association of Women Clerks and Secretaries (AWCS) leading a deputation to Bonar Law on 29 March 1919 to demand either suitable work or adequate maintenance payments.[54]

By April of that year, the Government had launched a programme enabling women to apply for training in any area which was not covered by the Treasury pledge. This pledge had been entered into by the Government, trade unions and employers during the war to protect their separate interests. This training programme resulted in the formation of the Central Committee for Women's Training and Employment (CCWTE); the Government contributed £50,000 towards women's training, with the proviso that the committee raised £100,000.[55] The initiative was regarded as totally inadequate by the women's industrial groups, who continued to lobby until they gained an extension of both time and money. Although these successes were small, they were helping to redress the balance to some extent. Women's groups were using their abilities to stem the flow of reaction as the LSWS had predicted was so necessary. They were also sustaining women's belief in themselves and their right to an economically independent future. Their sustained opposition was also acting as a barrier to policies which were curtailing all the economic progress which women had so far achieved.

The Pre-War Trade Practices Act

The first six months of demobilisation had largely affected industrial women workers. It was not until May 1919 that large numbers of professional women began to feel the pressure. The NUSEC was aware that women were insufficiently organised to withstand this onslaught, which became even more serious in June of that year with the introduction of the Pre-War Trade Practices Bill which had wide-reaching implications for all women in employment. By 2 June the bill had been rushed through its second reading and the women's movement had mobilised to resist it.

The bill was the legal fulfilment of the wartime Treasury agreement whereby employment practices in industry would be returned to their 1914 position. The bill ensured that it was illegal to employ women in any kind of engineering process or allied trade, whether skilled or unskilled, and on assembly work.[56] Apart from the loss of current and future employment opportunities, it meant a total disregard for all women's accumulated skills throughout the last four years. The Women's Engineering Society (WES) sought to challenge the bill, which was particularly injurious to the position of women in the engineering trades where many women had thrived during the war and gained great satisfaction from their new-found skills. In a period of redevelopment, when the country needed all its potential experience for the reconstruction process, women's contribution was being jettisoned. But in a wider political context it meant, as the WFL testified, 'a sinister attempt on the part of men trade unionists to legalise by Act of Parliament their pre-war practices of injustice to women'.[57] At a time when women had recently been accorded their political enfranchisement, it was a dangerous legislative development.

The Pre-War Trade Practices Bill had been dispatched with no attempt to include representative women in the consultation process; it was a further instance of the denial of women's right to be recognised seriously as valid contributors to the economic and political process. This was a position one woman had observed in February 1919 at the National Industrial Conference, where 'one had the feeling that to most of the speakers the question of women's work was a side issue'.[58] Part of the same process of denying women anything other than a supplemental role in the world outside the home, the new bill roused the full strength of the women's groups to defend their position:

> Women have opened the gate of opportunity, and they are not going to have it closed again. If we were equals and comrades during the war, we shall not rest as chattels and slaves after.[59]

The women's position, stated by Councillor Mrs Schofield Coates (WFL) embodied the League's policy. The league now proceeded to run a special campaign with open-air meetings in London parks, the distribution of propaganda at such venues as the Women's Co-operative Guild (WCG) Congress in Middlesborough and the Labour Party Conference in Southport. The Minister of Labour refused to see the League's deputation in July 1919, and they had to content themselves with sending him and the members of the House of Commons standing committee a written statement of their opposition.[60]

The women's service bureau, which was a part of the LSWS, and acted as an employment, training and advisory agency for women, was particularly active in opposition to the Bill. In June a letter of complaint regarding the manner in which the women's position had been discounted was sent to all MPs. Considering the Government's action 'unstatesmanlike', it condemned the attempt to deny women the right to choose their own work. It pointed out that in July 1918, out of the 792,000 women who had been employed in work covered by this bill, only 450,000 had been directly replacing men.[61] This was a vital point in the women's defence case. It underlined the fact that the process of dilution was being used as an excuse to impose wholesale bans on all types of employment for women except those regarded as 'women's work', in an attempt to return women to the home.

Ray Strachey, Parliamentary Secretary for the LSWS, having trained as an engineer at Oxford and helped to found the Society of Women Welders, took a great interest in this issue. She put forward the most common argument used by the movement, that most women worked for a livelihood and many had dependents: it was not a question of working for amusement. The LSWS and other groups were working on an amendment to the bill which would exclude new trades and processes from it, and state that sex alone should not operate to exclude a worker from employment. Strachey discovered on her return to London at the end of May that the Government was intending to put the bill through all its stages in one afternoon. Although it was not successful with this strategy, it did move quickly enough to make co-ordinated opposition by the women's organisations difficult. But the urgent work of Strachey and her secretary, Miss George, paid off to some extent when speeches she had written for two of the women's supporters, the MPs Acland and Major Wood, ensured a ten-day delay in the bill's proceedings. Although Strachey had been 'simply gasping with rage at not being able to make the speeches myself!'[62] One repercussion of this delay was that Strachey incurred the fury of the Labour Party, and she was certain that she had made some enemies for life in that camp.

The position of the Labour Party and the trade unions in relation to this bill, and their tradition of defence of women's rights, was a complex one. The trade unions were committed to the concept of a family wage, that it was a man's responsibility to maintain his wife and children. The Labour Party's relationship to the unions inevitably placed it in the position of sustaining this theory. But where did this leave the Labour Party in its defence of the position of women industrial workers when they were forced to support a policy which effectively undercut women's employment? To argue that by ensuring the safe employment position of men they were automatically protecting the financial position of the family and the women within it was simply not sustainable in the light of the post-war situation. It was a stick that *The Sunday Times* used to beat the Labour Party with in December 1918, when the restoration of the pre-war employment situation was under discussion: 'Advocating liberty for all, it is placing every conceivable obstacle in the path of the women who rendered victory possible'.[63] This also introduced a difficulty for Labour Party women who were in the position of defending women's need for an adequate standard of living, while remaining loyal to the class issues enshrined in Party policy. Although it should have provided no contradiction as:

> In the programme of the Labour Party the provision of adequate measures of social protection for those who are unable to protect themselves and are at the mercy of exploiters and profiteers of every kind is a feature. Many of these questions are of primary importance to women.[64]

This contradiction also impinged on the relationship between the industrial women's groups and the rest of the women's movement. The position in which Labour women now found themselves, having lost the independence of the separate women-only organisation of the Women's Labour League (WLL), was reported by the WFL from the Women's Section Conference of the Labour Party:

> It was very evident that the union of the Women's Labour League and the Labour Party was a marriage of the old sort – resulting in subservience and economic dependence of the wife. A certain enthusiastic section of the women were planning action to be endorsed by the Women's Conference, but the platform toned it down to a recommendation to the National Executive Committee of the Labour Party for their consideration. In reply to protests, their Chairman, Miss Lawrence, said: 'We cannot do anything of ourselves. We haven't the money'.[65]

It seemed that the misgivings voiced by some WLL members on their amalgamation into the Labour Party had been confirmed. Despite Margaret Bondfield and Miss Tynan being members on a joint committee from the National Industrial Conference, there had still been no consultation of Labour women as far as the new legislation was concerned. This 'burial' of women in the Labour and trade union movement was to arouse the antipathy of the non-party women and store up trouble for the future.

The women's societies had failed to halt the Pre-War Trade Practices Act or to introduce any amendments, but they had demonstrated once again that they were not prepared to tolerate such infringements of their liberty. It was also, as Ray Strachey attested, an episode through which more parliamentary experience was gained: 'I have... got further into the working of Parliament over this Bill than over any of the others'.[66]

The Attack on Government Employees

By the end of 1919 the steady decline in employment opportunities for women, with the attendant effect on women's lives, was increasing membership for women's employment organisations and other women's societies as women realised the value of representation and organisation. Affiliations between societies also grew and the AWCS recorded in their 1919 annual report their 'rapprochement' with manual workers in the spring and that they had begun to work with the NFWW, whilst their membership had doubled in that year.[67] In the early summer, together with the Federation of Women Civil Servants (FWCS) and the Civil Service Typists' Association (CSTA), the AWCS led a deputation to the Treasury to request employment concessions for clerical workers, and managed to have some of their requests conceded. The association had also begun to extend its participation in the women's movement by affiliating to the NUSEC.[68] Such new affiliations, made possible by the extension of the NUSEC's new constitution, had an invigorating effect on the NUSEC and demonstrated that young women who were 'keen and have definite views...'[69] were joining the movement.

In the latter part of 1919, the position of civil service employees came very much to the fore. The problems which were underlined by the demobilisation process for women civil servants represented the continuing employment battles which the women's movement had been dealing with for many years. The inequalities to which civil service women employees were subjected, and the ensuing campaign to combat them, were extremely complex; it is only necessary to outline the major features which had a bearing on the rest of the movement. This campaign assumed a high profile because the women's movement regarded the way in which the Government treated its own women employees as a reflection of its attitude towards the entire subject of women's employment. The issues which arose related to: the dismissal of trained and experienced female staff in preference to untrained men; equal pay; conditions of entry to the civil service; promotion opportunities; the type of work available to women; the employment of married women; and the representation of women on government committees which considered women's future employment conditions.

The nature of the demobilisation problem was different in the civil service because women had been established as permanent staff in the service for some years before the war. They had also been involved in ongoing disputes, such as equal pay, before the war. This was, therefore, unlike the position of women in engineering and the allied trades who had been accepted into non-traditional employment fields for women. However, in the civil service, large additional numbers of 'temporary' women workers had been recruited during the war. The problem was compounded in the demobilisation period by the differential treatment between the so-called 'temporary' staff and those regarded as permanent. It seemed that demobilisation was also being used as a way of imposing new conditions of service in order to undercut the position of the permanent women staff, or at the very least to impede their progress in the service. The women's groups were therefore attempting to defend both the rights of the temporary and the permanent staff. Peacetime and wartime issues had become interwoven in a complex web.

The basis for the defence of these temporary workers rested on arguments which were applicable to most other employed women. The women's advisory committee for the Ministry of Reconstruction in its interim report on women holding temporary appointments in government departments relayed a similar story to the industrial one. They stressed that these women were not, in the main, occupying reserved posts intended for ex-servicemen; rather the posts concerned new work entirely, or an extension of old work.[70] But little heed was paid to this information or the accompanying advice about the loss of skills and experience which would hinder service work, and large-scale dismissals went ahead.

Throughout the summer of 1919, resistance to the dismissal of women civil servants brought a good deal of customary abuse from the press, which christened these 'temporary' women workers 'Whitehall flappers' and 'chocolate dollies'.[71] In that November a protest meeting was held in London by the WIL, supported by the AWCS, on behalf of nearly 70,000 women clerks who had been dismissed without any financial or employment provision. Mrs Archdale (WIL) pointed out such jobs were being given to men regardless of their ability or training. This in turn forced women back into the sweated trades, with the consequent damage to their health, and the demand was made for the provision of adequate training to enable them to avoid such exploitation.[72] At another meeting on the training issue several days later, Lady Rhondda, President of the WIL, was reported as saying that 'the attitude of the Ministry of Labour appeared to be that there were only three forms of work available to women – tailoring, laundry work, and domestic service. The Ministry,' she added, 'must have been asleep during the war'.[73]

In the new year of 1920, the AWCS took up the case of over 700 War Office clerks who had returned to dismissal notices after the Christmas holiday. Their campaign took the form of a protest meeting followed by a deputation to Lloyd George with the intention of bringing new information to his attention. Representatives of several branches of the women's movement explained that these women had no unemployment donation, and many of them had no pre-war trade to fall back on. Any small income that some of them might have had was lost as a result of the war, and the possibility of support from male relations was also diminished. They protested that although the Civil Service Commissioners had orders only to employ ex-servicemen, there were many instances of men who had never been to war, or young men straight from school, being given these jobs. Women who had passed examinations were being replaced by men who had no qualifications or experience. The AWCS quickly made the connection:

> ... the 'fighting man' is made an excuse for the wholesale dismissal of women in favour of boys and men of any kind, just as 'patriotism' was made an excuse for persuading women to work for starvation salaries during the war.[74]

Without acknowledging the anomalies in the civil service hiring procedures which the women had detailed, Lloyd George launched into an attack on the very concept of employment equality and equal treatment, returning to the standard argument that employment for women is a part-time interim occupation until marriage, as opposed to the serious business of a career that it is for a man. He admonished the women's objective as wrong-headed, for 'anybody who places before women the prospect of absolute equality is doing something which is inconsistent with the nature of things'.[75] Jobs for returning heroes had been a convenient excuse to re-establish traditional practices to the satisfaction of employers and the unions and at the expense of women workers.

Whilst the 'temporary' clerks joined the sisterhood of the unemployed, the 'permanent' women civil servants were engaged in their own struggle. The matter of the re-grading of women in the civil service was being assessed by the re-organisation committee of the civil service national Whitley council. The Whitley councils had originated in 1916 to improve industrial relations between employers and employees. By 1920 there were 56 such joint councils, distributed among the different trades and occupations.[76] There was universal disapproval of this council by the women's movement as it was a board of civil servants – 'the very people whose vested interests would be upset by any changes'.[77] Although this re-organisation committee's brief was to discuss women's equality in the service, it included only four women among its 25 members. Its report, published in February 1920, set out five main provisions:

1 There would be a number of reserved places for women, whose appointment would be made by selection, not by competition as they were for male applicants.
2 Such positions would be in separate establishments.
3 The promotion procedure would also be separate from the men's.
4 There would be a different, and lower, pay scale.
5 All routine work on the lowest grade of writing assistant was to be allocated to women only.[78]

This latter provision, most indicative of all of the committee's bias, was rationalised as being work 'considered intolerable for men; women, it is said, suffer less from monotony owing to their capacity for leading a double life of phantasy'.[79]

Philipa Fawcett, the Secretary of the LSWS, had been a member of the women's advisory committee whose advice on 'temporary' women civil servants had been ignored, and now the LSWS was heavily committed to advancing the rights of the 'permanent' women staff. The LSWS reported that the Whitley council's recommendations could hardly be said to promote the concept of equality with which the women were concerned.[80] The movement united to fight against this principle of 'difference', and 1920 became almost the year of the civil service women. As Vera Brittain observed, the whole process constituted a 'degrading', as it effectively allocated all the higher grade posts to men.[81]

Marion Phillips wrote a report for the Labour Party executive on behalf of the SJCIWO, which strongly condemned the Whitley council's scheme:

This report makes proposals which so far as women are concerned are definitely retrograde and it appears likely that unless some strong protests are made by Labour this report will be accepted and the position will be worse than it is at present... (the report) cuts straight at the root of any attempt to get full equality.[82]

Women wanted to compete on a basis of equality with men, not on a separate road which invited the possibility of avenues of unequal and inferior treatment. This was a battle to be waged for all women workers, for as the LSWS perceived:

... so long as the wage is determined by the sex of the earner, both men and women workers will suffer, and from that suffering will spring increasing bitterness which will penetrate all classes of society and end by poisoning our national life.[83]

This equalitarian analysis of the feminist demand became applicable to many issues as the decade progressed.

A joint committee of organisations which had first met in 1919 now tackled the Whitley council's report. The committee consisted of 14 groups drawn from suffrage societies, professional associations and unions.[84] Although employing all the standard campaigning tactics, it placed its highest hopes on the amendment to the Sex Disqualification (Removal) Act[85] of 1919. This amendment guaranteed that any special regulation which concerned the admission of women to the civil service had first to be put before parliament for discussion. This, at least, guaranteed the joint committee an extension of time in which it could continue to press for change on the Whitley council's recommendations. However, as Zimmeck has described, the Treasury managed to totally circumvent the Sex Disqualification (Removal) Act, deciding that:

> As long as the 'spirit of the Act', providing an increased outlet for women, was observed, the Treasury could, it alleged, rightly retain 'a certain amount of discretion as to the manner in which that principle should be carried out'.[86]

The remainder of 1920 and 1921 witnessed the movement's consistent attack on these employment problems which were to remain on its agenda to some degree throughout the decade. In April 1920 the FWCS organised a Great Procession of Women Employees of National and Municipal Authorities which demanded equality of work, pay and opportunities and proved to be the year's campaigning highlight.[87] There were 3,000 women from all branches of the civil service, the suffrage societies and women's organisations in attendance, and the WFL maintained that 'Never since the height of the suffrage movement has such a procession of women been seen in the streets of London as that which marched from Hyde Park to Kingsway Hall...'[88]

The joint committee kept up the pressure throughout 1920 with ministerial deputations and another collective formed by the LSWS in May of that year, consisting of 20 women's organisations to deal with similar discontents experienced by women employed by the municipal authorities. The LSWS regarded the successful arrangement of these two committees as being 'an overwhelming testimony to the need of a non-party and non-sectional Society... to support the efforts of the women workers' own organisations'.[89] The National Union of Women Teachers (NUWT), which had campaigned steadily on equal pay since the early years of the century, worked with the LSWS on the municipal workers joint committee, as well as staging its own events as part of the municipal workers' campaign. An equal pay procession and rally in Trafalgar Square in November 1920 organised by the NUWT was also described as being reminiscent of the old suffrage marches.[90]

Although *Time & Tide* accused the older suffrage societies of continuing to use the traditional methods of 'educating by speech and propaganda' instead of using political action,[91] these 'old methods' still served a useful function for the movement. It was still important to keep women's issues in the public eye, and the publicity value of such events was no less important to this latest cause. Mass demonstrations had always consolidated and inspired the movement's membership, bearing witness to collective power and instituting confidence in their organisations, and in themselves. The FWCS saw the NUWT's November equal pay rally in this light, that 'Women themselves, perhaps, need to be reassured, by meeting together in their thousands, that the movement for equality is charged with more enthusiasm than ever before'.[92] The procession was also significant in that industrial and professional women were coming together to protest at a shared injustice.

Despite continued protest meetings and the sacrifices and persistence of the civil service women in the first half of 1921, no date had been set for the civil service changes to be debated by parliament. Women's unemployment continued to rise throughout the year, a year which was regarded by the LSWS as having 'something of a nightmare atmosphere'.[93] But August 1921 did yield a victory, when parliament finally debated the resolution drafted by the LSWS's joint committee concerning the Whitley council's report. By dint of the intense bombardment of MPs with information and propaganda by the movement in preparation for the debate, and with the support of their parliamentary friends, there was a large attendance in the Commons. Although the amendment was altered a great deal, several concessions were secured: that after a provisional period of three years, entry requirements for women would be the same as for men; that the conditions of service should be the same for women as for men; and that women's pay would be reviewed in three years' time.[94] With hindsight, this may seem to have been less a victory than a case of successful government procrastination. However, in such a hostile employment climate it was a considerable success which the women celebrated with enthusiasm. For it had, at the very least, used the provision of the Sex Disqualification (Removal) Act on the civil service to some good effect.

The Marriage Bar

There was little other cause for celebration in 1921 for the women's movement. The biggest blow that year was the escalation of the policy to get women out of the workplace and back to the home by the introduction of a marriage bar. The marriage bar was not a new strategy for controlling women's participation in the workplace: it had been in operation in some employment spheres since the latter part of the nineteenth century, as soon as large numbers of women began to enter traditional areas of male employment. In the Post Office it became customary from the 1870s that women would give up work on marriage, and the system was made official by 1894.[95]

In the autumn of 1921, the St Pancras Borough Council dismissed four women on their marriage. Dr Gladys Miall Smith's dismissal provoked the greatest outcry and sustained publicity as she was a Medical Officer of Health. The other three women were Mrs Reid, a baths attendant, Mrs Cook and Mrs Barrett, who were assistants at the Borough cleansing station.[96] These dismissals seemed nothing short of a flagrant breach of the 1919 Sex Disqualification (Removal) Act which had stated that neither sex nor marriage could be used to disqualify someone from employment. The WFL mounted a Married Women's Right to Work protest meeting on 25 November with Professor Winifred Cullis from the School of Medicine for Women, the lawyer Helena Normanton, Agnes Dawson (NUWT) and Professor Louise McIlroy, head of the women's unit of the Royal Free Hospital, as the main speakers. The right to marry was characterised as a basic human right and Professor McIlroy proposed that if the same rule had been applied to men 'there would have been a red revolution all over the country'.[97] A Conference of the Employment of Married Women followed in February 1922, called by seven of the leading women's organisations and attended by 34 societies.

Distressingly, this prohibition, which struck at the core of women's social condition, proceeded to gather momentum throughout the decade. As vehemently and vociferously as the women's movement campaigned for its removal, local authorities and other employers extended the bar against married women employees. The campaign against the marriage bar became, along with that for equal pay, one of the perennial issues of the 1920s and beyond.[98]

The Sisterhood of the Unemployed

Apart from the campaigns mounted for specific groups of women, a major preoccupation throughout the years from 1918 to 1922 was the campaign to improve conditions for all unemployed women. Their numbers increased and their benefits and training opportunities decreased as the four-year period progressed. Women's organisations were constantly proposing schemes and suggestions to the Government, as well as providing them with information and statistics, but none of these overtures was ever acknowledged.

The extreme economic crisis of 1922 brought the closure of the LSWS's women's employment bureau which had done so much to help address the issue of women's unemployment. During its last five and a half months in operation they had conducted 7,569 interviews with unemployed women, but had only been able to locate 566 vacancies. As the result of an urgent appeal, the LSWS was able to retain the training and general information section of the bureau so that at the very least it was able to refer women to possible sources of assistance.[99] Although the TUC report of September 1922 saw the Women Workers' Group, the Women's Department of the TUC and the SJCIWO all passing resolutions about training, women in the civil service and the employment of married women, by this stage 'The trade union movement was for the moment exhausted, and working class morale was being slowly sapped by unemployment and pauperisation'.[100]

Two major conferences on the subject of women and unemployment were held in 1922: one in February by the recently constituted Consultative Committee of Women's Organisations (CCWO) chaired by Nancy Astor, the first woman MP, the other by the Women Workers Group of the TUC in the following month. Both conferences were an urgent expression of the desperation of women's employment situation. By October 1921 unemployment for both men and women was at a record level, with 1,376,768 registered unemployed, besides the 395,000 who had exhausted their benefits and the unknown non-registered.[101] The worse men's unemployment became, the more desperate was women's position, as they suffered from the knock-on effect of more of their jobs being appropriated by men. By this time, even traditional 'women's work' was being adapted and given to disabled soldiers.[102] Nancy Astor was fighting for equal treatment for married women under the Unemployed Workers Bill. However, the ideal of female dependency was still current despite the fact that there were 200,000 war widows and 16,000 women whose husbands were severely disabled.[103]

The Conference of Unemployed Women held by the Women Workers' Group, as instructed by the general council, consisted of

234 delegates who were all unemployed. They covered a huge representative cross-section of women's employment, including chainmakers, cleaners, actresses and clerks. Margaret Bondfield chaired the meeting and a long list of speakers testified to their desperate financial suffering. Miss Froud (NUWT), Julia Varley (WWG) and Miss Maguire (AWCS, now affiliated to the SJCIWO), were some of the most well-known speakers. A deputation was sent from the conference to the Minister of Labour to plead the women's case, and at the close of the conference the women were urged not to rest until they had succeeded in getting the present Government out of office.[104]

The distinction between these two meetings marked the separation which began to take place between the non-party societies and those of the Labour and trade union movement. In 1920 the National Conference of Labour Women had passed a resolution concerning the need to gain extra power for the Labour Party and 'therefore urges all women in the industrial organisations to become members of the political Labour movement and to avoid dissipating their energies in non-party organisations'.[105] This endorsed the Labour Party's motive in annexing the WLL in 1918 to use the resulting Women's Sections to concentrate their efforts on strengthening the party. In 1921 the SJCIWO was invited by Nancy Astor to join the CCWO:

> ... but decided that it was not in accordance with the principles they had previously laid down with regard to non-party organisations, and therefore while expressing their readiness to co-operate for specific purposes, decided not to send representatives to the Committee.[106]

This was exactly why the non-party groups resisted any binding association with a political party, as it seemed almost inevitable that women's interests would become enveloped by the demands of party policy and the promotion of the party machine. Non-party groups could put women first, even if they were sacrificing the increased power which ought to have come from becoming part of the political establishment. Amalgamation with a male-dominated organisation was more likely to result in the fate which befell the NFWW:

> The most militant union in the history of women's organisations, which had existed for a mere 14 years and

organised more strikes than most unions do in a long history, became a 'submerged' district of the National Union. Far from the voice of women gaining the backing of a large industrial organisation, by 1930 it had been so effectively silenced that the National Union of General Workers did not send one woman delegate to the TUC conference that year.[107]

The women's movement had fought a long, hard battle on demobilisation with few major gains. But what might have been the long-term prospect for women's employment if it had not tenaciously defended every erosion of their hard-won advances? It had been important for women to make the point that their supposed position as dependents was in so many cases a practical impossibility and that, in addition, many women wanted to be economically independent. Also there had been some advances, as the WES noted:

> In the tumult of the present industrial upheaval it would seem almost impossible that any headway could be made in the establishing of women as engineers. Yet steady and substantial advance has been made during the past few months.[108]

Despite financial hardship, organisations continued to grow: the AWCS (which altered its initials to AWKS and adopted the bird of the same name as its emblem) alone, for instance, enrolled 8378 new members in 1921.[109]

While many Labour Party women believed that the principle of the vote having been won, it was now time to wage the fight of Labour against capital to achieve a socialist government, their suffrage sisters kept reiterating that those who believed that the fight was over were mistaken. The struggle was now on to keep 'the door open' and the optimism, despite the opposition of the past four years, was undaunted:

> The new girl, the new girl is steady, straight and strong,
> She knows she has a Union that is helping her along;
> She has a vote, she has a voice; MPs have cause to quake –
> When the Woman Clerk is speaking, 'Women, one and all awake!'[110]

Notes on Chapter 4

1   *The Woman Clerk*, March 1921, p 45
2   Seaman, L.C.B, *Post-Victorian Britain 1902-1951* (London, 1966, Methuen), pp 107-108
3   *Votes for Women*, 21 August 1914, front page
4   See Braybon, Gail, *Women Workers in the First World War* (London, 1981, Croom Helm) and Boston, Sarah, *Women Workers and the Trade Unions* (London, 1980, Davis-Poynter)
5   NFWW, Tenth Report for the Two Years Ended 31 December 1919, pp 12-13
6. *The Vote*, 8 March 1918, p 172
7   Mowat, Charles Loch, *Britain Between the Wars 1918-1940* (London, 1955, Methuen), pp 24 & 39
8   Seaman, L.C.B, *Post-Victorian Britain 1902-1951* (London, 1966, Methuen), p 108
9   Harrison, Brian, *Prudent Revolutionaries: Portraits of British Feminists Between the Wars* (Oxford, 1987, Clarendon Press), p 1
10 NUSEC, Annual Report, 1919, p 28
11 Quill, Gary, *The Labour World*, 26 October 1918, Gertrude Tuckwell Collection, 703/8
12 *The Position of Women*, SJCIWO, p 20
13 *The Vote*, 5 April 1918, p 207
14 *International Woman Suffrage News*, January 1919, p 50; LSWS Annual Report, 1918-1919, p 15; *The Common Cause*, 7 March 1919, p 565
15 *The Common Cause*, 6 June 1919, p 84
16 Zimmeck, Meta, 'Strategies and strategems for the employment of women in the British civil service 1919-1939' in *Historical Journal*, 27/4, p 910
17 FWCS, 'Equality' in *Association Notes*, January-March 1920, front page
18 Masson, Rosaline, 'Dark Stars (Unpaid) II. Unmarried' in Spender, Dale, *Time & Tide Waits for No Man* (London, 1984, Pandora Press), p 199
19 Gates, G. E., *The Woman's Year Book 1923-24* (London, 1924, Women Publishers Ltd for NUSEC), p 42
20 *The Common Cause*, 14 November 1919, p 392
21 WFL, Annual Report, April 1922-April 1923, p 6
22 LSWS, Annual Report, 1919-1920, p 7
23 'Premier's promise to women workers' in *The Daily*

Chronicle, 10 December 1918, Gertrude Tuckwell Collection, 702a/2; *The Vote*, 29 November 1918, p 475

24 McFeely, Mary Drake, *Lady Inspectors: the Campaign for a Better Workplace 1893-1921* (Oxford, 1988, Basil Blackwell), p 147

25 Boston, Sarah, *Women Workers and the Trade Unions* (London, 1980, Davis-Poynter), p 137

26 Graves, Robert & Hodge, Alan, *The Long Weekend, A Social History of Great Britain 1918-39* (London, 1985, Hutchinson), p 27

27 *International Woman Suffrage News*, January 1920, p 52

28 Brittain, Vera, *Testament of Youth: An Autobio-graphical Study of the Years 1900-1925* (London, 1978, Victor Gollancz), p 490

29 LSWS, Annual Report, 1919, p 17

30 An example of such praise appeared in *The Great War*, 3 November 1917, p 191: 'Women and girls who sacrificed one of the possessions a woman holds dearest – namely, her physical beauty – to dabble in dangerous, noxious commodities which stained her skin and hair and undermined her health at the same time. All these workers who worked thus loyally were national heroes no less than those who fought in the field of battle.'

31 See Braybon, Gail, *Women Workers in the First World War* (London, 1981, Croom Helm) and Marwick, Arthur, *Women at War 1914-18* (London, 1977, Fontana).

32 Nevinson, Margaret Wynne, *Life's Fitful Fever: A Volume of Memories* (London, 1926, A & C Black), p 278

33 The United Suffragists ran a regular feature in *Votes for Women* in which they contrasted light and heavy sentencing policy; invariably, crimes against women carried out by serving members of the military forces were given light or negligible sentences. See *Votes for Women*, 26 February 1915, p 183

34 Brittain, Vera, *The Women at Oxford* (London, 1960, George G. Harrap), p ix

35 They were Lady Emmott (LSWS), Gertrude Tuckwell (WTUL/NFWW) and Eleanor Barton (WCG). *The Vote*, 8 March 1918, p 172

36 Bondfield, Margaret, *A Life's Work* (London, 1950, Hutchinson), p 256

37 War Emergency: Workers National Committee, National

Conference on War Service, p 2

38   *The Labour Woman*, December 1918, p 95

39   Ibid.
      Sylvia Pankhurst congratulated the women on their action
      and thought it a sure sign of the emergence of 'workers' con-
      trol. *The Workers Dreadnought*, 23 November 1918, p
      1134

40   NFWW, Annual Report for the Two Years ended 31
      December 1919, p 13

41   *The Vote*, 11 April 1919, p 148

42   WES, Minute Book, 15 May 1919; *The Labour Woman*,
      April 1919, p 29; *The Common Cause*, March 1919, p 36

43   *The Labour Woman*, March 1919, p 36

44   LSWS, Annual Report, 1917-18, pp 12-13 had outlined that
      there was 'in these circumstances an opportunity for
      vigorous and constructive work in the defence of women's
      right to work'.

45   *International Woman Suffrage News*, January 1919, p 50

46   Gates, G. E. (ed.), *The Woman's Year Book 1923-24*
      (London, 1924, Women Publishers Ltd for the NUSEC),
      p 352; TUC Report 1922, pp 217-218

47   LSWS, Annual Report, 1919-1920, p 14; LSWS, Annual
      Report, 1922, p 8; Gates:*The Woman's Year Book*, p 352

48   The WTUL became the Women Workers' Group of the TUC
      in 1922

49   *The Common Cause*, 27 December 1918, p 441

50   NFWW, Annual Report for the Two Years Ended December
      31 1919, p 16

51   NUGW, Women Workers' Section First Report for the Year
      Ended December 21 1921, p 26

52   *The Labour Woman*, April 1919, pp 39-40

53   *The Common Cause*, 28 March 1919, p 615

54   AWCS, Annual Report, 1919, p 2

55   Gates, G. E. (ed.), *The Woman's Year Book 1923-24*
      (London, 1924, Women Publishers Ltd for the NUSEC), p 353

56   LSWS, Annual Report, 1919, p 11

57   *International Woman Suffrage News*, July 1919, p 137

58   *The Common Cause*, 7 March 1919, p 568

59   WFL, Annual Report, May 1919-April 1922, p 4

60   *International Woman Suffrage News*, July 1919, p 137;
      International Woman Suffrage News, August 1919, p 154

61   Section on the Pre-War Practices Bill, Folder 2, 1919, Smith
      Collection, Oxford, pp 3-5,

62 Ibid., p 18
63 'The Woman's Lead' in *The Sunday Times*, 8 December 1918, 702a/1, Gertrude Tuckwell Collection, p 6
64 *The Labour Woman*, April 1918, p 282
65 *The Vote*, 4 July 1919, p 245
66 Folder 2, 1919, Smith Collection, Oxford, p 18
67 AWCS, Annual Report, 1919, p 2
68 AWCS, Annual Report, 1919, p 3
69 NUSEC, Annual Report, 1919, p 42
70 Ministry of Reconstruction, women's advisory committee, report of the sub-committee to consider the position after the war of women holding temporary appointments in Government departments, Section 1
71 *The Common Cause*, 11 November 1919, 702a/13, Gertrude Tuckwell Collection; *The Woman Clerk*, December 1919, p 2
72 'Discharged woman clerks' in *The Times*, 19 November 1919; 'Women in Whitehall' in *The Morning Post*, 20 November 1919, 702a/13, Gertrude Tuckwell Collection
73 *The Morning Post*, 29 November 1919, 702a/14, Gertrude Tuckwell Collection
74 *The Woman Clerk*, January 1920, p 15
75 *The Woman Clerk*, February 1920, p 33
76 Mowat, Charles Loch, *Britain Between the Wars 1918-1940* (London, 1955, Methuen), p 37
77 LSWS, Annual Report, 1919-1920, p 8
78 Ibid., pp 8-9
79 Brittain, Vera, *Women's Work in Modern England* (London, 1928, Noel Douglas), p 119
80 LSWS, Annual Report, 1919-1920, p 8
81 Brittain, Vera, *Women's Work in Modern England* (London, 1928, Noel Douglas), p 119
82 Phillips, Marion, *Women in the Civil Service and the Whitley Council: Report for the Executive of the Labour Party*, March 1920, p 1
83 LSWS, Annual Report, 1919-1920, p 8
84 LSWS, Annual Report, 1919-1920, p 9. Some of the organisations were the NUSEC, NCW, AHM, FBUW, FWCS, AWCS
85 See Chapter 9 for a full account of this legislation.
86 Zimmeck, Meta, 'Strategies and strategems for the employment of women in the British civil service 1919-1939' in *Historical Journal*, 27/4, pp 901-924
87 'Equality Supplement' in FWCS Association Notes, January-

March 1920

88   *The Vote*, 7 May 1920, p 42. Some of the organisations represented were the WFL, the NFWT, the LSWS, the NUSEC, the CWSS, the AWCS

89   LSWS, Annual Report, 1919-1920, p 12

90   Phipps, Emily, *History of the NUWT* (London, 1928, NUWT), p 60

91   *Time & Tide* 25 February 1921 quoted in Spender, Dale, *Time & Tide Wait for No Man*, (London, 1984, Pandora Press), p 173

92   FWCS, Association Notes, October 1920, p 270

93   LSWS, Annual Report, 1921, p 6

94   LSWS, Annual Report, 1921, pp 9-11

95   Clinton, Alan, 'Women and the union of postal workers' in *Post Office Workers: A Trade Union and Social History* (London, 1984, Allen & Unwin), p 426

96   *The Vote*, 2 December 1921, front page

97   Ibid.

98   The marriage bar was finally abolished for teachers in 1944. In October 1946 the Labour Party abolished it for the whole of the civil service. Although there were variations in practice; my mother worked in the civil service and had to ask her manager's permission to get married in 1939 to ensure that she could continue to work after marriage.

99   LSWS, Annual Report, 1922, pp 11-12

100   Seaman, L.C.B, *Post-Victorian Britain 1902-1951* (London, 1966, Methuen), p 146

101   *The Vote*, October 28, 1921, p 658

102   McFeely, Mary Drake, *Lady Inspectors: The Campaign for a Better Workplace, 1893-1921* (Oxford, 1988, Basil Blackwell), p 149

103   Folder 2, 1919, Smith Collection, Oxford, p 15

104   'Conference of Unemployed Women' in *The British Trades Union Review*, April 1922, Vol III, No 9, pp 9-13

105   Report of the National Conference of Labour Women, 21-22 April, 1920

106   SJCIWO, Report, 1921, J.S. Middleton Collection, p 2

107   Boston, Sarah, *Women Workers and the Trade Unions* (London, 1980, Davis-Poynter), p 150

108   *The Woman Engineer*, March 1921, 1/6, p 55

109   AWCS Annual Report, January 1920-March 31 1921, p 2

110   'The Old Order Changeth' in *The Woman Clerk*, August 1921, front page

Chapter 5
Legislative Campaigning

Any historian recording women's struggle for equal opportunities... has to leave the neatly-defined realms of legislation for a complex scene in which custom and prejudice decide the rate of advance.[1]

There was a vast catalogue of legislative reform planned by the women's movement for the years from 1918 to 1922. Apart from the primary concern of franchise extension, the issues requiring legislation fell broadly into three categories: those pre-war issues which had been exacerbated by the war and had a high priority, such as housing, infant mortality, maternity welfare, the equal moral standard and equal pay. Second, were those issues arising from the war such as the representation of women in the peace process, the nationality of married women and the continuation of a women's police force. The final category included those demands which had gained significance since the franchise achievement concerning the equal guardianship of children, the rights of married women, income tax and married women's property, endowments for mothers, widows' pensions, access to the legal profession and public service professions.

Whatever the campaign, an important element dominating the movement's attempts to claim equality for women was the scale of the prejudice which fuelled the opposition to attempted reforms. Lady Rhondda (Margaret Haig) maintained that after the war the women's movement was engaged in two battles, to achieve legislative progress for women and to change public opinion.[2] Indeed, it was the barrier of public prejudice which provided the original motivation for Rhondda establishing her paper, *Time & Tide*, in May 1920 as a vehicle for change.

The very nature of the prejudice made it difficult to counteract. Vera Brittain understood that 'Much less responsive to revolutionary pressure are personal and social competition, economic status, moral tradition, and long-accepted habits which Virginia Woolf once called "tough as roots but intangible as sea-mist"'.[3] Combating such prejudice was rendered more complex because the movement was fighting on so many fronts. In 1919 the National Union of Societies for Equal Citizenship (NUSEC) prioritised its three major areas of concern as promoting women's participation in the Peace Conference and the League of Nations, gaining new legal rights for women and alleviating the employment problems of demobilisation. Additionally, it had numerous other items on its agenda but was aware that with 'the present deplorable attitude towards women... The public need education in sex equality quite as urgently as they did before the vote was won.'[4]

Such prejudice may have come as a shock to many women who imagined that their war-time contribution and partial enfranchisement had placed them within striking distance of total emancipation. Such continued antagonism heightened awareness of the necessity to extend the franchise to the 6 million women excluded from the 1918 legislation as the only way of ensuring equality. Despite the climate of opposition, the movement was optimistic about the feasibility of gaining entry to professions now closed to women. This confidence had been encouraged by an electoral statement signed by Lloyd George and Bonar Law as part of the Coalition Government's election manifesto in November 1918 which declared that 'It will be the duty of the New Government to remove all existing inequalities of the law as between men and women'.[5] The Women's Freedom League (WFL) was not going to allow Lloyd George to forget this declaration and printed it monthly, bannerlike, on the front of its paper *The Vote*, and announced that, 'Our new power, we have been urged to use, is a power to be reckoned with; no longer can women be pushed on one side as negligible'.[6] This was another reminder to Lloyd George of his 1918 general election speech to a woman-only audience that women's equality would only be achieved if they demanded it through the use of their vote. The WFL fully intended to use his advice as a stick to beat the Government with.[7]

Campaigns of 1918

Apart from the campaign to enable women to stand as prospective parliamentary candidates, there were two other struggles occupying women's groups during the course of 1918 which had successful outcomes. The first protest was a continuation of the equal moral standard campaign and concerned the sanctioning by the British military authorities of 'tolerated brothels' for the use of British soldiers in France and the army's issuing of prophylactics to soldiers. The movement did not share the opinion of the Under-Secretary for War that it was a good thing to provide 'clean women' to satisfy 'human nature', and a mass meeting called by the Association for Moral and Social Hygiene (AMSH) in March 1918 called for a single moral standard for men and women.[8] Less than a month after the start of the campaign the Government announced that British soldiers were now forbidden to visit such brothels. *The International Woman Suffrage News* pointed out triumphantly that 'Josephine Butler had to work 17 years for the abolition of regulation in garrison and seaport towns. Now that women have votes things move more quickly.'[9]

The second successful campaign concerned equal pay. At the beginning of March the Board of Education recommended to local authorities a differentiation in salaries for elementary school teachers, with higher pay scales for men. Having only a few days to act before the London County Council (LCC) met, the National Federation of Women Teachers (NFWT), supported by the WFL, launched a protest against the differentiated pay scale. As a result, the LCC rejected the Board of Education's recommendation and the women's movement proceeded to challenge the new Education Bill, which also sought to establish unequal pay scales. This campaign was strategically important because it was an example of the indivisibility of the women's struggle, enabling success by one group to induce a sense of achievement among them all at a time when women were looking forward to protecting their wartime gains.

The Legislative Agenda

Post-1918 legislative gains by no means embraced all the provisions which the women's movement sought, nor were they achieved without a great deal of persistent effort over many years. As the Birmingham Society for Equal Citizenship and Women's Citizens' Association reported at the end of 1920:

> ... we still find, as we expected, that sex disabilities and injustices do not quickly fall to the sound of feminist trumpets, but must be patiently undermined and destroyed, albeit with far more effective instruments than of old.[10]

Legislation such as the Maternity and Child Welfare Act of 1918, for instance, was the result of long years of work by and on behalf of women originating with the infant mortality movement at the end of the nineteenth century.

One such piece of legislation which fell far short of the movement's expectations was the Sex Disqualification (Removal) Act, which became law on 23 December 1919. It provided for the admission of women to the legal profession, the eligibility of women householders for jury service and extended entrance to the civil service. However, the opening statement of the act also seemed to offer leverage for future campaigns, specifying that:

> A person shall not be disqualified by sex or marriage from the exercise of any public function, or from being appointed to or holding any civil or judicial office or post, or from entering or assuming or carrying on any civil profession or vocation.[11]

The act had originated as an opposition Emancipation Bill to extend the franchise to all women, and had been hijacked and emasculated by the Government.[12] It was hardly surprising that women's organisations were less than enthusiastic about it despite their appreciation that the act opened more doors to women. In the ensuing years women wrote with barely concealed contempt and dissatisfaction about the act when its limitations manifested themselves with dispiriting regularity.

Major Hills, a Coalition Unionist, and Lord Robert Cecil, an Independent Conservative, gained some improvements to the act, one of which was an amendment enabling Oxford and Cambridge

Universities to award degrees to women. Previously women could follow courses at these universities but were not entitled to degree status even if they had attained the required standard. Oxford now chose to allow women entry to all degrees, apart from those of Bachelor of Divinity and Doctor of Divinity. Vera Brittain realised that 'The national changes which had given women the vote, and made them eligible for Parliament, spared the University authorities any disturbing suspicion that their revolutionary behaviour was, in fact, revolutionary'.[13]

Other legislative campaigns of the early 1920s which met with repeated rebuffs reinforced the movement's fears that 'our work for equality is not yet at an end'.[14] The campaign to gain entry into the legal profession predated the provisions of the 1919 Sex Disqualification (Removal) Act and had been on the WFL and the NUWSS's programmes from the beginning of 1918. Activists such as Helena Normanton (WFL) had tried throughout 1918 to gain admission to the Middle Temple to study law. The NUSEC relaunched its campaign for the Women Solicitors' Bill in spring 1919 as the WFL lobbied for support, and with little tangible progress recorded, the WFL was pushing the Government to enable the Barristers' and Solicitors' (Qualification of Women) Bill to become law.[15] Eventually, legislation authorising women to enter the legal profession came into force with the 1919 act. The continuous pressure of the women's groups ensured the inclusion of those measures in the act and certainly prepared the ground for an acceptance of the concept of women in the legal profession.

As well as the creation of new rights, campaigns sometimes sought to re-establish lost ground, as with the nationality of married women. Until 1870 a woman who married a foreigner retained her own nationality, but in that year the law was changed forcing a woman to take the nationality of her husband.[16] This legislation echoed the concept of coverture, the loss of legal identity on marriage, which the women's movement had resisted for decades. Their new legal status caused great distress to British women married to men regarded as enemy aliens during the war,[17] and the post-war consequences were little better:

> Her property may be confiscated to pay the war debts owing by the enemy state to her own land of birth. In other words, the British government has seized the British property of 2000 British-born women because Germany went mad in 1914. It would be humorous if it were not so tragic.[18]

This issue was addressed through the British parliament but also via the League of Nations and the International Woman's Suffrage Alliance, as it affected women throughout the British Empire.[19] Although the Government promised a committee of enquiry in 1918, by 1935 the indignities persisted, as experienced by Ray Strachey's (LSWS) daughter, Barbara. Having married a foreigner and automatically taken on his status, she had to obtain a visa in order to remain in Britain![20]

During the immediate post-war years a pattern emerged in the movement's method of effecting the introduction of legislation into parliament. Organisations with specific legislative goals, such as the National Council for the Unmarried Mother and her Child (NCUMC), took responsibility for drafting a proposed bill and taking the preliminary initiative. Often, a large organisation such as the NUSEC would make the preliminary moves or the NUSEC would take over a bill when a smaller group like the NCUMC enlisted its support if its own first attempt had not succeeded. The NUSEC could then use its larger resources, enlisting its affiliates and other sections of the movement to contribute their expertise in promoting the bill.

Diana Hopkinson outlined the process which her mother, Eva Hubback, used as parliamentary secretary of the NUSEC.

> Before the new legislation could be placed on the statute book, a long and laborious campaign had to be planned. In the first place, Eva was responsible for informing the local societies about the proposed changes, and for collating the suggestions that came from them. She had to make provincial journeys to speak at meetings of the societies and of other sympathetic organisations. At these meetings she heard women's opinions on the necessary changes in the law and collected the case histories of those who suffered under its existing form. When she felt sufficiently knowledgeable... she summarised the information. With the help of lawyers and one or more Members of Parliament... she drafted the relative Parliamentary Bill.[21]

Having completed the drafting stage and organised supporters in the House of Commons, the next step was a campaign to put pressure on the Government to introduce a bill. More usually, a supporter in the Commons would try and draw a slot to introduce a private member's bill. This was a route strewn with obstacles, with minimal chances of success. However, the process enabled the societies to create an opportunity to propagandise the House and attest to existing public feeling on the subject while attracting publicity and support to exert pressure on the Government. It gained maximum attention, putting the subject on parliament's and the public's agenda. With only two women MPs and no women in the Lords, it also provided a means for women to access and utilise the political machinery.

One such long-running battle to effect favourable legislation concerned the attempted establishment of an equal moral standard for men and women, in a campaign to repeal legislation relating to the control of vice and prostitution. The women's societies hopes that Regulation 40D of the Defence of the Realm Act would be repealed immediately after the armistice failed to materialise. Alison Neilans of the AMSH relaunched the wartime opposition campaign in November 1918 with a joint protest meeting in London attended by members of 54 organisations.[22] In the spring of 1920, the AMSH issued guidelines for the use of feminist societies which recommended them to oppose any legislation containing tenets:

a) which make of women, or of any women a special class liable to special penalties, or special health regulations.
b) which tend to place women under police control other than that commonly exercised over all persons equally.
c) which permit either police or medical officers to enforce compulsory medical examination of women for venereal disease.[23]

In the summer of 1920 three bills relating to the equal moral standard claimed the movement's attention: the Criminal Law Amendment Bill (No. 1) of the Bishop of London, raising the age of consent for girls from thirteen to eighteen; the Criminal Law Amendment Bill (No. 2) from the Home Office introducing compulsory 'rescue' homes; and a Sexual Offences Bill.[24] After considerable protests by representatives of over 58 women's organisations, for the strength of feeling on this issue was as marked as ever, a government bill was introduced in 1922. It was 'nursed' through its parliamentary stages by a joint committee of five women's organisations and supported by the MP Margaret Wintringham. The Criminal Law Amendment Bill became law at the end of July, raising the age of consent to sixteen. Although far from securing all the conditions desired by the women's societies, it did provide a measure of protection for young girls.[25]

There were three major pieces of welfare legislation which the women's societies tried to introduce during this period: pensions for civilian widows with children, the Equal Guardianship of Children Bill, later the Guardianship of Infants Bill, and the Bastardy Bill, which later became the Children of Unmarried Parents Bill. Even a brief outline of their parliamentary progress serves to highlight this arduous process and the problems accompanying the movement's attempts to press for women's reforms.

Women's groups were concerned that civilian widows had to face identical problems to servicemen's widows of trying to support a family under the post-war rise in the cost of living and a lack of suitable employment. Unlike servicemen's widows with children, civilian widows had no pension. The NUSEC had drawn up a bill in 1919, but it was not until 1920 that the Labour Party, supported by Nancy Astor, introduced the bill into the Commons.[26] The Government contested that the country could not afford to implement the measure because of enormous war debts and the economic crisis.[27] By 1921, after three years of work, the NUSEC conceded the Government's justification, although it reiterated its concern that such economies were being made at the expense of society's most disadvantaged sector, children.[28] The NUSEC did not abandon the campaign but continued lobbying in order to build support for a more auspicious opportunity.

In 1919, the NUSEC also completed its preparations for the Equal Guardianship of Children Bill to award the mother the same rights and responsibilities as the father. In July 1920, it was introduced as a private member's bill but having passed its second reading and been referred to a standing committee, it 'died' at the end of the parliamentary session.[29] Reintroduced in 1921 as the Guardianship of Infants Bill, it was lost because of the large number of amendments which had the effect of making the bill too controversial to stand any chance of becoming law.[30] There were many ways to obstruct women's progress, and when the WFL reported on the 'wrecking' of three of the women's legislative hopes in 1921, it saw the only remedy to such government tactics as 'that of extending the suffrage to women on equal terms with men, and of securing a far greater number of women in Parliament'.[31]

The NCUMC Bastardy Bill, which it introduced in May 1919, suffered the same fate. It was concerned with the payment of maintenance to support the illegitimate child and to ensure that the child should become legitimate on the subsequent marriage of the parents. Although it passed its second reading with a large majority, the standing committee managed to nullify most of its major provisions and what remained failed to complete all stages before the end of the parliamentary session. In 1920 the NUSEC took it over and redrafted it, basing it on the Bastardy Bill but calling it the Children of Unmarried Parents Bill.[32] By 1921 it still had not found a place in the ballot and the NUSEC decided to support a similar proposal which had. This measure passed twice through all stages in the Commons but was eventually thrown out by the Lords. There was no capitulation on the part of the women's movement, and the NCUMC formed a joint consultative committee of groups wishing to continue work on the parliamentary campaign.[33]

In the face of so so many defeats Ray Strachey surmised that:

> It is a question of tactics. Some cry, 'all or nothing,' and it is only too likely that 'nothing' will be the result. A study of Parliamentary tactics is to be recommended to those who speak for the organised women today.[34]

But even skilful tactics and support were no guarantee of enduring success. There were several instances where progress had seemingly been achieved, yet women found themselves waging the struggle repeatedly to sustain that progress. Two notable examples during this period were those of women jurors and women police. The Sex Disqualification (Removal) Act had made provision for women to become jurors operational from the beginning of 1921.[35] Almost immediately, opposition to women jurors began to manifest itself, and the act enabled such prejudice to take a tangible form. The act gave judges and local councils the power to exclude women jurors from the courts by appointing men-only juries. The reverse case was also possible but it was always the refusal of female jurors which was operated. The justification for this exclusion was that women's delicacy and sensitivity made them unsuited to the rigours of the kind of evidence which many cases involved. The option not to use women jurors was invariably exercised in cases such as those involving sexual attacks on women and young girls, incest and divorce, where the defendants were predominantly male. Elizabeth Macadam of the NUSEC felt that:

The motive for this campaign is not too difficult to penetrate, but disguised as it has been beneath a cloak of professedly chivalrous desire to protect women from hearing unpleasant details, shocking to their delicate susceptibilities, it has succeeded in awakening some sympathy among the less thoughtful and more sentimental sections of the public.[36]

But it was precisely in such cases that the women's societies felt that women jurors should be present.

Margaret Nevinson (NUSEC), the first woman Justice of the Peace in London, wrote of the country which had drawn up the Magna Carta yet failed to see the illogicality of its position with regard to women and the law. Until 1919, it had been men who 'take them, handle them, try them, sentence them, imprison them (without one woman present, not even in the jury), even hang them by the neck until they are dead'.[37] Now there were men trying to perpetuate that unrepresentative system.

By the summer of 1921, two male MPs were attempting to nullify the legislation relating to a woman's right to serve as a juror, suggesting that women's jury service should become optional and there should be a referendum of women on the subject. The NUSEC began a campaign to defend the position of women jurors, drafting a Women Jurors' Bill which aimed to redress the exclusion provision of the Sex Disqualification (Removal) Act and to enable more women to sit on juries.[38] At its 1921 conference, the WFL called upon the Government to pass an amendment to the act and to bring about the reforms demanded by the NUSEC with special emphasis on establishing equal numbers of women jurors.[39] There was no further legislative success, and the discriminatory provisions against women jurors were added to the movement's reform agenda.

Another manifestation of prejudice found in the legal world was directed at women police. After the war, in November 1918, in recognition of the valuable work which women police had performed during the war, a group of 100 women was chosen by the Metropolitan Police as an experimental force. Known as the women patrols, they were under the command of a Mrs Feo Stanley. Lilian Wyles recorded the reception which the women had received in 1918 from their male colleagues:

... they proclaimed their distaste of the idea loudly and forcibly. That the Home Secretary and the Commissioner must be completely deranged, they were certain... Women to invade the Police Force: it was laughable; it was grotesque.[40]

Although women had 'stormed' another male stronghold, it was by no means a complete victory. The reservation was made that the women patrols were only an experiment, and if the experiment failed (what constituted failure was not made clear), they would be disbanded. Gradually the work of the women patrols was extended and although the hostility of their colleagues was much in evidence, their work was enormously appreciated by women. By 1922 women officers were dealing with the majority of sex offences, escorting women prisoners, caring for attempted suicides and many other aspects of welfare work related to women and children.[41] However, in February 1922, the first part of the committee on national expenditure's work, the Geddes Report, was published. In the light of the country's financial crisis its remit was to recommend cuts in public expenditure. One of the savings it suggested was the disbanding of the women police patrols. Interestingly, no women had been involved in contributing evidence to the Geddes committee.[42]

An immediate campaign was launched by the National Council of Women (NCW), with Nancy Astor and Margaret Wintringham fronting the parliamentary fight. A deputation to the Home Secretary on 20 March 1922 supported by 59 women's societies testified to the appreciation of the valuable work performed by the women police.[43] The Home Secretary demonstrated the kind of prejudice directed at women's issues faced when he defined the women's work as welfare work, not police work. As such, he could not justify spending public money designated for police work to fund the continuation of the women patrols.[44] This was a classic devaluation of women's work which derived from the tradition of welfare work being voluntary in nature and performed by women. It used male criteria to establish a code of societal values and was indicative of the continuing failure of parliament and the Government to place women and children's issues on the nation's agenda. In the face of such a dismissive attitude towards women's welfare issues, the fate of the three welfare bills can be better understood.

Yet again, the women's movement refused to yield, despite the fact that the dismissals had already taken place. It was now a double battle of reinstatement and retention, a more difficult position to be fighting from. But the campaign continued, and by June 1922 a measure of success was achieved when it was announced that a force of 20 women would be retained within the metropolitan force.[45] This was sufficient to sustain the principle of women police, and for the remainder of the decade Nancy Astor in particular worked for the expansion, improvement and consolidation of the concept of a women's police force. The issue of women police was important for several other reasons, not only to open up another employment opportunity for women but to prove women's ability and desire to be competent in traditional male occupations, within the normal demands of peace time. The concept of women being able to work within the most unpleasant and dangerous conditions could contribute towards dispelling the traditional Victorian image of womanhood. It was also an example of women's progress from the voluntary to the professional sector, which was part of the 1920s movement's goal to upgrade the status of women's work to give them credibility on a broader scale within society.

There were also two issues in the medical world which were of concern to the women's movement at this time: the lack of representation of women on hospital governing boards, campaigning on which was part of the wider campaign to increase women's representation on all public bodies, and the training of women doctors. The latter was another example of regressive action, where hospitals which had opened their doors to female medical students during the war were reversing the decision by 1921 with the excuse that it had only been a wartime expedient. As with women jurors, the decision was based on the grounds of 'delicacy'. Again, what was particularly worrying was the spreading revival of bars on women from the professions and public involvement in society, which left women to restage a battle which they had imagined had been won. This was why the Sex Disqualification (Removal) Act was so important, and why the women's organisations' disillusion with it became so great when it repeatedly failed to do its job and, more disturbingly, when it actually served to undermine the position of women.

Helena Normanton (NUSEC) expressed much of the anger and sense of betrayal which was felt in the movement when in the late spring of 1921 a government paper was published which set out further restrictions relating to the Civil Service's employment of women. All diplomatic and consular posts were reserved for men, and this also applied to government appointments made in Britain to the colonies. Women were barred from the Indian Civil Service and, finally, all vacancies in the Trade Commissioner Service and the Commercial Diplomatic Service, with the exception of some chief clerkships, were reserved for men. In the light of all these exclusions, Normanton felt that:

> The Sex Disqualification Act is all done away with, except for the admission of women to the legal profession and justiceship of the peace... I return to the Government election pledge... And this is how HM Government carries it out![46]

Lady Rhondda declared that the 'removal' of discrimination in the act had never managed to get outside its brackets! She was convinced that such opposition stemmed from the belief that:

> When a being of a class which throughout the ages has been considered to be in certain directions inferior... has been regarded as belonging to the permanent serfdom of the race – gets into a hitherto barred profession... it lowers the whole prestige attached to entering that particular profession... the whole standard of values is lowered.[47]

Whereas women were attempting to raise their status, some men perceived the women's rise as a diminution in status for men. That was part of the prejudice, this perceptual gap which was extremely difficult to overcome. It must have seemed sometimes as if men's support for women's emancipation did not extend beyond an admittance of the principle, exemplified by Margaret Nevinson's experience of 'the eternal assertion: "I don't mind women having the vote, but I hope they won't want to sit in Parliament," made me aware of the prejudice we were up against'.[48]

There was an expectation by the women's movement in the post-war reconstruction period that within the agreed limits of necessary economic restraints the way would be clear for them to seek and achieve progress in line with their new status as citizens. What value did that new status represent, if it was not a recognition of their right to be accepted and acknowledged within the mainstream of society as having a contribution to make? The reality was that in whichever direction it turned the women's movement was confronted by prejudice and opposition within the very institutions to which it had so recently gained admittance. It was forced to utilise the energy it wanted to dedicate to completing the emancipation process in struggling to avoid having recent gains reversed. Yet by dint of its tenacity and the power of its networking it was able to stand its ground remarkably well. Even more surprisingly, it was able to make small advances. The importance of this caucus of women lay in its refusal to accede to the forces of reaction, to 'keep the flag flying' in readiness for more propitious times and to support those women who were not in a position to fight for themselves, but were immersed in the basic task of survival.

What was certain, as the WFL maintained at the beginning of 1922 in an article entitled 'Deliberate Betrayal', was that they had nothing to thank the then Government for. Detailing the Government's persistent obstruction of the women's legislative agenda, the WFL demanded, 'What reason have women to support this Government or any of its representatives at the coming General Election?'[49]

Notes on Chapter 5

1   Brittain, Vera, *Lady into Woman: A History of Women from Victoria to Elizabeth II* (London, 1953, Andrew Dakers), p 95
2   Rhondda, Viscountess, Margaret Haig, *This Was My World* (London, 1933, Macmillan), p 299
3   Brittain, Vera, *Lady into Woman: A History of Women from Victoria to Elizabeth II* (London, 1953, Andrew Dakers), p 95
4   NUSEC, Annual Report, 1919, p 27
5   *The Vote*, 9 May 1919, front page
6   *The Vote*, 3 January 1919, p 35
7   *The Vote*, 13 December 1918, pp 12-13
8   *The Vote*, 8 March 1918, p 173
9   *International Woman Suffrage News*, 1 April 1918, p 109
10   Birmingham Society for Equal Citizenship and Women Citizens' Association, Annual Report, 1919-1920, p 19
11   Sex Disqualification (Removal) Act, 23 December 1919, Section 1
12   See Chapter 9 for a full account.
13   Brittain, Vera, *The Women at Oxford* (London, 1960, George G. Harrap), p 151

14 NUSEC, Annual Report, 1921, p 3
15 *International Woman Suffrage News*, March 1919, p 78; *The Vote*, 9 May 1919, front page
16 *The Vote*, 4 July 1919, p 242
17 WFL, Report, October 1915-April 1919, p 12
18 Normanton, Helen, 'Who Would be a Married Woman?' in *Woman Magazine*, July 1924, p 382
19 *International Woman Suffrage News*, 1 April 1918, p 108; 1 August 1918, p 172
20 Interview with Barbara Strachey, 12 June 1989, Oxford
21 Hopkinson, Diana, *Family Inheritance: A Life of Eva Hubback* (London, 1954, Staples Press), p 87
22 Arncliffe-Sennett Collection, Vol 28, 1918-1938, 6 November 1918
23 *International Woman Suffrage News*, April 1920, p 105
24 NUSEC, Annual Report, 1920, pp 7-8
25 NUSEC, Annual Report, 1922, p 16
26 NUSEC, Annual Report, 1920, p 9
27 The post-war economic situation was that Britain had lost £300 million in investment terms, the Government had lent £1825 million to the Allies and borrowed £1340. The country also owed approximately £850 million to the United States.
28 NUSEC, Annual Report, 1921, p 15
29 *International Woman Suffrage News*, August 1920, p 177
30 NUSEC, Annual Report, 1921, p 14; *The Vote*, 28 October 1921, p 658
31 *The Vote*, 9 December 1921, front page
32 NUSEC, Annual Report, 1920, p 8
33 *The Vote*, 9 December 1921, front page; NUSEC, Annual Report, 1921, p 12
34 *International Woman Suffrage News*, February 1921, p 75
35 NUSEC, Annual Report, 1921, p 17
36 *International Woman Suffrage News*, March 1921, p 92
37 Nevinson, Margaret Wynne, *Life's Fitful Fever: A Volume of Memories* (London, 1926, A & C Black), p 252
38 NUSEC, Annual Report, 1921, p 17
39 WFL, Report, May 1919-April 1922, p 17
40 Wyles, Lilian, *A Woman at Scotland Yard* (London, 1952, Faber & Faber), p 12
41 Ibid., pp 81-83
42 *The Vote*, 22 February 1922, p 52

43 *The Vote*, 3 March 1922, front page
44 *The Vote*, 24 March 1922, p 94
45 AMSH, Annual Report, 1922, p 16
46 *The Vote*, 6 May 1921, front page
47 Rhondda, Viscountess, Margaret Haig, *This Was My World* (London, 1933, Macmillan), p 277
48 Nevinson, Margaret Wynne, *Life's Fitful Fever: A Volume of Memories* (London, 1926, A & C Black), p 284
49 *The Vote*, 17 February 1922, p 52

Chapter 6
Women and Parliament

It is historically accurate to say that British politics, even after the enfranchisement of women, has been predominantly about, by and for, men.[1]

Access to the House of Commons

An immediate concern, after the 1918 partial franchise success, was to establish women's entitlement to stand for parliament. As there had been no government statement expressly barring women from standing as parliamentary candidates, Nina Boyle (WFL/WWSL) seized the initiative by standing in the Keighley by-election in April 1918 as a test case, with Mrs Marion Holmes (WFL/WWSL) acting as the first female election agent. Failing any parliamentary intervention, Boyle's candidature hinged on whether she would be accepted by the returning officer on nomination day, 19 April. Her candidacy was duly accepted, although there were found to be errors in her nomination papers and she was disqualified on a technicality.[2] Not until four months later, in response to questions in the House of Commons, did the Prime Minister, Bonar Law, state that women were not entitled to be parliamentary candidates. An immediate campaign was launched by the women's societies to secure this right in time for the post-war election. A motion debated in the Commons in October was carried by a majority of 249; a bill was introduced and became law on 21 November 1918 giving the movement another success to celebrate.

Entry to the House of Lords

While the right to stand as a prospective parliamentary candidate for the House of Commons was achieved relatively smoothly, entry to the House of Lords proved more challenging. At the end of 1920, Lady Rhondda tested the validity of the opening statement of the Sex Disqualification (Removal) Act when she submitted her claim as a peeress to sit in the House of Lords in her own right. By March 1922, the suffrage papers were congratulating Lady Rhondda on winning the case, breaking down another barrier for women.[3] However, in May of that year, the Lords' committee for privileges reconsidered the case and by a vote of 20 to 4 found against Lady Rhondda's claim. Proceedings were directed by the Lord Chancellor, Lord Birkenhead,[4] and Lord Cave outlined the grounds upon which Lady Rhondda's claim was rejected:

> In my opinion the common law gave no right or title to a Peeress to sit in this House... It was not the case of her having a right which she could not exercise. I think she had no right... the Act of 1919 while it removed all disqualifi-cations, did not purport to offer any right. If the right to sit in this House is to be conferred on Peeresses, it must be done by express words.[5]

Lord Dunedin elaborated that while the act removed a disability, it did not create a right.[6]

This case is significant for what it revealed about the mixed feelings towards the 'woman question' within the Lords and how, in the final analysis, the reactionary forces could overcome the opinion of more liberal peers. What is also of interest is the way in which the act was interpreted; not only in the precedent which it set for the future, but in the way it demonstrated how the spirit of an act could be undermined by the political will of the opposition. This also raises the issue of how innovative legislation without a corresponding change in social consciousness can reduce the legislation's efficacy. It confirmed how accurate the women's societies were in their belief, expressed ironically enough by Lady Rhondda for one, that what was needed most was a change in people's attitudes towards women. It also indicated the remaining strength of the opposition to women's total emancipation and provided tangible evidence for the movement's suspicions of the inadequacy of the Sex Disqualification (Removal) Act.

Because entry to the Lords concerned only an elite group of women, Lady Rhondda's campaign, which she continued throughout the 1920s, should not be dismissed as being of minimal interest or importance. It was important on a wider scale than that of the personal attainment of peeresses; it represented a symbol of women's entry to the ultimate seat of traditional political power. The Lords not only initiated legislation, but as the second legislative chamber could provide women with another channel for introducing and influencing women's legislation in parliament. It could make a contribution to the aim of securing places for women in all prestigious public institutions and, with only two women MPs in the Commons, women in the Lords could have provided Astor and Wintringham with additional support. Although not all peeresses would have claimed this new right and not all would have necessarily used their power in the women's Cause, nevertheless increasing the number of influential women at such a time would have constituted an advance. Enlarging the number of women as a physical presence, giving them visibility in another influential institution, would have contributed to dismantling the barriers against the presence of women in public fora. One of Lady Rhondda's many contributions to the movement was her insistence on testing the viability of operating a right when it had been won. She appreciated that the value of winning rights was claiming and utilising them.

Political Education

Suffrage societies were eager to institute a crash programme of political education for women into the rights and responsibilities of citizenship. At the first post-war election, 6 million women would be entitled to vote, many of whom had no understanding of political matters or procedures. If this new right was to be used to maximum advantage to improve women's lives, there was an urgent need to increase political awareness among women voters. Most significantly, the possession of political power signalled the necessity for a considerable psychological transformation, making the adjustment from excluded observer to citizen. Grace Hadow, a previous Women's Social and Political Union (WSPU) member, pinpointed the difficulty in the changed self-perception which she thought the vote would bring: 'We shan't know ourselves in any other role other than a derided minority'.[7] Women had to learn a new role, and suffrage papers prefaced all campaigns with urgent reminders of the imperative for women to be active citizens.

The NUWSS understood that:

Deprived for so many years of every means of approaching public service, she can hardly be expected immediately on her enfranchisement to develop knowledge of Parliamentary procedure or any great enthusiasm for those politics which she has always been told are 'not her business'.[8]

Such political education needed to address basic processes of forming independent opinions, as economic powerlessness coupled with 'sex' oppression had been a potent recipe for silence.

Towards the end of 1917, when the partial franchise success seemed secure, some societies began work on such political education. One of the most extensive education programmes was originated by the National Union of Women Workers (NUWW) and the National Council of Women (NCW).[9] A committee was drawn up from members of the NUWW's executive and from 49 affiliated societies, and this committee decided upon the formation of a network of Women Citizens' Associations (WCA) throughout the country which should be open to women from all other societies. Once again the movement's enthusiasm for ensuring women's successful political participation unified its diverse elements with suffrage societies, professional and industrial groups, political organisations as well as welfare associations working together on this educational project.[10]

Despite franchise eligibility being restricted to women over thirty, membership of a WCA was to be open to all women over sixteen, either through their existing membership of another women's society or solely in a WCA. The WCAs were to operate as non-party, non-sectarian democratic groups, whose objects were to 'foster a sense of citizenship in women. Encourage the study of political, social and economic questions; secure the adequate representation of the interests and experience of women in the affairs of the community.'[11] In the year following partial enfranchisement many local suffrage societies and branches of larger suffrage societies amalgamated with other local women's groups. They changed their status to re-form as local WCAs, believing these to be more appropriate to the needs of the day.

The London Society for Women's Suffrage (LSWS) was a good example of the rapid and efficient way in which women's organisations anticipated the need for new methods evolving from the experience and structures already in existence. By November 1917, it had published a leaflet on *Applied Suffrage* in which it suggested how societies could use established wartime networks to promote women's awareness of their political potential. Such committees could ensure that all local public and legal affairs were equitably conducted, as well as setting up women's bureaux to provide information, education and training on political issues and a register of key public vacancies for public appointments for which women could volunteer.[12] Ray Strachey, Chairman of the employment committee and her sister-in law, Philippa, LSWS Secretary, both stressed the importance of sustaining wartime links for future expansion. Charlotte Despard (WFL) also urged the maintenance of the increased co-operation of the war to form constituency associations which could provide a platform for women to discuss politics and learn from visiting speakers.

The political education campaign, instigated in the spring of 1918, was crucial to the continuing political emancipation process. It specifically aimed to enable women to understand their entitlements and how to put them into practice, in preparation for a forthcoming election. The baffling complexity of qualification and procedure of the Representation of the People Act was decoded by National Union of Women's Suffrage Societies (NUWSS) publications such as Chrystal Macmillan's *And Shall I Have a Parliamentary Vote?* Leaflets such as *Six Million Women Can Vote*, *The New Privilege of Citizenship* and *How Women can Use the Vote* explained who had an entitlement, the political implications for women and how to register within the specified time limit.

Being entitled to the vote and claiming that right are two very different things, as enfranchised women were about to discover. One difficulty likely to be encountered was registering to vote. Maud Arncliffe-Sennett made four attempts to register, three in writing and one in person. She finally sent a telegram to the President of the local government board responsible for administering the election, asking him what further steps should she take to become registered.[13] Arncliffe-Sennett was an accomplished businesswoman with many years campaigning experience in the women's movement, but nevertheless, she encountered this bureaucratic obstruction, as did her niece:

> Mrs Smith and I spent all morning trying to find the place to vote (i.e. to register) without success. Everyone we asked was so nasty I can quite understand how beastly it must have been to have had that wall of insulting prejudice against one in every turn if they are like this now that it is won![14]

How much more difficult the process must have been for women with little or no education, vulnerable to the intimidation of authority.

Such widespread prejudice obstructing women's public participation illustrated Winifred Holtby's later insight that 'Political emancipation is a condition of freedom; it is not freedom itself'.[15] Legislative success was only the first step in the emancipation process. Such rights only serve to gain access to power when accompanied by machinery to facilitate the use of those rights and foster sufficient public awareness to give substance to those rights. The suffrage societies now faced the task of countermanding the prejudice of a system which they had not devised and were not controlling. Distributing procedural information was one important part of encouraging and supporting women in the battle to take on the system by claiming their new electoral right.

The 1918 General Election

The November general election of 1918 gave women their first opportunity to participate in the representative process and gain direct access to political power in their own right, both as voters and as parliamentary candidates. There were 8.5 million women over thirty who had won the right to vote, and the 1918 Parliament (Qualification of Women) Act enabled women over 21 to stand for parliament. The parliamentary anomaly now existed of enabling women who did not have the vote to become prospective parliamentary candidates and, if successful, members of parliament. Standing as parliamentary candidates also presented many problems which would take time to solve, but the most immediate difficulty in 1918 was the election timetable. The date of the election had been announced on 14 November but the enabling act had not become law until 21 November. Nomination day for candidates was nine days later on 4 December and polling day came only ten days after that on 14 December. Although the circumstances of this election were exceptional, any women's organisations involved had only 23 days in which to select candidates, locate contestable seats, enter the nomination, choose an election agent, finalise election policy, enlist voluntary support, raise additional funds, organise a schedule of meetings and arrange publicity.

But the suffrage societies already had much of their election machinery in place. They had been drawing up policy and encouraging women to come forward as prospective candidates since enfranchisement, in expectation of their inclusion in an election. Nevertheless, this was still a challenging task to undertake with any hope of success. Ray Strachey's mother recorded that 'They scarcely expected to be elected, so new was the idea of women MPs... But those who had fought for the political enfranchisement of women felt that even unsuccessful candidates were worthwhile.'[16] It was important to make as significant a showing as possible, for there were gains to be made in fighting the election other than those of winning seats. The Women's Freedom League (WFL) stressed the historic, symbolic nature of the election and the need for women to demonstrate their capability of carrying the responsibility they had fought for.[17] This meant demonstrating that they were not intimidated by the political process and were more than capable of utilising the electoral machine. In such a way they might contain some of the criticism which could hinder their political progress.

Despite all the handicaps, the women's movement launched its campaign with the usual degree of optimism and fervour in this 'coupon election'. All Coalition candidates who had the support of Lloyd George, the Coalition leader, and Bonar Law, the Unionist leader and Lloyd George's ally, received a letter from them which endorsed the recipient's candidature. (The Labour Party had withdrawn from the Coalition before the election and campaigned independently.) This letter became somewhat derisorily known as a 'coupon' and was largely distributed among Conservative candidates, virtually ensuring election success.[18]

The 17 women candidates ranged across the political spectrum,[19] with non-party women predominantly standing as Independents, although there were some exceptions. Charlotte

Despard, the WFL President, as a lifelong socialist and ILP member, stood as a Labour candidate. Emmeline Pethick-Lawrence (WFL) used the Labour Party's invitation to stand as an opportunity 'to explain publicly the reasons why I believed that the only chance of permanent peace in Europe lay in a just settlement after the war'.[20] This was a courageous stand, as the 'khaki' election, as it was also known, was characterised by the slogans, 'Make Germany Pay' and 'Hang the Kaiser', emanating from Lloyd George's promises for German reparation in the peace settlement. Such tactics did not improve Lloyd George's image with the women's movement, which had been struggling for so long to promote peace and internationalism. It was hardly surprising that with a large number of the women candidates standing on a feminist, which meant a pacifist platform, they were not afforded the guarantee of a 'coupon'. Seven women candidates had been involved in working for peace or in emphasising the need for a non-punitive peace settlement, whilst others had supported alien refugees. The last thing that the Coalition leader needed was to have such women in parliament exposing the folly of his extravagant claims for the peace where Germany would stand the cost of the war and there were 'dreams of wealth for the country in which all would share'.[21]

Despite the hostile election mood, neither the women candidates nor their supporting societies made any attempt to adapt or tone down their message. Some of the women candidates had a rough reception when campaigning because of what was interpreted as their pro-German sympathies. Ray Strachey, standing as an Independent for Chiswick, suffered from such accusations, her meetings were disrupted and she was 'greeted with hisses and catcalls'.[22] Charlotte Despard was accused of treachery and heckled,[23] whilst Emmeline Pethick-Lawrence realised by a strange, but understandable, irony that it was not the women but the soldiers who were her supporters because for the women 'this election was their chance of "doing their bit" and they were all "going over the top" to avenge their husbands and their sons'.[24] The only woman candidate who received Lloyd George's 'coupon' was Christabel Pankhurst, standing for the Women's Party as the patriotic candidate for Smethwick and supporter of the Coalition. Not only did she have the guarantee of a coupon, but the alternative Coalition candidate had been withdrawn in her favour. This support for nationalism and an aggressive peace settlement illustrated how estranged the Pankhursts and their few followers had become from the main body of the women's movement. There were some women who wanted to stand, like Selina Cooper of the NUWSS, who could not find a seat[25] or like Arncliffe-Sennett, who had been offered a seat in Edinburgh but had to decline because of her husband's objections.[26] Although Margaret Wynne Nevinson had been in the movement for many years, she had previously refused to work in election, on the basis that 'I myself not being held fit to have a vote'.[27] Now she was prepared to campaign and canvass.

In view of their non-party philosophy and limited resources, the suffrage societies had the problem of who to support during the electioneering. The NUWSS chose the truly non-party, feminist solution by supporting all the female candidates irrespective of party affiliations. However, with only 17 women candidates contesting 706 seats, it was also supporting any good male candidate who supported the feminists' demands. However, as a suffrage society, it felt that its first priority was to support the women candidates. Whilst approving all the women's candidatures and giving them all a degree of help, it specifically concentrated on working for two members of its executive, Ray Strachey, its honorary parliamentary secretary, and Margery Corbett Ashby, who was standing as a Liberal in Birmingham. The NUWSS was pleased to be able to re-open its pre-war election fighting fund which could now be allocated for the first time for the use of women candidates.[28]

Similarly, the WFL worked for three of its members: Charlotte Despard, who was contesting Battersea; Miss Phipps, standing as an Independent in Chelsea on behalf of the National Federation of Women Teachers (NFWT), of which she was an ex-president; and Mrs How-Martyn, an Independent for Hendon. The WFL also gave as much encouragement as possible to the other women candidates. In constituencies where there was no woman standing, the WFL urged voters to support any male candidate who supported the equality platform. The WFL candidates were specifically promoting equal political rights for men and women, equal pay, the abolition of Regulation 40D and the equal moral standard. Both Charlotte Despard and Miss Phipps had a particular interest in welfare rights for women and children, in addition to improved educational opportunities.[29]

Apart from seeking to get as many women as possible elected, the suffrage societies were also emphasising the active participation of women voters. They portrayed voting as an active function for women to perform, rather than as a passive role of being 'acted upon' by candidates and political parties. The emphasis was on citizen rather than subject. As such, the women's organisations sought to involve women in the process more directly, by instructing them on how they might participate more fully during the campaign. Of course, as a by-product of such active participation, women were educating themselves politically. The emphasis lay on responsibility, that women should make themselves responsible for ascertaining the candidates' position on women's issues. Election campaigns were largely conducted through public meetings, familiar enough terrain for suffrage workers, but not for a large number of women. Women's societies attempted to assist and encourage such women who wanted to get involved by publishing lists of questions which might be used to interrogate candidates at public meetings to determine their position in relation to women's emancipation issues. The NUWSS issued a document to every constituency in which the 15 demands to be made of candidates embraced all aspects of the union's policy, including the appointment of women among the official government delegation to the peace conference.[30]

The Women's Local Government Society (WLGS) also joined the NUWSS to compile another list of seven questions covering equal pay, the equal moral standard, the removal of restrictions on women's careers, equal opportunities in education and training and the need for women on government committees.[31] Other societies like the Women's Political League (WPL), formerly the Belfast Women's Suffrage Society (BWSS), also produced such plans, and the WFL published their 'Candidates' Catechism' which was a 15-point questionnaire dealing with the franchise extension, women's entry into the legal profession and other feminist demands.[32] In such a way, the women's groups managed to detect large areas of possible discriminatory practice. It was a timely opportunity to use concerted pressure to place women's issues back on the political agenda and in the public domain: yet another important by-product of the election campaign. But there was also real hope of success for some of the women candidates. Mary Macarthur was an official Labour Party candidate, representing the needs of working women in Stourbridge where 'the voters included a number of the chainmakers and hollow-ware makers for whom she had fought in the early days of the Trade Boards'.[33] There were also high hopes for Mrs Despard, who had the advantage of having lived and worked for 30 years in Battersea where she was well-known and much-loved, while the male opposition candidate was totally unknown.[34]

Such hopes made disappointment all the more acute when the Coalition won the election by a landslide and only one woman, Constance Markievicz, won a seat. Sister to the suffragist, Eva Gore-Booth, Markievicz was involved in the Irish struggle for independence and was a member of Sinn Fein. This involved refusing to take the oath of allegiance as a gesture of protest to the British crown, and this therefore prevented her from taking her seat in parliament. Such a result was a cruel irony for the women's movement's election hopes.[35]

Analysing the Results

After the publication of the results on 28 December, the women's movement analysed its performance in the face of this disappointment. The 1918 general election, popularly represented as a failure for the women's Cause, was more accurately a triumph against virtually insuperable odds. The movement had not succeeded in getting a woman elected to parliament, but it had achieved a good deal in laying down groundwork for the future. It had shown that it was equal to the challenge of preparing and mounting a vigorous campaign at short notice when both funds and energy were low. At a Lyceum Club celebration dinner for all the women candidates, many organisers and candidates gave positive and optimistic accounts of their experiences. Mrs McEwan, who had stood as a Liberal in Enfield, stressed the educative value of the campaign for the candidates, the voters and the movement.[36] That sentiment had also been expressed by the NUWSS which was keen to use this experience as a foundation for future political education.[37]

Some of the handicaps which the women faced have already been dealt with: the inadequate amount of time in which they had to prepare, not having Lloyd George's official endorsement, lack of money, the small number of women candidates, no previous experience of direct participation in elections and the difficulty of registration, but there were many others. One glaring example of individually experienced prejudice was the case of Mary Macarthur. Having only recently married, she did not use her married name of Mary Reid Anderson, for she was known to all in the industrial and Labour world by her unmarried name, which was how she registered her candidacy. However, the returning officer, despite many protests, insisted that legally she must use her married name; consequently, that was what appeared on the ballot paper. Margaret Cole, in Macarthur's biography, pointed out that this effectively lost Macarthur many votes. The unfamiliarity of the name to many of the women workers, large numbers of whom were illiterate, plus the fact that they had never voted before, led to confusion. They did not realise that Anderson and Macarthur were the same person.[38] At a celebration dinner at the Pioneer Club, Macarthur relayed how she had accused the returning officer of:

> ... robbing me of my good name – for had I been nominated as Mary Macarthur I should have secured many more votes than I did as Mary Reid Anderson. I regarded the result of the election... as a remarkable victory, and I still so regard it.[39]

Macarthur had still polled 7587 votes, to the winner's 8920, in a contest where she had been strongly favoured to win.

Another disadvantage for Independent candidates, who relied solely on the women's societies for electioneering support, was that they did not have the extensive machinery of the political parties backing their candidature. Although it often seemed that political party support for women could be less than enthusiastic and, still in its early years of development, often there was 'next to no Labour organisation'.[40] But lack of resources apart, the intention of political parties had been to use women to increase the power of the party, not to empower women. The WFL had also attempted to reduce other disadvantages, such as those experienced by housebound mothers, by recruiting an army of volunteers to baby-sit, enabling women to get out and vote. Apart from such specific material factors affecting women's ability to participate, the WFL also noted that the rapidity with which such changes had come about had meant that the significance of enfranchisement and its attendant responsibilities were yet to be fully realised by many women.[41] It has also been suggested that a particular section of women did not exercise their right 'for fear of revealing their age; in those days excessive delicacy was still observed in the matter of mentioning a woman's age'.[42]

There were factors to be considered which affected the nation as a whole, and, although not confined to the women candidates' situation, must have contributed to their results. The NUWSS felt that the majority of women had voted Conservative, as had the men, because of the influence of the 'khaki' propaganda. Despite the thrill that the women's movement understandably felt at this historic opportunity, it was only to be expected that, exhausted by war and with little time to consider the issues, many women were ignorant about the entire proceedings.[43] It was also generally accepted that despite the rancour and passion that the campaign aroused, there was also a mood of apathy which meant that the election turnout was under 60 per cent. This did not, however, apply as extensively to women. It would seem that these women were not so much voting against the women candidates, as for the Coalition which had promised them revenge on Germany, new homes, plenty of work and a better life.

The WFL declared that the existing party organisations had given women little support and, most significant of all, no 'safe' seats. They acknowledged their disappointment, even their despondency, at the results but, like the National Union of Societies for Equal Citizenship (NUSEC), they saw the key issue as the education of the electorate, both male and female. Mrs Despard forecast success if only the movement maintained its integrity and its loyalty to the Cause. The WFL, radical as ever, even suggested that as an act of good faith, the Government should reserve a number of safe seats for women.[44]

The few women candidates must almost have been lost in the sea of male candidates and Coalition promises, while the women candidates promoted a more realistic and painful analysis, that people did not want to hear, by insisting that peace terms designed to punish the German people could only result in laying the foundation for future conflict. After years of deprivation it was not a comforting message, but the women's movement had yet to learn the political art of dissembling:

> We are proud of such women candidates; they have set an example in electioneering which is full of promise for the future. They avoided personalities, but dealt fair and square with essentials; they disdained tricks but upheld truth.[45]

The matter of how significant a part gender had played in the results was another factor in the post-election analysis. Edith How-Martyn (WFL) thought that being a woman would not ensure success, but in being a good woman candidate, the fact of their 'womanhood' would be an advantage. Margery Corbett Ashby (NUSEC) believed that her sex had not lost her the election, rather she had lost the party vote and had gained the votes of women who wanted to be represented by a woman.[46] The NUWSS was confident that it was the principles for which the women fought which generated criticism, not their sex.[47]

This concern about the influence of sex was a key issue, especially in the light of press allegations that it was impossible to convince women to vote for women candidates and that this had been a significant reason for the women candidates' failure. In view of the enormous obstacles they had faced, their results could not be regarded as a negligible achievement. The factor which contributed most to the women's defeat and to the success of the Coalition was enshrined in the distribution of the 'coupons'. As a result, those who challenged the Coalition message were regarded as unpatriotic to the point of treachery.

The Coalition had secured 484 members from a possible total of 706, with the Labour Party as the largest opposition group with 59 MPs. The composition of this new parliament meant that it was largely an unknown quantity to the women's movement. As the NUSEC estimated in its 1919 annual report, there were only 120 MPs left in the House who were known to have an interest in women's issues, which was to be of great significance to the women's Cause in the following years.

Alternative Avenues of Power in Public Office

After the disappointment of the 1918 election the WFL vigorously promoted women's participation in the London County Council and provincial county council elections in March 1919.[48] The encouragement of women candidates for local government elections, which was often a more accessible method of gaining political power for women, was part of the drive to put women representatives in key political positions. One of the WFL's members, Rose Lamartine Yates, an ex-WSPU member, gained a seat on the LCC, and another, Edith How-Martyn successfully contested a seat on the Middlesex County Council.[49] Women were also encouraged to stand for parish and urban councils, as well as for the Board of Guardians for the administration of poor law relief. The WLGS was also in the forefront of this campaign, and in 1919 published a list of nearly 60 women who had been elected as town councillors all over the country, many of whom were prominent in the movement. Millicent Fawcett (NUSEC), who was also a member of the National Federation of Women Workers (NFWW), had gained a seat for Labour in York; Mrs Barton (WCG/WFL), also Labour, had won in Sheffield; Mrs Schofield Coates (WFL) took a seat in Middlesborough for Labour; and Mrs Rackham (NUSEC) stood as an Independent in Cambridge. In London, 121 women had gained seats, giving Labour just under 50 women councillors.[50]

Under the Sex Disqualification (Removal) Act women were now able to become magistrates and in December 1919, the Lord Chancellor announced the appointment of the first seven women magistrates, lifting the barrier to another avenue in public life.[51] In July 1920, 234 additional women magistrates were appointed and, as with the councillors, many of them were also active in the women's movement. In fact out of 31 newly-appointed magistrates in London, 21 of them were members of one or more of the women's organisations.[52] One of the functions of the movement as a training ground for public office was producing results. Also the contention made over the years by women's organisations that women who were being tried by the judicial system should be represented in it was at last beginning to be recognised.

Women in the House of Commons

It was ironic for the movement that the first two women to become members of parliament gained seats which had previously been held by their respective husbands. Nancy Astor became the first woman MP as the result of a by-election, fighting her husband's Plymouth seat in consequence of his inheriting the family title. She was joined by Margaret Wintringham who succeeded in winning her husband's seat after his death. Melville Currell has analysed this phenomenon of 'male equivalence', why women have been tolerated and what the expectations of them are:

> The crucial point is that the woman stands in a derived position, as an alter ego rather than solely in her own right. The woman is expected to carry on the man's work... acting almost as a projection of him.[53]

If that was indeed the way in which male MPs viewed Astor, it did not make her first two years, from taking her seat in December 1919 to being joined by Mrs Wintringham in October 1921, any easier. Many MPs totally ignored her, refusing to communicate with her.[54]

Whatever their private apprehensions, the women's societies congratulated and welcomed Astor, and she demonstrated very rapidly that 'Her sympathies were warmly with these champions of her sex'.[55] Astor was wealthy, a society hostess and a Conservative, on the face of it not an auspicious start for a women's champion. But in her post-election speech she declared her intention of working in the Commons for women and children. A day after taking her seat, she circulated a letter to the women's societies:

Since I am the first woman to take her seat in the House of Commons, I feel that I have a special opportunity of helping Women's Societies, and I am therefore anxious to be thoroughly in touch with their opinions and wishes... I am determined to do my best to be useful to the causes and interests of women. I hope and beg that your organisation will back me up in so far as it politically can. What I hope is that we women will be able to act up to our beliefs irrespective of party politics. I see no political salvation until we do.[56]

The bulging folders of correspondence which she received from women's groups testify to the response which her letter produced.[57]

The first woman MP was an opportunity not to be wasted by the movement, and two days after Astor's election success, Ray Strachey, the LSWS's parliamentary officer and a 1918 parliamentary candidate, offered to act as Astor's political secretary:

It is so important that the first woman MP should act sensibly; and she, though full of good sense of a kind, is lamentably ignorant of everything she ought to know as a Member of the House... I have two objects in doing this. First of all to make sure that the first woman MP doesn't break down somewhere, and then to help her to be of the maximum use to all the things that we want to get done... My second object is purely selfish. I want to get further into political things, and this I should have a real opportunity of doing...[58]

Strachey felt she would have a freer hand if she acted in an unpaid capacity, although she wanted Astor to pay for Strachey's own secretary. Astor's wealth was a great advantage in her work for women: it meant that she could afford as many paid staff as were necessary to get the job done. She had an accountant, a constituency agent, a personal secretary (Hilda Matheson, later to be head of talks at the BBC), and two typists.[59]

Strachey saw her own role as being to 'write her memoranda and speeches, watch events for her, prepare her parliamentary questions, see her deputations, select what invitations she must accept, and so on'.[60] Strachey worked for Astor in the lady member's room of the Commons every afternoon. As Strachey was a member of many women's committees, she was in a key position to assist all of them through Astor. Because of her wide network of contacts and interests, she was probably one of the most suitable women to have been in this position to maximise Astor's potential for the movement. Naturally, the movement was eager to ensure that Astor did not remain the sole woman MP for long.

The issue of support for women candidates was imperative and as soon as the 1918 election was over, the WFL was urging its members to form more election committees to begin the education process and increase the support for future candidates.[61] Simultaneously, the NUSEC, in partnership with the NCW, launched a campaign to raise public awareness, and that of the political parties, of the need for women candidates.[62] A public meeting in February 1920, chaired by Mrs Ogilvie Gordon of the NCW, launched the campaign. It was addressed by Nancy Astor, Eleanor Rathbone and Mrs Lloyd George, representing her husband. Astor outlined the immense task that one 'isolated' woman had of trying to deal with every aspect of women and children's concerns in parliament. The question of how they should solve the problem of the lack of support for women candidates led Eleanor Rathbone to argue that it would be impossible to establish themselves without the assistance of the political parties if they wanted 'a chance to fight for seats, not only for forlorn hopes'.[63] This might have seemed a surprising point, coming as it did from the president of the largest non-party women's organisation, but it was a pragmatic approach to changing circumstances and recognition of the need to spread the net of co-operation.

This February meeting led to the formation of a NUSEC/NCW joint committee, with input from the WFL. It 'aroused interest' through its extensive network of branches, held meetings nationwide, compiled a list of women from all political parties, arranged deputations to the party whips and instigated an appeal fund. In April 1920 it worked for the candidature of Margaret Bondfield when she stood in the Northampton by-election.[64] The NUSEC also held election classes for both prospective parliamentary candidates and constituency workers, using the expertise of political strategists like Philippa Strachey, president of the LSWS and Marian Berry, secretary of the WLGS. This was all essential preparation for building a strong infrastructure for the future.

Party and Non-Party Organisations

The emphasis on the maintenance of a non-party position by suffrage societies was asserted with its inclusion in each of the societies' constitutions. The betrayal of the women's Cause in 1884, when so many of their supposed Liberal allies had voted against the women's suffrage amendment of Gladstone's Reform Bill, highlighted their position as outsiders in relation to party politics. As the suffragist Mrs Wolstenholme Elmy had commented, 'I think it a mistake on the part of any woman to be a party woman first and a suffragist only in the second place'.[65] Now that a section of women were within the political arena, the issue of placing sex allegiance before that of a particular political ideology was ripe for re-examination. Consequently, the pages of suffrage papers held many debates concerning their non-political stance, while the women's party political groups attempted to alert women to the necessity for giving their allegiance to a specific party to ensure the success of women's objectives.

The renewed interest of political parties in capturing women as both voters and party members in the 1920s echoed the need there had been to enlist their aid in the early 1880s, when the increased size of the electorate and the passing of the Corrupt Practices Act resulted in the formation of women's groups within the Conservative and Liberal Parties. The political parties needing their help in electioneering work, women joined in large numbers and often, as a result, such women became politicised in the women's Cause. They were thus able to capitalise on the skills they had acquired in electioneering on behalf of the men for their own ends. It also raised women's political awareness because 'The contrast between the anxiety of politicians for women's assistance at elections and their indifference to women's suffrage once safely elected could hardly pass unnoticed'.[66]

Similarly, the politicians' eagerness to enlist women as party members, now that they were voters, gathered momentum during the 1920s as general elections followed one another in rapid succession. The struggle for supremacy of the three major parties became more acute in the wake of the fall of Lloyd George's Coalition Government in autumn 1922. The knowledge that an additional 8 million voters were there to be 'captured' led male politicians into trying to solve 'the problem of the woman voter'.[67] The Labour Party realised in 1922 that 'It is true to say that at this election women hold the key of the situation. With their support Labour will win. Without it Labour cannot win.'[68]

Arthur Henderson's directive concerning the establishment of women's sections in 1918 was seen by non-party women and many Labour Party women to be part of the renunciation of independent political action for Labour and industrial women. The energies of Labour women were needed to strengthen the party as it came under attack for its supposed Bolshevism, and by assisting with its expansion, to secure its position as the second major party on the electoral scene. The amalgamation of the NFWW and the Women's Trade Union League (WTUL) seemed to complement this process, marking Labour and industrial women's absorption into the male-dominated political party proper, and delineating between Labour women and the rest of the movement, a delineation which the declining economic fortunes of working class women served to emphasise.

As far as the Labour Party was concerned, the instigation of the women's sections had paid massive dividends: in the four years from 1918 to 1922, the party had attracted 100,000 women members.[69] Barbara Ayrton Gould, ex-WSPU, founder of the US and Women's Industrial League (WIL) member, spelled out the particular importance of the women's vote for Labour:

> It is large; it is going to become larger; and it is new. Consider the importance of that. Men voters are still bound fast in the hoary and Tory traditions of the old-established Parties... Women... simply because they are newcomers to politics are free from this constraint.[70]

Time & Tide in June 1923 noted how astute the Labour Party was in attracting women to the women's sections by declaring the party's dedication to women and women's rights.[71] Rallies were held across the country at which this message was proclaimed. There were full-time regional organisers whose main task was to establish women's sections, as well as giving talks, distributing propaganda and acting as a conduit from the regions to party headquarters. Dr Marion Phillips, as chief woman organiser, held ultimate responsibility for the women's sections and was tireless in her promotion of the Labour Party.

There was a tension for the Labour Party's women's sections with regard to women's education for citizenship. For instance, at both the Newark and Sittingbourne women's sections this process involved regular lectures from male and female party members covering topics such as women's part in the labour movement, the suffrage movement, social and economic issues. At the same time, the inaugural meeting of the Sittingbourne group in November 1922, addressed by a Mr Wells, revealed the clear intentions of the party when he emphasised how vital the women's particular role was in elections and how sorely missed that assistance had been in the recent election.[72] This was certainly reminiscent of the political cry of the late 1890s. Six months later, Mr Wells was asking the Sittingbourne women to take up this special women's work as 'canvassing was work which could well be done by members of the women's sections'.[73] Miss Taverner, a women's section organiser, whose district covered London, the home counties, Kent, and nine other counties, was regularly beseeching Sittingbourne women to promote the Labour movement by assisting male candidates in elections.

This 'special' women's contribution often involved menial routine chores, for the women's sections were regarded as a supporters' club whose main priority was to provide the storm troops for male candidates at elections, rather than to educate and encourage potential women candidates to fight for their own rights. However, there was a return for women who had joined a political party: they became politicised, could use their position to promote the women's Cause, could practise public speaking, rehearse arguments and develop a feeling of solidarity and strength as women. But many women found this division by sex a contradiction, seen against the equality for which they had fought, to have such a separation operating within a mixed organisation, where the real power was held, by and large, by men. Non-party groups, even those with mixed membership, were women's organisations, with the power held, and the policy determined, by women.

But the crux of the growing divide between Labour Party women and non-party women rested with Labour women's priority to defeat capitalism in the fight against increasing poverty, in a post-war world where the prosperity had been promised. Such desperate poverty, which doubly disadvantaged women and their children, increased the priority of class for socialist women. Labour women were prepared to invest so much of themselves in the Party for the promotion of class solidarity: as Ellen Wilkinson believed, 'the woman who earns her living, whether as wife or wage-earner... is suffering mainly from the wrongs that afflict all her class'.[74] However, she was also able to understand the shortcomings of party political organisation with regard to the women's sections. She saw how work they had done had not been appreciated, that by segregating women within the Party their existence had been trivialised by 'regarding the women's sections as a butt for the chairman's jokes, or a useful institution for organising whist drives'.[75]

Ellen Wilkinson's socialism did not prevent her from being an avowed feminist. She was not afraid to work within the House of Commons on a cross-party basis for women and with non-party groups outside the House. This did not mean either that she shrank from being in contention with other women members when party ideologies were at issue. Wilkinson operated in much the same way as Nancy Astor, who, more like a Liberal than a Conservative, could almost have been viewed as a Woman's Party candidate, if there had been one, because of her determination to work across party lines to represent women's concerns. In much of Astor's correspondence with women's organisations she made a favourable response to non-party groups, which she treated generously with time and money. She had made her all-party stance abundantly clear in her adoption speech in 1919:

> If you want a party hack don't elect me. Surely we have out-grown party ties. I have. The war has taught us that there is a greater thing than parties and that is the State.[76]

Her biographer, Sykes, also noted that despite her refusal to be a 'sex-candidate' she couldn't live up to this resolve and always greeted new women to the House irrespective of party affiliation.[77] Wilkinson and Astor certainly had their moments of conflict rooted in party difference, but they also sustained a friendly co-operation used to good effect for the promotion of women's issues in the House.

Less flexible was the attitude emanating from Marion Phillips, categorised by *Time & Tide* as of the 'my party, right or wrong' school. *The Woman's Leader* based its analysis of the conflict between party and non-party factions on Phillips' hard-line stance against non-party groups. The Standing Joint Committee of Industrial Women's Organisations (SJCIWO), led by Phillips, sent a letter to all its branches and affiliated societies in 1920 purporting to give 'advice' on the position of Labour Party women's affiliation to non-party organisations. The SJCIWO warned its members about the Women Citizens' Associations (WCAs), which were largely middle class in nature and consisted of such societies as the NUSEC and the WLGS. The letter suggested that Labour Party women refuse any WCA's invitation to join its ranks, on the grounds that:

> ... action cannot be taken without introducing party politics, and therefore the WCAs will either fail to do anything but talk, or they will be led on to run special Women Citizen Candidates for local authorities and even for Parliament.[78]

The concern for the Labour Party was that such women did not support the aims of the working class, and represented a rival for parliamentary power.

Phillips enforced this position with a resolution at the Labour Women's Conference later in 1920, which was reported in *The Woman's Leader*:

> That this Conference of working women recognises that the time is now come for a great effort to secure full political power for Labour, and therefore urges all women in industrial organisations to become members of the political Labour movement, and to avoid dissipating their energies in non-party political organisations.[79]

The discussion which followed illuminated the problems of such a prescriptive resolution, as well as the resistance of all delegates to accept it. Many socialist feminists also belonged to a wide range of non-party groups which were active in working for different aspects of women's rights, and they questioned the definition of a non-party group. They pointed out that even the chairman, Mary Macarthur, worked on committees of non-party associations and could not be said to abide by such a stricture. Phillips justified Macarthur's position by insisting that the term 'non-party' did not apply to groups which were formed on a temporary basis to achieve a specific object. But delegates decried her definition by pointing out that:

> This description would cover a multitude of political bodies, such as, for instance, Women's Suffrage Associations, Temperance Leagues, the League of Nations Union – in fact it might apply to almost all political organisations, which, after all, are all temporary in the sense that they exist only until their object is attained.[80]

Delegates demanded clarification from Phillips, exhibiting some sarcasm when they demanded whether they should only belong to other political organisations as long as they did not use up too much energy, or not at all? It was an exasperated Mary Macarthur who ruled that delegates could put their own interpretation on the resolution and act accordingly.

This was an important debate, because it emphasised the difficulty of trying to impose rulings on a membership with wide inter-organisational allegiances, which reflected the breadth of its commitments and concerns and which could not always be neatly contained within the limitations of party dogma. It also high-lighted the difference between theory and practice, the need for flexibility in the interests of pragmatism. This was what the suffrage societies were in a position to do, untrammelled as they were by party political considerations. Suffrage societies had always maintained that their non-party stance enabled them to appeal to women from all parties and persuasions for the collective good of all women. Again, this turned upon the belief in the sustainability of a representative 'community of interest'.

In 1923 the debate was revived in the pages of *The Woman's Leader* when Marion Phillips, in a speech to the Monmouthshire Labour Women's Advisory Council in February 1923, counselled her audience to have nothing to do with groups which 'come to them in the guise of friends and ask them to co-operate in regard to certain individual points in the Labour Party's programme'.[81] She specifically cited the NUSEC and the National Federation of Women's Institutes (NFWI) as examples of such organisations. Helena Auerbach had been a member of the LSWS, an executive member of the NUWSS, vice president of the NUSEC and was also the honorary treasurer of the NFWI. She defended the NFWI on the grounds that there was no clash of interests between party and non-party women. The NFWI was founded in 1915 as an organisation for women in isolated rural districts, and by 1923 it had 2600 branches.[82] Auerbach protested that working for specific political ends did not exclude the consideration of women's other needs, that the two were complementary:

> If Dr Marion Phillips would carefully study the democratic constitution of the NFWI she would realise that the educational work which is done by the WI Movement must render women not less, but infinitely more capable than they have ever been before of taking part in every kind of responsible Political work.[83]

Grace Hadow, the ex-suffragette and Vice-President of the NFWI pointed out the following year there had been an incorrect analysis of the term 'non-party'. Hadow believed that to be non-party did not forbid an interest in politics, but presented a wider interpretation: 'I fail to see how anyone can take even the most elementary interest in children and cooking without inevitably taking an interest in politics'.[84]

The Woman's Leader was at a loss to understand why the NUSEC had been singled out for condemnation in this way when it advocated many policies which were of interest to women of all parties. The NUSEC felt that Labour were losing the opportunity of making contact with a new audience which, through ignorance of Labour Party policies, might sustain anti-Labour feelings. It also maintained that Labour women could also be nourished by contact with other sections of women.[85] This more opportunistic perception, of appreciating the opportunities which might accrue from working with women from all spheres, contrasted sharply with Phillips's separatist response, when she dealt with:

> ... the dangers of organisations which dealt with women's questions that were not the most important and urgent matters for working women, and dealt even with them from a more or less superficial standpoint, because fundamentally the women who belong to such organisations hold differing views on social and economic arrangements.[86]

In conclusion, she explained that Labour women wanted their ideas translated into action (as if non-party groups did not) and that this could best be done by concentrating their efforts within their own camp, only liaising with others on specific demonstrations or campaigns. It was the notion of a singular purpose which was bounded by strict party ideology.

Phillips's position, based on a class analysis, was comprehensible in terms of political expediency for a young party which was desperately concerned to gain maximum representation and power to redress the economic gulf between the classes. In the early years of the 1920s unemployment continued to rise and the working class was suffering greatly, living in appalling conditions. The dole had been cut and the only redress for many was the irregular handouts of local poor law relief. Throughout this period *The Labour Woman* detailed the degradation which people suffered, especially that of women and children.[87] Aware of such desperation, it was hardly surprising that socialist women concentrated their efforts on the defeat of capitalism. Little wonder, when viewed from this perspective, that although middle class herself, Marion Phillips's resolve to achieve social justice made her somewhat wary of middle and upper class women whose freedom to participate in politics rested on their private incomes.

Phillips was also secretary of the SJCIWO, and this purist line had been demonstrated on many occasions with the SJCIWO's refusal to co-operate with non-party groups. Such had been the case in 1919 with the WIL and the Women's International League.[88] In 1920, they withdrew from the council for the representation of women in the League of Nations,[89] and after attending an initial meeting, they declined to participate in the consultative committee of women's organisations initiated by Nancy Astor.[90] *The Woman's Leader*, in an article on sex loyalty, suggested that 'Labour women may feel more conscious of the economic social differences which divide, than of the feminist affinities which unite'.[91]

Individual Conservative Party women were also members of many non-party feminist organisations, but the Women's Unionist Organisation (WUO), formed in 1918 after the passing of the Representation of the People Act to organise women electors, was far from being part of the women's movement. Nevertheless, it tried to intervene in the party versus non-party controversy. The WUO's reaction to the non-party issue resulted from the Labour Party women's sections success, rather than from any genuine interest in the merits of the debate. The Unionist obsession with the 'red menace' gained fervour in proportion to the Labour Party's increased percentage of the vote at each election, and the WUO saw non-party groups as being in danger of infiltration by socialists.

WUO members were eager to prevent such a take-over, reinforcing their efforts against the Labour Party by direct appeals to non-party women. They attempted to undermine the links between non-party groups and the Labour Party by reminding women's groups that:

> Non-party women's interests have been hopelessly disappointed and betrayed by the Socialists. They have not given, as promised, equal franchise, equal rights in the home, widows' pensions, nor equal pay for equal work.[92]

This attack followed the Labour Government's brief term in office in 1924. What is interesting is that the WUO was still reacting to Labour women's influence, rather than attempting to attract non-party women to the WUO by virtue of what it had to offer as the organisation which 'defends the home and the family'.

Despite the damage which seemed to have been done to the close working relationship which Labour and suffrage women had established prior to the war, there were many women who maintained joint loyalties and were intent on sustaining the duality of being both party and non-party women. Muriel Matters Porter retained her WFL and Labour Party memberships, and as a parliamentary candidate intended to maintain her independence should she win:

> I could be relied upon not to follow tamely the crack of the Party whip when questions which can never be made purely Party issues are under discussion. I recognise that Party organisation is necessary... I believe that the Labour Party's programme promises to this country those things which to me mean so much for the welfare of all... if I go into the House it is to urge and vote upon issues the furtherance of which is more to me than the Party.[93]

Porter was testifying to the non-party credo summed up by the phrase first used by Charlotte Brönte and later by Mrs Fawcett, of 'being your own woman'.[94]

Older feminists within the post-war women's movement had been members of non-party women's organisations for far longer than women had been allowed to participate in party politics. As outsiders, they believed it was the most advantageous position to be in, with greater freedom to negotiate with the party machine from a safe distance. One commentator also considered the practical implications where 'One first-class loyalty is a heavy enough responsibility. More than one is an intolerable burden.'[95] In defence of the non-party position, Edith How-Martyn (WFL) believed there was no easy solution and that 'Women should join the society, party or otherwise in which they will be happiest, as then they will do their best work'.[96]

Edith Picton-Turbervill, who sustained dual allegiances, was also representative of women who were cautious of 'grinding the Feminist axe too freely'[97] in this post-war world. Now that women operated in a wide sphere of activities and institutions, it was an inappropriate label, which was restrictive and caused suspicion among political parties, delaying women's progress.

All through the 1920s, the suffrage societies had plenty of occasion to caution against placing too much faith in political parties, as promises were broken and women's issues cast aside. It was felt that feminist solidarity was more likely to build strength and co-operation than the divisiveness engendered by party politics. But *Time & Tide* had quite a different perception of the efficacy of the non-party system and believed that:

> ... it is the strength of the non-party women's organisations rather than the number of women attached to the party organisations which is likely to decide the amount of interest taken by the parties in women's questions.[98]

Faith in their own organisations, coupled with an understanding of the many forces at work in the new post-war political scene, assured the LSWS of their ability to resist any schisms:

> Political work is more complex than it was in the days of the Suffrage fight... Party feeling which was not always easily overcome even when we were voteless, is a stronger force among us today, but so long as the Society holds to its non-party traditions, and is swayed by no consideration save that of forcing upon all parties the advancement of the object for which it exists, differences of political opinion among its members will continue to be not only no drawback, but positively advantageous.[99]

Notes on Chapter 6

1   Smith, Malcolm, *British Politics, Society and the State Since the Late Nineteenth Century* (London, 1990, Macmillan), p 65

2. *The Vote*, 12 April 1918, p 24; 19 April 1918, p 222; 26 April 1918, p 226

3   *The Vote*, 10 March 1922, front page

4   The fact that Lord Birkenhead directed this case is somewhat ironic as he 'allowed himself to be eager for postumous fame... on the part played by him as a law reformer', (DNB, 1922-39, p 787), but evidently not when it came to women!

5   Proceedings and Minutes of Evidence taken before the Committee for Priviliges, Margaret Haig, Lady Rhondda, House of Lords, 1922, p clxxv

6   Ibid., p clxxvi

7   Brittain, Vera, *The Women at Oxford* (London, 1960, George G. Harrap), p 146

8   *International Woman Suffrage News*, December 1918, p 32

9   The NCW consisted of representatives from the branches and affiliated societies of the NUWW.

10 *Women Citizens Asociations*, NCW pamphlet, approx. date 1917-1918, p 1. Affiliates involved included the CLWS, CUWFA, AUWT, WIC, FWG, WLGS, FWGC, MU.

11 Ibid., p 3

12 Strachey, Ray, *Applied Suffrage*, LSWS pamphlet, November 1917, p 2

13 Arncliffe-Sennett Collection, Vol 28, 1918-36

14 Ibid.

15 Holtby, Winifred, *Women and a Changing Civilisation* (London, 1934, John Lane, Bodley Head), p 34

16 Smith, Mary Pearsall, unpublished draft biography of Ray Strachey, Smith Collection, Oxford, p 5. Mary Pearsall Smith was Strachey's mother.

17 *The Vote*, 29 November 1918, p 274

18 Mowat, Charles Loch, *Britain Between the Wars 1918-1940* (London, 1955, Methuen), p 3

19 *International Woman Suffrage News*, January 1919, p 49

20 Pethick-Lawrence, Emmeline, *My Part in a Changing World* (London, 1938, Victor Gollancz), p 332

21 Ibid.

22 Smith Papers, Oxford, January-November 1918, p 2

23   Mulvihill, Margaret, *Charlotte Despard – A Biography* (London, 1989, Pandora Press), p 125

24   Pethick-Lawrence, Emmeline, *My Part in a Changing World* (London, 1938, Victor Gollancz), p 332

25   Liddington, Jill, *The Life and Times of a Respectable Rebel* (London, 1984, Virago), pp 295-8

26   Arncliffe-Sennett Collection, Vol. 26, 1918-36

27   Nevinson, Margaret Wynne, *Life's Fitful Fever: a Volume of Memories* (London, 1926, A & C Black), p 249

28   *International Woman Suffrage News*, December 1918, p 32

29   *The Vote*, 29 November 1918, p 474

30   *International Woman Suffrage News*, January 1919, p 48

31   *International Woman Suffrage News*, December 1918, p 32

32   *The Vote*, 6 December 1918, p 3

33   Cole, Margaret, *Women of Today* (London, 1938, Nelson & Sons), p 125

34   *The Vote*, 6 December 1918, p 2

35   *International Woman Suffrage News*, January 1919, p 49

36   *The Vote*, 17 January 1919, p 53

37   Ibid.

38   Cole, Margaret, *Women of Today* (London, 1938, Nelson & Sons), p 125

39   *The Vote*, 17 January 1919, p 53

40   Pethick-Lawrence, Emmeline, *My Part in a Changing World* (London, 1938, Victor Gollancz), p 331

41   *The Vote*, 13 December 1918, p 12

42   Graves, Robert & Hodge, Alan, *The Long Weekend, A Social History of Great Britain 1918-39* (London, 1985, Hutchinson), p 21

43   *International Woman Suffrage News*, January 1919, p 49

44   *The Vote*, 3 January 1919, p 35

45   *The Vote*, 20 December 1918, p 18

46   *The Vote*, 17 January 1919, p 53

47   *International Woman Suffrage News*, January 1919, p 49

48   *The Vote*, 2 February 1919, pp 98-99

49   *The Vote*, 14 March 1919, p 117

50   *The Labour Woman*, December 1919, p 142

51   They were the Marchioness of Crewe, the Marchioness of Londonderry, Mrs Lloyd George, Elizabeth Haldane, Gertrude Tuckwell (SJCIWO), Mrs Sidney Webb and Mrs Humphrey Ward. See *The Daily Express*, 24 December 1919, p 1

52   *The Vote*, 23 July 1920, p 113

53   Currell, Melville, *Political Woman* (London, 1974, Croom Helm), p 167

54   See Collis, Maurice, *Nancy Astor, an Informal Biography* (London, 1966, Faber & Faber), p 77 for the story of why Winston Churchill ignored Astor in the Commons despite the fact that they were old friends.

55   Ibid., p 56

56   *International Woman Suffrage News*, January 1920, p 58

57   The Astor archive contains numerous folders of correspondence from women's groups requesting her assistance; there were few that she refused to help. See MS 1416/1/1:822-828: Societies IV – Women's Associations 1922-29; MS 1416/1/1:829-833: Societies V – Membership or Office Accepted.

58   Smith Papers, Oxford, 20 November 1919, p 32

59   Ibid.

60   Ibid.

61   *The Vote*, 3 January 1919, p 36

62   NUSEC, Annual Report, 1919, p 33

63   *International Woman Suffrage News*, March 1920, p 88

64   NUSEC, Annual Report, 1920, pp 6-7

65   Rubinstein, David, *Before the Suffragettes: Women's Emancipation in the 1880s* (Brighton, 1980, Harvester Press), p 140

66   Ibid., p 157. See also *International Woman Suffrage News*, 1 February 1918, p 70

67   *The Labour Magazine*, November 1922, p 308

68   Ibid.

69   *The Labour Woman,* 1 June 1922, p 85

70   *The Labour Magazine*, December 1922, p 344

71   *Time & Tide*, 15 June 1923, p 608

72   Sittingbourne Labour Party Women's Section Minutes, Friday 24 November 1922

73   Ibid., 31 May 1923

74   *The Vote*, 4 July 1924, front page

75   *The Labour Magazine*, January 1925, p 398

76   Grigg, John, *Nancy Astor, Portrait of a Pioneer* (London, 1980, Sidgwick & Johnson), p 74

77   Sykes, Christopher, *Nancy, the Life of Lady Astor* (London, 1972, Collins), p 230

78   *The Labour Woman*, March 1920, p 37

79   *The Woman's Leader*, 30 April 1920, p 290
80   Ibid.
81   *The Woman's Leader*, 2 March 1923, front page
82   Jenkins, Inez, *The History of the Women's Institute Movement of England and Wales* (Oxford, 1953, OUP), p 38
83   *The Woman's Leader*, 16 March 1923, p 55
84   *The Woman's Leader*, 1 August 1924, p 215
85   *The Woman's Leader*, 2 March 1923, p 34
86   *The Woman's Leader*, 9 March 1923, p 46
87   See for example *The Woman's Leader* 1 March 1922, p 40
88   SJCIWO, Minutes, 7 January 1919, pp 1 & 4
89   SJCIWO, Report, 1921, p 2
90   Ibid.
91   *The Woman's Leader*, 2 March 1923, p 34
92   *Home & Politics*, November 1924, p 5
93   *The Vote*, 12 September 1924, front page
94   *The Woman's Leader*, 4 January 1924, p 395
95   *The Woman's Leader*, 2 March 1923, p 34
96   *The Woman's Leader*, 15 June 1923, p 157
97   *The Vote*, 1 February 1924, p 35
98   *Time & Tide*, 15 June 1923, p 608
99   LSWS, Annual Report, 1921, pp 7-8

Chapter 7

General Election Campaigns:
1922-1924

——————————————

But if we belong to the sex which can only aspire to the
privilege of voting after attaining the age of thirty, by one of
the eight or ten complicated methods provided to test our
more mature intelligence, it is certainly time we set ourselves
to the study.[1]

The women's movement contested three general elections between
1922 and 1924, and these stretched the movement's resources to
the limit. This period provides an opportunity to examine the
movement's campaigning operation and its results, which indicate
the progress women were making both with regard to the parliamentary process and their own political development. It also
demonstrates the operational implications of the rival party and
non-party ideologies and what effect they were to have on the
future direction of the movement as it progressed towards the
middle years of the decade.

The 1918 election had not provided women with sufficient time
to mount an adequate campaign, and had been little more than
an opportunity to mark an historic event. The 1922 November
general election was the first opportunity for women to present a

serious challenge as political contenders. Unlike the 1918 election, the women's societies had advanced warning of the 1922 election.[2] Although both Liberal factions[3] were united with the Conservatives against the growing Labour Party, there was increasing distrust of the Coalition leader, Lloyd George. The Conservatives feared that in the interests of his personal political survival, which was somewhat precarious, Lloyd George might attempt to split the Conservative Party, just as he had the Liberals. After repeated rumours of an election throughout 1922, which made it difficult for the women's groups to carry on with their normal parliamentary activities, the Conservatives forced the issue in the autumn and voted to withdraw from the Coalition. The election was called for 15 November 1922.

The suffrage societies swung into action, determined at the very least to retain the seats of the two existing women MPs, Nancy Astor in Plymouth and Mrs Wintringham at Louth, but also to return more women for the massive task of wresting full equality from a reluctant House. There was also great concern within the movement with regard to the two women MPs' burden of work, as both women rarely refused any request which the women's organisations made of them. Apart from this practical consideration there was the glaring injustice of the lack of representative numbers of women in parliament.

No sooner had the suffrage societies analysed the 1918 election results than planning began for the next election: raising election fighting funds, setting up party machinery, encouraging women to come forward as candidates, running education classes and propagandising members, the public and parliament on the necessity for more women MPs. The suffrage societies had always appreciated the value of publicity and placed great faith in the communication of information, disseminating innovative ideas via the distribution of leaflets, pamphlets and newspapers. The 1922 general election was no exception: public prejudice against women candidates had to be overcome and confidence in the individual candidates inspired, as well as the education and encouragement of the female electorate undertaken. This was a critical function of the non-party organisations' work, providing a catalyst for action by furthering discussion of ideas, keeping those ideas in the public gaze and paving the way for public acceptance and support.

Choosing which candidates to support depended firstly on the availability of resources, then on the societies' consideration of the candidates' commitment to the aims of the women's movement as well as the specific policies of the supporting society. The use of questionnaires to elicit the views of prospective candidates on women's issues was a popular electioneering tool employed by many women's organisations to determine its allocation of candidate support. The National Union of Societies for Equal Citizenship's (NUSEC) questionnaire was issued to all candidates, male and female. Sixteen questions covered equal franchise, equal pay and opportunities, unemployment, the equal guardianship of children, the equal moral standard, the League of Nations, women in the House of Lords, illegitimate children, women police, separation and maintenance orders, women's nationality, women jurors, widows' pensions, the admission of women to Cambridge University, the taxation of married women and proportional representation. The first six issues were designated as of greatest importance.

The Women's Freedom League (WFL), however, sent out different questionnaires to male and female candidates. The one devised for men contained five sections, subdivided into subsections which covered the franchise, women in the Lords, equal pay and opportunities, raising the age of consent for boys and girls, equal status for married women and equal training and relief for the unemployed.[4] Other societies sent out questionnaires with general questions relating to equality issues, as well as more specific enquiries relating to their members' interests. The professional and clerical women's election questionnaire sent out by the Association for Women Clerks and Secretaries (AWCS) covered public administration, the protection of office workers, transport and housing, unemployment, equal citizenship and general health topics.[5] Candidates were inundated with such questionnaires. Mary Grant, suffrage worker and Liberal candidate, received 100.[6] As well as being sent to individual candidates, they were also sent to the headquarters of the political parties, to ascertain official party policy on women's issues.

Having discovered the supposed attitude of candidates to women's emancipation issues, major support was allocated first to women candidates, and more specifically to those women who were members of the particular organisation involved. Although it was more often a question of how much support was allocated, rather than a matter of denying assistance totally to non-members. Considering the limits of resources, the women's societies offered some kind of assistance to nearly all the qualifying female candidates. The NUSEC, with its vast organisational network, was able to use its regional groups to help women candidates in their own districts and also 'did excellent work in reaching voters who could not have been approached from the party platforms'.[7]

The London Society for Women's Service (LSWS) had entered into an agreement with the NUSEC to take responsibility for election work in its own district which covered most of the metropolitan boroughs, createding problems such as:

> ... nine (women) stood for constituencies within the Society's area. It was obviously impossible to give adequate help to all these, especially as some of them were standing against men who were old friends of the society and constant supporters of the women's causes.[8]

It was this type of dilemma which made the non-party stand problematic on occasion, as societies could hardly afford to neglect or offend sitting male candidates who had previously supported the women's Cause. With only 33 women standing, compared to over 1400 men, it was essential for the parliamentary survival of the women's Cause that they continued to support sympathetic male candidates. The problem, as ever, was the scarcity of resources.

Another difficulty was that of party affiliation. Of the 33 women standing in 1922, only two, Eleanor Rathbone and Ray Strachey, who were NUSEC members, were standing as Independents. The NUSEC concluded:

> The Committee gave help quite impartially to all parties, but the preponderance of Liberal and Labour over Conservative women who were brought forward as candidates inevitably led to a large measure of support for these parties.[9]

This apparent party preference was accidental, for as a non-party association it was not the political party which qualified a candidate for support but the manner in which they had responded to the society's questionnaire. The WFL were, as with the NUSEC and other organisations, 'specially supporting the women who are known to us as standing for the full equality of the sexes'.[10]

Although the WFL appealed to its supporters to work for 21 of the candidates, as an organisation it was placing its maximum assistance at the disposal of just four women. It stressed that resources permitting, it would have supported all the women candidates, but that it was simply a question of priorities.[11]

The questionnaires had two other important functions. Firstly, the results were published and used as propaganda to advertise and promote those candidates who were supporters of the women's Cause, which was especially valuable for the new women voters who wanted to know who they should support to maximise the use of their vote to women's advantage. Secondly, the WFL stressed the need to keep all such information for future use in by-elections, when candidates who did not succeed in this election might reappear in the future.[12] Such accumulated information functioned as an information bank for future campaigns. It was always made clear to candidates completing such forms that their views would be made public within their constituencies and would remain on file. *Time & Tide*, the paper linked to the militant Six Point Group (SPG), devised another method of publicising MPs' views to assist voters. It drew up 'black and white lists' of MPs which were compiled on the basis of previous record on women's issues in the House of Commons. It informed its readers that additional information was available on request from the SPG. It was an ingenious tactic, presented in a readily comprehended format, and had the advantage over questionnaires of being compiled without actual recourse to the MPs.[13]

After the 1922 election, *The Labour Woman* cast doubt on the value of the non-party organisations' questionnaires:

> We suggest to these women that it was a waste of time to get pledges from members of the Anti-Labour Parties. Experience has amply proved that promises given by any of them before an election are of little value afterwards.[14]

This was rather an unhelpful and partisan perception which ignored the good offices of many Conservative MPs, such as Robert Cecil, as well as the Liberal supporters of the Cause. The education of women voters was regarded by the women's societies as a crucial part of the election process in the exercise of their citizenship: after all, for women with no political experience it was a bewildering process. At the very least, the information gleaned from questionnaires provided some guidelines to candidates' anticipated performance, as well as pointing women in the direction of the issues which needed to be addressed. The NUSEC appreciated the educative value of elections for both candidates and electorate, and its long-term benefits for inculcating concepts of citizenship.[15] Canvassing, setting-up local information shops, distributing election literature, getting maximum press coverage, holding meetings and arranging deputations to individual candidates were all methods of accomplishing this dual function. It was also an invaluable opportunity for increasing membership.

In constituencies where there was a woman candidate, the WFL advised women to vote for her, otherwise it counselled them:

> ... to put aside all party prejudices and predilections, and to vote for the candidate who, she honestly believes, will be the greatest help to women in the new House of Commons. The only way to secure the reforms we have worked for is by making the best and wisest use of the political power which most of the women over thirty years of age now possess.[16]

It was easy to see from such advice why some Labour Party women were not over-enthusiastic about working with or lending support to the non-party sector. Such political opportunism, as recommended by the WFL, demonstrated an ability to abandon adherence to the party line in favour of expediency. The NUSEC propounded a similar policy where running a non-party campaign meant using every opportunity to secure the return of members who would adopt its programme of reforms. In this, the second election in which women could directly participate, there was a great deal at stake, and it was imperative for women to find the most influential method of increasing their power. While approving the Liberal and Labour manifestos, in which both parties professed the intention of implementing equality between the sexes, the NUSEC counselled that:

> ... we cannot trust solely to any such general professions of faith from Party Headquarters... Every candidate should be questioned on these reforms by the women voters, and should be made to feel that women are in earnest in demanding them.[17]

It amounted to women voters having to prove the seriousness of their intentions by establishing their political credibility. In this way, women voters could smooth the path for women candidates to be accepted as representatives of the whole electorate, not just as sex representatives. Part of this process involved rebuffing the inevitable accusations of sex interest which could follow from recommendations such as the NUSEC's to hold women-only meetings which emphasised the need for women electors to return women candidates.[18] Measures which would improve the efficacy and collective strength of the women's campaign might also alienate women from the mainstream political process.

Of the 33 women standing in the 1922 election, only eight had neither suffrage society nor party political membership, but had gained their experience of public affairs in philanthropic, church or social work. Of the remaining 25, eight had only party political affiliations, while seven had solely non-party connections. There were a further 10 who had memberships or affiliations of both political parties and suffrage societies. Such combinations meant that there were 17 non-party women and 18 party women standing as candidates. Women like Dr Ethel Bentham, who was a Labour Party activist, was standing for Labour, but had also been a member of the Women's Social and Political Union (WSPU), the National Union of Women's Suffrage Societies (NUWSS) and the Women's Labour League (WLL); or Margery Corbett Ashby, who was a lifelong Liberal, had worked for the WFL and was now also on the NUSEC executive and was President of the International Woman Suffrage Alliance (IWSA). Eleanor Barton was a Co-operative Party candidate and a WFL member, along with Commandant Mary Allen, who had always been firmly identified with the WFL, yet was not standing as an Independent, but as a Liberal.

That the overwhelming percentage of women candidates emanated from one or other branch of the broader women's movement was hardly surprising in the light of its contribution to women's political development. But this organisational profile emphasises the interdependence of party and non-party organisations and the importance of both branches in constructing a broad church from which women could launch their campaigns. It might have been difficult for Labour women to appreciate why avowedly non-party women remained resolutely outside the party machines, but during these three election years Labour Party women candidates benefitted from and duly appreciated the assistance which their non-party sisters were able to give them. Margaret Bondfield was a staunch Labour Party woman, but the NUSEC, while acknowledging that she was 'not exactly "one of ourselves"'[19] still sent some temporary organisers to assist her in the Northampton constituency during the campaign.[20] In this way it demonstrated the reality of its non-party theory and their hope that 'feminist solidarity' would unite party and non-party women.[21]

Women candidates had to be particularly careful in their election speeches to avoid falling into the frequent pitfalls which the prejudices of the press and male politicians were willingly constructing for them. Nancy Astor, who had been a Conservative MP for three years, had been identified as 'the fiercest feminist of them all'[22] and convincingly steered the path between party and non-party. She was also trying to avoid being stereotyped as a woman's MP by demonstrating that as the first woman MP it was necessary that she would be concentrating on issues concerning women and children, while also giving time to questions which involved men as well as women.[23] Winifred Coombe-Tennant (NUSEC), standing as a National Liberal, voiced the fear of many women candidates that 'I do not want anyone to vote for me solely because I am a woman – nor to vote against me solely for that reason'.[24]

The greatest difficulty must have been experienced by Independent candidates, for although free of party policy, they did not have a party label to use as shorthand for establishing their identity with the electorate. They had to work hard to construct that political identity and, as Ray Strachey discovered, they were liable to all kinds of misinterpretation, whether deliberate or accidental. It was noticeable with the women candidates' election addresses that they were careful to present a balanced viewpoint. References to their feminist beliefs and parliamentary intentions for women were cautious, as demonstrated by Strachey's address in 1922:

> I do not approve of extremes in politics. I distrust Revolution on the one hand and Reaction on the other, and I believe we ought to pursue a middle course. I see, however, a serious danger in class bitterness... I am a woman, but if you elected me I should, of course, endeavour to represent the men as well as the women in the Division.[25]

It was necessary for non-party workers to adopt similar discretion when they were campaigning on behalf of women candidates. Because of the suffrage societies' desire to get as many women as possible into parliament, they were often in a position of working for women whose party political views were at odds with their own beliefs. However, the NUSEC avoided the possible problem of conflict by neutralising the situation with the formation of equal citizenship committees which worked on strict non-party lines.[26]

The suffrage societies paid attention to the smallest detail to maximise the women candidates' chances of success.

Women electors, no less than women candidates, were singled out for special attention by the press as there was great speculation as to their collective electoral behaviour, magnified by their political novelty value. The pressure on women who had to perform in such an atmosphere was sufficient justification for political circumspection. Strachey noted how some male candidates treated women electors as if they were less intelligent than male voters, and would be content with a 'political sop'.[27] It was even more important in these circumstances for women candidates to expose such behaviour, while encouraging confidence in their own ability to respond to the women electors' priorities and defeat the undoubted tendency for women to cast their votes in the same way as their husbands or male relatives.

With their customary optimism, the women's organisations felt that despite such obstacles the 1922 campaign had gone well, and Elizabeth Macadam (NUSEC) went so far as to forecast that six to eight women would be elected.[28] But despite the undoubted ability of many of the women candidates and the tremendous amount of hard work, skilful organisation and planning, no new gains were made: only Nancy Astor and Mrs Wintringham retaining their seats. The election was a Conservative Party triumph, with Bonar Law becoming Prime Minister and the Labour Party taking second place, increasing its seats from 59 to 142.[29]

A Post-Election Analysis

In a post-election pamphlet the NUSEC suggested that any attribution of failure being due to their sex was a 'rash' assumption.[30] Prior to the election the press remarked that the small number of women candidates was proof that the majority of women were evidently not interested in the political process. The WFL retorted that as men had been involved in the political process since 1265 and women for only four years, 33 candidates was not an inconsiderable number,[31] especially as the barriers to women's political participation were still deep-rooted. Margaret Wynne Nevinson, in the movement for many years, refused to stand because:

Coming late into the possession of a vote and after my long experience of the fight to get it, I could never be an

> enthusiastic party politician, and to stand as an Independent
> is to court disaster... To waste all that money and energy,
> and not to get in, offends my sense of economy.[32]

To stand any chance of success necessitated full-time dedication to the campaign with a view to long-term commitment as an MP. It was a particularly resilient and confident woman who could place herself in the public forum in this way. Dr Christine Murrell, chairman of the Women's Election Committee (WEC), which had been formed to support any woman candidate who stood on the equality platform, pointed out that lack of money prevented many women from standing.[33] In 1922, the candidate's deposit alone was £150, which represented an annual wage for many men; women were far less likely to be in possession of such a sum, let alone the expenses that running a campaign entailed. Working class women, if they were experienced enough, could spare neither time nor money. Even middle and upper class women might not be in a position to acquire the necesssary funds for candidature.

Dr Murrell also noted that prospective candidates' lack of money also dissuaded some political parties from adopting women in constituencies where they might otherwise have considered a woman.[34] As Eleanor Rathbone realised:

> It is much rarer to find women than men who can afford to
> spend lavishly on nursing and fighting a constituency; also
> they are less able to cultivate friendly and natural relations
> of the "come and have a drink" sort with the men it would
> be useful to cultivate.[35]

She also maintained that the older suffrage women in the non-party societies were too far removed from the party political machines to be able to make any demands on such political groups, while younger feminists were concentrating all their time and energy on cultivating their professional careers. An ex-candidate offered a further explanation for the lack of women candidates:

> I stood as a candidate at the last General Election (1922) for
> a hopeless seat... When the present Election came along I
> decided I would not fight any seat which had not a fair
> chance of being won because I felt that if women candidates
> in numbers accepted hopeless seats from their Parties it
> would tend to establish the legend that 'Women never get in'.[36]

Several feminist journals protested at the fact that in the 1922 election not one woman had been given a safe seat by her party. Worse than that, 'Of the defeated 31, only one, Lady Cooper, was standing for a seat previously held by a candidate of her own political party...'[37] Such treatment from all parties was hardly conducive to securing the loyalty of women candidates or electors. If anything it confirmed the non-party societies' suspicion of the party system.

Rathbone both posed and answered the question:

> One may ask why women do not succeed in securing fairer play from the party organisations?... Women have only recently come into this field, the party organisations are officered mainly by men, who have men's prejudices and, wanting to win, are afraid of experimenting with the unknown. They probably believe the press nonsense about women being jealous of women.[38]

This was the assessment of a non-party woman. But there also seemed to be good cause for George Bernard Shaw's fury on Margaret Bondfield's behalf, that despite her reputation as a dedicated and hard-working Labour Party member, she was still not given a safe seat to contest:

> You are the best man of the lot, and they shove you off on a place where the water is too cold for their dainty feet just as they shoved Mary (Macarthur) off on Stourbridge, and keep the safe seats for their now quite numerous imbeciles.[39]

The WFL thought that with all these factors to consider having as many women candidates as they did was an achievement.

Edith Picton-Turbervill, who first stood for Labour in 1922, wrote of the sheer determination required to travel round the country, often alone, to badly-attended meetings, and of the difficulties which beset a rural candidate:

> How dismal – oh, how dismal very often is the nursing by Labour candidates of villages in country constituencies. The fear of being seen by landlord, or others in authority, going to a Labour Party meeting whether it is justified or not still hinders many of the village folk of England attending such meetings.[40]

Local constituencies which had selected a woman would not expend great resources on a seat which stood little chance of being won, despite this being rather a circular argument. These were the cases in which the non-party societies were essential in providing even a limited measure of support to all women candidates, whatever their party. In this sense, party and non-party women shared a common experience of fighting poor seats with few resources. Even Nancy Astor and Margaret Wintringham, in addition to other candidates, thanked the WEC for their 'valuable help', and Professor Winifred Cullis reported to the annual meeting in 1923 on 'the enormous amount of work which had been done with a minimum of expense'.[41] Once again, the years of sustaining a movement on a minimal income were turned to positive account. It was, after all, only an advantage to have the backing of a political party if that party had the belief and confidence in the candidate which it was willing to translate into tangible assistance. Otherwise, as *Time & Tide* attested, political parties were paying little more than 'lip service to the proposition that it is desirable to have women in Parliament'.[42]

The prejudice which Rathbone wrote of was spoken of by one of the unsuccessful candidates at a WEC meeting in December 1922. Mary Grant, who had been a suffrage worker before the war and then joined the women police, had stood as a Liberal in Leeds and considered that prejudice against women was a definite factor to be considered in their failure, especially in connection with certain subjects. The hostility from male audiences had been very evident, for example, when she spoke about equal pay. She also believed that religious differences in some districts accounted for a loss of votes for women. But she also reasoned that the experience had been put to good use in the amount of propaganda that each candidate had generated for the women's movement.[43] Ray Strachey had been the object of what her mother termed, 'deleterious rumours' started by her opponents. As a result she was forced to issue a leaflet to counteract them:

PLEASE NOTE: Mrs Oliver Strachey is NOT a Bolshevist, an Atheist or a Communist. Her husband was NOT a Conscientious Objector and her children are NOT neglected.[44]

Of course, the drawbacks which handicapped the women candidates were not only directly related to their position as parliamentary candidates: other difficulties concerned the electoral machine itself. The obstacles of the registration process was one,[45] and the method employed for vote allocation was another: both of these had been on the movement's agenda since 1918. Many of the post-election reviews by women's groups concentrated on the unrepresentative nature of the relationship between the votes polled and the seats gained. Proportional representation was a part of the NUSEC's and the WFL's policy, Millicent Fawcett being an active supporter of the Proportional Representation Society. The WFL insisted that:

> We must make no mistake about it; if we want women MPs, and we do, then we must get PR... We have only to look at those places where PR is used, to see the difference it has made in the composition of their Parliaments.[46]

In Germany, Holland and Ireland there was a higher percentage of women MPs because of proportional representation. The WFL computed that on the votes cast in the 1922 election, Margaret Bondfield, Lady Cooper, Ray Strachey, Mrs Burnett Smith, Eleanor Rathbone and Dame Gwynne Vaughan would all have won seats under this system.[47] The frustration of the 1922 election had been that although they had not won any new seats, the women's share of the vote had doubled since the 1918 election. Considering their handicaps, their results had been creditable, with only four women losing their deposits. In total, the women had polled 230,356 votes, yet they had only two MPs. As the NUSEC demonstrated,[48] the narrowness of some of the women's defeats was a heartening outcome: with proportional representation there might have been real cause for celebration.

The General Elections of 1923 and 1924

Barely a year later, on 6 December 1923, an election was called by Stanley Baldwin. Supposedly as a response to mounting unemployment, Baldwin had decided to introduce trade protection to replace the traditional Liberal policy of free trade, and was going to the country for support for his new policy. It was a surprise move, and the suffrage societies swung into operation again, rather sooner than they had anticipated.

Perhaps as a result of the brief interlude between elections, the number of women candidates only increased by one to 34. Of these, 12 had stood in 1922 and there was an increase in the number of women standing for Labour.[49] The Independent Labour Party had recently given instructions to its divisional councils that more women should be encouraged to stand,[50] and this had immediately resulted in three more Labour candidates. However, the old complaint of the nature of the seats which the parties had allocated to women was still as relevant, and prompted the non-party groups to assert that women would only improve this state of affairs by working outside the political parties. The difficulty was how to break the chain of disadvantage, although the Six Point Group (SPG) had no doubts as to the inadvisability of women accepting 'party leavings':

> When the women get defeated... the parties who have thus used them are the first to turn round and say: 'There is no use putting up women candidates, they only get defeated'... It should be remembered that there is no generosity in offering a woman the chance of fighting a hopeless seat on condition that she pays her own expenses.[51]

The campaign was waged in a similar fashion to that of 1922, with the NUSEC noting that on this occasion there was also a demand for its speakers by male candidates. With only 258 seats, the Conservatives were still the largest single party in the Commons, although outnumbered by the joint total of Labour and Liberal seats at 349 (191 Labour, 158 Liberals). Both the Conservatives and Liberals came to a similar conclusion about an effective way in which they might utilise the situation to defuse the rising threat of Labour:

> a 'merely tactical' alliance to keep Labour out would only strengthen it for the future, whereas in office 'it would be too weak to do much harm but not too weak to get discredited'.[52]

So Asquith supported Labour's claim, and in January 1924, the first Labour Government took office, with the Conservatives opportunely blaming the women's vote for their fall,[53] rather than Baldwin's lack of judgement.

The women's Cause seemed to profit by Labour's rise, with three Labour women taking seats for the first time: Margaret Bondfield, Susan Lawrence and Dorothy Jewson. However, it was the overall result for the women candidates which gave cause for excitement, with the return of eight women MPs. The other five were made up of three Conservatives, Nancy Astor, the Duchess of Atholl and Mrs Hilton Phillipson, along with Margaret Wintringham and Lady Terrington, the two Liberals.[54] Although, ironically, the Duchess of Atholl had been an anti-suffragist and Mrs Hilton Phillipson could hardly be classified as a feminist, to have eight women in the House of Commons after only three elections was an important achievement. It would now be a matter of experience as to how this group of women could work together in the Commons to achieve maximum benefits for women. Astor aligned herself with the women's societies as 'women who put reforms ahead of party'.[55] Mrs Wintringham's relief for Nancy Astor, herself and the future effectiveness of the women's Cause was evident when she declared that 'It is difficult for anyone except those two to realise how sorely we have needed more Women Members, whatever their party, and what a relief to us their coming will be'.[56] The non-party faction were not naive enough to believe that women should work together at all times on the basis of sex. On some occasions party would dominate and at others women's issues would unite them. Although the Duchess of Atholl believed that a woman's party would be far more divisive than class or party, she also believed in cross-party action: 'I tried to make clear to my women colleagues of all three parties that I was ready to co-operate with them wherever possible, on non-party questions of special interest to women'.[57]

Helen Fraser, a 1922 NUSEC candidate, believed that it was possible to achieve a fusion of both working within their party and together as women. Otherwise, if women worked as Independents within parliament they would, in essence, function as a Woman's Party which was not a desirable goal. She anticipated women's involvement would develop:

> These points of view on national, international, financial, social, and industrial policies are neither masculine nor feminine – they are human, and will be modified and changed as we develop and women get into parties, just as men do, because they belong there by conviction and temperament.[58]

Women's motivation for entering parliament were surely the key to how they would function once they had gained a seat. But ideology aside, it was necessary for them to establish themselves within an institution where they had no recognised place.

All such debate and speculation ended abruptly less than ten months later with the fall of the Labour Government and another election on 29 October 1924. The women's movement was distressed, for it meant the probable end of the Government which had been its political ally and from which they had expected so much. It was also the end of a term of office in which the eight women MPs could consolidate their position and guide through legislative changes for women. Three elections in three years also meant that the movement's resources were at full stretch, not having had any sustained period of recovery from the war and the reconstruction period. These factors contributed to an emotional and physical exhaustion at a time when it was necessary to instil enthusiasm into a contest that no-one was eager to fight.

The women's movement must also have been dismayed by the manifestos which the parties produced: Labour, with *A Word to the Women*, two short paragraphs largely praising what they had achieved in office. The Conservatives' one paragraph, *Women and Children*, concentrated on aspects of crime, and the Liberals' manifesto did not contain one reference to women's reforms. After five years of citizenship, the party politicians' attention to women's concerns was less than a nod. Little wonder that the WFL responded with 'A Plague on all Your Parties'.[59]

In 1924, there were 39 female candidates: 21 for Labour, six Liberals, eleven Unionists and one Independent, Mary Richardson.[60] Of these 39 candidates, 22 had stood in previous elections. Despite their electioneering experience and another increase in the votes polled for women to 387,573, only four women were returned to Westminster. These were Nancy Astor, the Duchess of Atholl, Mrs Hilton Phillipson, and a new MP who had been an NUWSS organiser, an ex-Communist now standing for Labour, Ellen Wilkinson.[61] There was great distress at the reversal of the women's fortunes, especially as Margaret Bondfield and Margaret Wintringham had failed to be re-elected.

The Zinoviev Letter[62] sealed the fate of the Labour Party, which lost ground with only 152 MPs and ensured a Conservative landslide with 415 seats, while the Liberals were at their lowest ebb with 42.[63] The women candidates had reaped the reward of their parties, but despite their low numbers, Ellen Wilkinson worked with the energy of ten and proved an invaluable addition to the House.

Conclusion

The period from November 1922 to October 1924 was certainly a political baptism of fire for the women's movement. It was a demanding period for any party to withstand, but for a movement so recently introduced to the political mainstream, it was more than challenging. Despite its erratic success in gaining parliamentary seats, its electoral showing over those three years was a positive one. The number of votes cast for women had risen from 58,976 in 1918 to 387,573 in 1924, a more than sixfold increase in six years. From 17 prospective parliamentary candidates in 1918, the number had risen to 39, with an average of nearly 10,000 votes cast per woman in 1924, compared to less than 3,500 in 1918. This had all been achieved with maximum support from the women's suffrage societies, which had depleted resources, a very minimum of support from the political parties and a barrage of discouragement from the press.

Party political women were disadvantaged: although they were tied to the fortunes of their party, their sphere of influence was restricted and they did not receive support in proportion to the contribution they made to the party. They were also circumscribed by a male agenda and were not benefitting from the advantages which being allied to an official party machine was supposed to bring. The reverse was the case where a Labour woman was given the opportunity to stand for a promising seat by her colleagues because she was a woman.[64] Non-party women operating successfully as Independent candidates would never bring any large-scale influence to bear on legislative change. Perhaps the best solution was Helen Fraser's suggestion of combining political party membership with sustaining separate women's organisations as all-party groups. The idea of an all-party women's group within parliament had been difficult for women MPs even to experiment with as there had been too few of them in the Commons and insufficient parliamentary time to establish working procedures for such a group.

How such a group might have acted as a strategic power base for women in the Commons is one of many speculations in this process of women entering political institutions, seeking to increase their power and efficacy, whilst attempting to sustain their feminist credentials and working with female colleagues who were not feminists. How they functioned as individuals, party members and part of a group of women, how far they were able to contribute to the proceedings of the House on women's issues, what reaction they prompted from male MPs and how, if at all, they influenced the Commons' work culture provide departures for further research.

Notes on Chapter 7

1   *The Woman's Leader*, 3 February 1922, p 3
2   Mowat, Charles Loch, *Britain Between the Wars 1918-1940* (London, 1955, Methuen), p 136
3   The Liberal Party became split in 1916 when David Lloyd George displaced Asquith as Prime Minister. Having no official party machine to support him, although followed by 140 Liberal MPs, Lloyd George promoted the idea of a Coalition Party.
4   *The Vote*, 3 November 1922, p 349
5   *Professional and Clerical Women's Election Questionnaire*, AWCS pamphlet, 1922, J.S. Middleton Collection
6   *The Vote*, 15 December 1922, p 397
7   NUSEC, Annual Report, 1922, p 8
8   LSWS, Annual Report, 1922, p 7
9   NUSEC, Annual Report, 1922, p 9
10   *The Vote*, 3 November 1922, p 349
11   *The Vote*, 10 November 1922, p 357
12   Ibid.
13   *Time & Tide*, 8 November 1922 in Spender, Dale, *Time & Tide Waits for No Man* (London, 1984, Pandora Press), p 136
14   *The Labour Woman*, 1 December 1922, p 183
15   *How to Conduct a Non-Party Election Campaign*, NUSEC pamphlet, October 1922, p 3
16   *The Vote*, 10 November 1922, front page
17   *Manifesto to the Women Voters of Great Britain*, NUSEC pamphlet, 1922, p 2
18   *How to Conduct a Non-Party Election Campaign*, NUSEC pamphlet, October 1922, p 3
19   *International Woman Suffrage News*, December 1922, p 43
20   NUSEC, Annual Report, 1922, p 8
21   *The Woman's Leader*, 23 November 1923, p 338

22   Stocks, Mary, *My Commonplace Book* (London, 1970, Peter Davies), p 145
23   *The Woman's Leader*, 10 November 1922, p 324
24   Ibid.
25   Ibid., p 325
26   *How to Conduct a Non-Party Election Campaign*, NUSEC pamphlet, October 1922, p 1 gives details on how potential conflict can be minimised at meetings.
27   Smith Papers, Oxford, Folder II, December 1922
28   *International Woman Suffrage News*, November 1922, p 26
29   Mowat, Charles Loch, *Britain Between the Wars 1918-1940* (London, 1955, Methuen), p 145
30   *Why Women Candidates were Defeated at the General Election of 1922*, NUSEC pamphlet, 1923, p 1
31   *The Vote*, 10 November 1922, front page
32   Nevinson, Margaret Wynne, *Life's Fitful Fever: A Volume of Memories* (London, 1926, A & C Black), p 284
33   *Time & Tide*, 6 July 1923, p 697
34   Ibid.
35   Strachey, Ray (Ed.), *Our Freedom and its Results by Five Women* (London, 1936, Hogarth Press), p 32
36   *The Woman's Leader*, 30 November 1923, p 347
37   *International Woman Suffrage News*, December 1922, p 43. The others were *Time & Tide*, *The Vote* and *The Woman's Leader*.
38   Strachey, Ray (Ed.), *Our Freedom and its Results by Five Women* (London, 1936, Hogarth Press), p 31
39   Bondfield, Margaret, *A Life's Work* (London, 1950, Hutchinson), p 245
40   Picton-Turbervill, Edith, *Life is Good*, (London, 1939, Frederick Muller), pp 160-161
41   *Time & Tide*, 2 March 1923, p 253
42   *Time & Tide*, 17 October 1922 in Spender, Dale, *Time & Tide Waits for No Man* (London, 1984, Pandora Press), p 135
43   *The Vote*, 15 December 1922, p 397
44   Smith Papers, Oxford, Folder 1, 1922, p 19
45   See Chapter 6 for further details.
46   *The Vote*, 24 November 1922, front page
47   Ibid.
48   *Why Women Candidates were Defeated in the General Election of 1922*, NUSEC pamphlet, 1923

49   *The Labour Woman*, 1 December 1923, p 188
50   *The Woman's Leader*, 24 August 1923, front page
51   *Time & Tide*, 16 November 1923 in Spender, Dale, *Time & Tide Waits for No Man* (London, 1984, Pandora Press), p 146
52   Mowat, Charles Loch, *Britain Between the Wars 1918-1940* (London, 1955, Methuen), p 169
53   *The Labour Magazine*, January 1924, p 400
54   *The Vote*, 14 December 1923, p 395
55   *The Woman's Leader*, 14 December 1923, p 369
56   Ibid.
57   Atholl, Katharine, Duchess of, *Working Partnership* (London, 1958, Arthur Barker), p 138
58   *The Woman's Leader*, 15 June 1923, p 156
59   *The Vote*, 12 October 1924, p 333
60   This was 'Slasher Richardson' (WSPU) who had attacked the painting the Rokeby Venus in 1914; she had previously stood for Labour.
61   *The Woman's Leader*, 7 November 1924, p 326
62   The Zinoviev or Red Letter was a forgery which implicated the Labour Party in plans for the mobilisation of the working class for a future revolution; it appeared two days before the election.
63   Mowat, Charles Loch, *Britain Between the Wars 1918-1940* (London, 1955, Methuen), p 190
64   *The Vote*, 27 April 1923, p 132

Chapter 8
Old and New Feminism

It is not easy, as one pushes through the day-to-day cross-currents of the women's movement, to sense clearly and unmistakably the drift of the tide – or even to proportion the significance of events as they emerge haphazard, and with the ink still wet... from the time machine.[1]

As the women's movement continued to develop, its theoretical base became more sophisticated and two ideologies seemingly gained prominence, new or welfare feminism and old or equalitarian feminism. Whether these two strands of thought were as distinct as has previously been attested, how they developed, what effect they had on the campaigns in hand, and how the theories related in practice to the organisations and the membership of the women's movement are significant areas of inquiry.

The combination of women's electoral participation, Nancy Astor's crusading performance in the Commons and determined lobbying by the women's movement ensured that welfare issues relating to women and children were given more serious consideration in parliament. Success varied: the Matrimonial Causes Act, equalising divorce; Astor's Intoxicating Liquors (Sales to Young Persons Under 18) Act; and the National Council for the Unmarried Mother and her Child's (NCUMC) Bastardy Act, all passed in 1923, presented a sharp contrast to the barren year of 1924.[2] The tenacity and hard work of the women's organisations ensured achievements such as the passing of the Guardianship of Infants Act in 1925 after six years' work by the National Union of Societies for Equal Citizenship (NUSEC) and its supporters. In the same year the Summary Jurisdiction (Separation and Maintenance) Act became law, along with the Widows, Orphans and Old Age (Contributory Pensions) Act. Such continuous campaigning was powerful evidence of the accumulative influence of the movement as a catalyst for the growth of social justice and welfare provision.[3]

By the middle of the 1920s the emergence of two areas of operation in the shape of welfare and equalitarian feminism was gaining ground. However, adherence to these philosophies was neither rigidly confined to distinct organisations, nor operated as consistent policy. The major issues which highlighted the debate on old and new feminism were those of family endowment, restrictive or protective legislation and birth control. The first two issues were the most prominent, as they involved women's economic emancipation, embracing unemployment, the status of single and married women workers, equal pay and the industrial organisation of women.

Family Endowment

The trigger for the 1920s exposition of a dual definition of feminism lay with the family endowment or family allowance movement led by Eleanor Rathbone. Rathbone's experience during the war as the administrator of separation allowances through the Liverpool branch of the Soldiers' and Sailors' Families' Association made her realise that:

> Of course family allowances were the answer to the 'equal pay' impasse: to the anti-feminist conception of motherhood as an occupation without independent economic status; to the anxiety of the overdriven mother and the malnutrition of the neglected ex-baby when a new mouth claimed its share of an inelastic unresponsive family income.[4]

Believing that she had found a strategic economic key to many women's problems, Rathbone set up the Family Endowment Committee (FEC) in 1917. Three fellow National Union of

Women's Suffrage Societies (NUWSS) colleagues, Kathleen Courtney, Maude Royden and Mary Stocks were members of the committee, together with a number of socialist colleagues.[5] The report produced by them in September 1918 recognised that 'There can be no real independence, whether for man or woman, without economic independence'.[6] The focus of the argument concentrated on one of the main planks of feminist emancipation, that of establishing equal pay where men and women were doing the same work. This attempt was continually being rebuffed by the Government and trade unions' claim that as a man's wage was intended to keep a family, equal pay was an impossibility. This position ignored the reality of women entering the labour market because of their husband's low wages, sickness, disability or death. In such circumstances women were forced to accept sweated wages which had the effect of depressing all women's wage levels.

The FEC maintained that a family allowance would provide multiple benefits to married women with families, by giving them economic independence with their own 'wage'. It would also accord women status by recognising the value of women's work as wives and mothers, remove them from the labour market and depressed wages, thereby facilitating equal pay. In turn this would end poverty and the neglect of children in those families where women were forced to go out to work. The FEC concluded that 'It means, in short, an approach to the humane maxim, "To each according to his need"'.[7] Despite the expert discourse of Rathbone's 1924 work, *The Disinherited Family*, the extent of the opposition from all political parties evidenced the controversial nature of the subject. Opposition to the scheme came not only from political parties and male-dominated trade unions but also from inside the women's movement. On the publication of its report, the FEC became the Family Endowment Council (FECl) and published a number of pamphlets. One, written by Rathbone and Stocks, specifically aimed at encouraging women's organisations to adopt the scheme and attempted to answer the catalogue of objections, as well as explaining how the scheme might be financed.[8]

Conflict surrounding family endowment was also emerging within the NUSEC, of which Rathbone was President. At the 1925 annual council meeting she moved a resolution for the union to adopt family endowment as part of its policy. After an impassioned speech, the vote went in Rathbone's favour but, as a result, Millicent Fawcett, a fierce opponent of family endowment, resigned from the editorial board of *The Woman's Leader*. Fawcett believed that:

> It is also probable that if parents are relieved of the obligation to support their children, one of the very strongest inducements to submit to the drudgery of daily toil would be withdrawn.[9]

She felt that the concept of family endowment was nothing less than a declaration of socialism. Her Liberal heritage of personal responsibility was unmoved by the poverty and destitution of many women and children which motivated Rathbone.

In a written response to Fawcett's article, Rathbone admitted that the implementation of her scheme 'is not at present, nor probably will be for many years, within the sphere of practical politics'.[10] However, she was anxious to elicit a commitment to the principle of family allowances by political parties and women's organisations, rather than an outright rejection on the basis that a perfect scheme had not yet been devised. The reservations by the Labour movement were many and complex, and the 1923 Labour Women's Conference followed the party line by rejecting it. However, Rathbone's insistent campaigning over the years brought acceptance, and by 1926 the NUSEC could report that the Women's National Liberal Federation (WNLF), the National Council of Women (NCW), the International Woman Suffrage Alliance (IWSA) and the Independent Labour Party had all passed resolutions concerning family allowances.[11] By 1927, the Family Endowment Conference was reported as 'a successful affair which at least demonstrated the life and vigour of the movement. A large and heterogeneous selection of societies was represented...'[12] The Standing Joint Committee of Industrial Women's Organisations (SJCIWO) also reported its approval of the adoption of the principle at the 1927 Labour Women's Conference, welcoming its adoption by the Labour Party's annual conference.[13]

Rathbone's solution for addressing the problem of family poverty, which she believed had been vindicated by the improvement in women's and children's health during the war through separation allowances,[14] also brought with it a radical shift in feminist perspective. Stocks later revealed that Rathbone had felt that the equalitarian interpretation of feminist demands was too narrow for the post-war world, and that a different emphasis was needed with a fresh approach.[15]

Women's organisations had already revised their constitutions and aims, but this next step was a major reappraisal of their philosophy. The essence of the new ethos for Rathbone emerged in her speech to the 1925 NUSEC annual council when she claimed that:

> At last we have done with the boring business of measuring everything that women want, or that is offered them by men's standards, to see if it is exactly up to sample. At last we can stop looking at all our problems through men's eyes and discussing them in men's phraseology. We can demand what we want for women, not because it is what men have got but because it is what women need to fulfil the potentialities of their own natures and to adjust themselves to the circumstances of their own lives.[16]

This statement reflected a new confidence from women who had been citizens for seven years. Welfare feminism was a recognition of the importance of the function of the wife and mother, of the distinctions between the sexes. It was an attempt to gain recognition and status for this essential role and its implications for the economy and the health of the nation.

Taking the larger view, her scheme was an attempt at an economic reappraisal which embraced all women in its recognition of the economic interdependence of the family, employment and equal pay. The ensuing debate between welfare and equalitarian feminists uncovered a range of interpretations which produced new dimensions in the theoretical analysis of women's lives.

The review of 1926 in *The Woman's Leader* remarked on the introduction in that year of the expression 'new feminism', and gave its definition of the respective positions:

> There is the feminism of pure equality, and the feminism of equivalent opportunity... And there is the feminism which says: women have a certain specialised part to play in the world, let us see that they play it with the same measure of consideration which men regard as necessary when they have a specialised part to play. The programmes are not mutually exclusive. They are not necessarily antagonistic. But they do involve... a difference of emphasis... New feminism... accuses old feminism of a slavish acceptance of masculine standards, while the old feminists cherish the conviction that the new feminists are at heart mere 'social reformers'.[17]

This emerging duality promoted questions concerning a re-appraisal of the nature of equality, what the necessary conditions were for the practice of equality and what effect the two interpretations would have on the feminist agenda in hand. The most contentious point lay in the acceptance by the new feminists of the 'special' role of women. They maintained that although all issues were of concern to both men and women, there were some which were of greater interest to women:

> It follows inevitably that questions such as birth control, family allowances, housing, smoke abatement, though they affect both sexes, do not affect both sexes equally... There is probably scarcely a department of human activity in which the physiological differences... have not some effect... upon the outlook of the two sexes. To those who hold this view, 'equal citizenship' means something more than a knocking down of barriers and a removal of disabilities.[18]

Equalitarians perceived this as playing into the opposition's hands. Suffragists had struggled to escape from the confinements of the 'woman's sphere' and establish that the interests of men and women were identical in order to accord women the right to an equal place in the world. This had been the purpose of the feminists' insistence on their designation as 'human beings' in order to claim their rights. Now welfare feminists were qualifying and compromising that position, claiming special interests for women in which it would mean men who would be marginalised.

The lines along which this debate were drawn were by no means rigid, existing not only between organisations, but within them. Rathbone's definition of equality was countered by Elizabeth Abbott, who was also a member of the NUSEC. Abbott believed that the welfare feminists were spawning arguments which were little more than a linguistic distraction:

> Theoretical discussions on 'what is equality' are valueless – another red herring across the equalitarian track. The issue is not between 'old' and 'new' feminism. (There is no such thing as 'new' feminism, just as there is no such thing as 'new' freedom. There is freedom and there is tyranny.) The issue is between feminism – equalitarianism – and that which is not feminism.[19]

But the new feminists claimed that they were extending the agenda of female values: 'It is a poor kind of feminism which adopts unquestioningly the standards of a man-made social philosophy'.[20] They described the equalitarians' position as that of aping male values and thus restricting feminism to an unimaginative duplication of the male position which would never be able to fulfil the needs of women's lives.

The controversy was heightened when Kathleen Courtney, another executive member of the NUSEC, branded the equalitarian school of thought as the 'me too' feminists. Likening them to a little girl chasing her older brother and continually crying, 'Me, too', Rathbone contested that the need for such tactics was over. It was no longer necessary to make such demands for:

> All this has been won. There are still a few analagous rights not yet secured... To the new school, the habit of continually measuring women's rights by men's achievements seems out of date, ignominious and boring... Now that we have secured possession of the tools of citizenship, we intend to use them not to copy men's models but to produce our own.[21]

Understandably, the equalitarians bridled at the 'Me, too' reduction of their theory, calling it a 'cheap jibe'.[22] In counteracting it, Abbott emphasised the universal nature of the equalitarians' stance, which made it seem as if it was the welfare feminists' theory which was the narrow one:

> The demand for equality has been a demand that such rights, liberties, and opportunities as the State allows to its citizens shall not be withheld from women; a demand that wherever and whenever the State sets a value upon its citizens, it shall not set an inferior value upon women; a demand for the removal of every arbitrary impediment that hinders the progress, in any realm of life and work, of women. That is equality.[23]

The equalitarian Six Point Group (SPG), which prided itself on its practical grasp of politics, had previously criticised the NUSEC for continually expanding its agenda to include issues, such as smoke abatement, which the SPG thought had nothing to do with the Cause.[24] Such activity only served to weaken its case for equality issues and squandered resources which should be concentrated on what was within practical reach of success. With the advent of welfare feminism the SPG clung more adamantly than ever to its belief that feminism's prime aim was the complete political emancipation of women. When the NUSEC espoused family allowances as part of its new feminism, *Time & Tide* asserted that this position displayed a lack of seriousness towards the current franchise campaign. SPG members such as Vera Brittain and Winifred Holtby wrote of their adherence to equalitarian values. Holtby's explanation attacked Rathbone's contention that the equalitarian approach was outdated:

> ... while the inequality exists, while injustice is done and opportunity denied to the great majority of women, I shall have to be a feminist, and an Old Feminist, with the motto Equality First. And I shan't be happy till I get it.[25]

And in a 1927 SPG pamphlet, Brittain explained that:

> Feminism still lives in England today because the incompleteness of the English franchise represents but one symbol among many others of the incomplete recognition of women as human beings... Recognise our full humanity and we will trouble you no more.[26]

By the mid-1920s it was also clear that this polemic was mitigated by many different shades of opinion between the two feminisms which reflected the varied experiences of individual women. If Rathbone's family endowment scheme had provided the platform for these new ideological explorations within the movement, then birth control and restrictive/protective legislation developed the grounds for extending the debate.

Birth Control

Birth control was one of the considerations which Rathbone designated as of particular concern to women, and part of the welfare package which could improve women's lives. Dealing with the economic position of women, family endowment logically embraced birth control as an indirect means of addressing the acute poverty of working class women. In the light of this debate the article in *The Women's Leader* of October 1925 tackled the nub of the matter when it posed the question, 'Is Birth Control a Feminist Reform?' It began by defining its feminism as being 'The demand of women that the whole structure and movement of society shall reflect in a proportionate degree their experiences, their needs, and their aspirations'.[27] It was then able to apply such a definition to the role which occupied the majority of women, that of motherhood.

Dora Russell and Leah L'Estrange Malone, Labour Party members, were two of the founders of the Workers' Birth Control Group (WBCG) who in 1924 devised the campaign slogan that 'It is four times as dangerous to bear a child as to work in a mine, and mining is men's most dangerous trade'.[28] This industrial analogy was taken up by *The Women's Leader* demanding that the 'occupation' of motherhood be guided by stringent regulatory standards just as the most dangerous male employment was. It called for 'maximum freedom to determine under what conditions she will or will not perform her function, and how far by reasonable "limitation of output" she may improve the standard of her "product"'.[29]

Viewing the government population policy, of a high birth rate balanced by a high death rate, as a degradation to women and the society which permitted it, the NUSEC insisted that the provision of birth control information to married women was an essential feminist reform. In the light of the controversial nature of the subject, it qualified its statements by maintaining that this was not, however, a demand for the general provision of birth control. The NUSEC had worded the resolution which it had passed earlier in the year very carefully:

> That this Council calls upon the Ministry of Health to allow information with respect to methods of Birth Control to be given by medical officers at Maternity and Child Welfare Clinics in receipt of Government grants, in cases in which either a mother asks for such information or in which, in the opinion of the Medical Officer, the health of the parents renders it desirable.[30]

This cautious approach was a realistic anticipation of the attacks that could follow at a time when it was illegal for state-funded clinics and centres to give birth control advice, and where doctors and nurses who had done so had been dismissed.[31] To openly discuss women's sexual behaviour and campaign for choice in working women's lives were still little short of revolutionary.

The political sensitivity surrounding the subject was one of the reasons given by the SPG for shunning the issue and insisting that it should not be a feminist claim. That a reform which could enable women to have greater control over their sexuality, improving their health and economic circumstances, should not be regarded as a feminist goal seems a perverse judgement. However, it was made in the light of the two societies' differing interpretations of the feminist ideal. The SPG's adherence was to the primacy of equal civil and political rights as the cornerstone of female emancipation, rather than economic and social rights: 'They (family endowment and birth control) may of course be valuable social reforms for quite other reasons... but they are not, except for this reason, feminist reforms'.[32] The divisions which have been interpreted in this new versus old feminism conflict can be seen to be rather more a matter of a differentiation in the means to the end, rather than an implacable ideological rift.

The controversial birth control campaign threw up deep concerns from other feminists, women's groups and individual women, which did not necessarily place them in the equalitarians' camp. The St Joan Social and Political Alliance (SJSPA) objected on religious grounds, while many feminist doctors such as Letitia Fairfield (NUSEC) and Mary Scharlieb (SPG) protested on the grounds of health risks or morality.[33] But the SPG's main concern was that this controversial NUSEC campaign was diverting attention from the powerful public agitation for the final, concerted effort for the franchise which was being launched in 1926. It was very firmly a tactical objection, based on the advisability of featuring such a contentious issue at a time when it might overshadow and damage their primary campaign of franchise equalisation.

Another interesting aspect of this argument was the low profile which the Women's Freedom League (WFL) took. There was no mention of the rival philosophies in its annual reports, and references to the key issues of family endowment and birth control in its paper, *The Vote*, were largely limited to accounts of conferences. The main tenor of the WFL's ardent campaigning at this time was a focused attack on the attainment of equal political rights, and it remained detached from what became, in the correspondence pages of *Time & Tide*, a vigorous exchange.

However, Rathbone and her supporters correctly gauged the strong appeal for working class women of the birth control campaign. Indeed, Rathbone must have felt that her position was vindicated when a meeting she chaired in April 1926 on birth control methods was filled to capacity. There were nearly 40 women's organisations represented as well as associated interest groups and individuals.[34]

It has already been noted that after initially rejecting the concept of family allowances, the women of the Labour movement gradually came to approve the scheme. Similarly with the birth control issue, Labour women were cautious in their initial response. This stance was probably a result of the subject's controversial nature, for there was no doubt of working women's desperate need for the kind of relief which had been available to middle class women for many years. There were several concerns relating to the position of women within the party which made their reserve understandable and demonstrated another inhibiting feature of being part of a political party. Early in 1924, seven Labour Party women interested in the promotion of birth control (including Dora Russell and Leah L'Estrange Mallone) wrote to *The Labour Woman* reminding the party that the 1923 Labour Women's Conference had promised that a sub-committee would discuss the issue. The letter was asking for renewed support and activity throughout women's branches.[35] In the same issue, an article, 'Birth Control: A Plea for Careful Consideration', dealt with some of the party's major reservations. Dora Russell pointed out[36] that the Labour Party had always relied a good deal on the Catholic vote and a young party building up its support could not afford to alienate such a large section of the electorate. *The Labour Woman* emphasised the party's reluctance to air the debate because the religious and moral beliefs of its diverse membership meant that 'even discussion of the subject' was contentious.[37]

There was also considerable resistance within the party to the idea that birth control could be a solution for working class poverty. It ran counter to the ideal of founding working class prosperity on a reorganisation of society on socialist principles. Endorsing the supposed economic link with family size was not only a betrayal of its policies but an underwriting of the opposition's policy. Labour believed that the Liberal Party was integrating birth control into its economic thinking 'because the Liberals do not want to make any drastic changes in the distribution of wealth'.[38] This mixture of motives which fuelled Labour women's and the party's opposition was represented by members such as Miss Quinn of the Tailors' and Garment Workers' Union. Miss Quinn was a Catholic, and as well as her membership of the Labour movement had been a WSPU member, imprisoned five times. At the 1925 Labour Women's Conference she caused quite a stir with an impassioned accusation that birth control was 'filth'. By 1927, when Labour had accepted the policy of birth control, she used an alternative tack to characterise it as 'a complete capitulation to capitalism, a philosophy of cowardice and a policy of despair'.[39]

The 1923 Report of the SJCIWO detailed how a birth control resolution had been deferred and that the SJCIWO had formed a committee to investigate the issue, with the membership representing Labour and suffrage interests.[40] But it was in 1924 that the issue really began to gain favour, perhaps because it was the year of the Labour Government and women both inside and outside the party had great expectations for the implementation of women's reforms. At that year's Labour Women's Conference, there were eight resolutions on the necessity for birth control information and success was achieved in the launch of the women's birth control group, with Dorothy Jewson, the Labour MP and WFL member as its President.[41] After three years' discussion, having avoided the accusation of haste and avoided dissension, the SJCIWO recommended to the Labour Party in 1925 that the state should enable doctors and poor law services to provide birth control information on request.[42]

Labour Party women had reconsidered their position, but the men were not yet ready to risk adopting such a disputatious issue. However, with the massive weight of support from the women's sections, there was some pressure on party men to reach a compromise. The 1925 conference, whilst denying that the subject was a political party issue, acknowledged that members should be 'free to hold and promote their individual convictions'.[43] This executive resolution might be construed as a skilful evasion of a party commitment to the needs of working women; a further indication of Labour women's containment within the corral of the women's sections.

Restriction or Protection? Industrial Legislation for Women

The third issue which fuelled the debate between welfare and equalitarian feminists was one in which Labour women had been involved for many years, and was largely the provenance of industrial women. The issue of restrictive or protective legislation caused considerable factional conflict involving organised women in a confusion of allegiances.

Non-party women believed that legislation governing the working conditions of women in industry was used by trade unions and employers to limit women's employment opportunities, hence their alternative nomenclature of 'restrictive' legislation. It was a means of retaining well-paid work for men, whilst hiving women off to an unskilled, low-paid industrial ghetto. Feminists claimed that legislation governing health and safety conditions should be determined on the basis of the work involved, not on the sex of the worker. Industrial women insisted that such protective legislation was an additional weapon in their arsenal to guard women employees from industrial exploitation. They argued that only by instituting such protection initially for women workers would protection be applied, in time, to men also. But non-party women regarded such male 'protection' as a cynical manipulation of sentiment engendered by strictly economic motives. They contested that if such legislation was necessary, then it was necessary for all workers, both male and female.[44]

The advent of proposed additions to the Factories Acts in 1924 revived what had not been an issue since the 1842 Coal Mines Act. Before the non-party organisations could mount any opposition, the general election campaign intervened. However, publications such as *The Vote* and *The Woman's Leader* seized the opportunity to air their case against such restrictions while *The Labour Woman* put the alternative view. Barbara Drake did not spare her sisters' feelings when she wrote that:

> Industrial women are as sound as middle class feminists on the question of 'equal laws', but, unlike these arm-chair philosophers, they are far more concerned for the practical results of legislation than for its mere conformity with the abstract principle of sex equality.[45]

Drake had put her finger on the reason why, as the SJCIWO had resolved, it was only possible for suffrage women and industrial women to work together on isolated campaigns of joint interest, rather than acting as a consistently unified force.

The position of Labour women MPs in parliament emphasised the divide when, for instance, the NUSEC organised a deputation to Susan Lawrence in April 1926 exhorting her to support the NUSEC stance. Speakers represented a variety of women's organisations, Dr Winifred Cullis (WNLF/SPG/WEC), Miss Barry (SJSPA), Chrystal Macmillan (NUSEC), Philipa Strachey

(LSWS), Anna Munro (WFL) and Mrs Betty Archdale (WIL/SPG), editor of *Time & Tide*. However, although Susan Lawrence was now a member of the WFL and supported equality of the sexes, 'she felt unable to give practical support to the immediate demand'.[46]

Diametric opposition between Labour women and non-party women was supplemented by internal divisions in the women's societies which reflected the welfare and equalitarian debate. The most significant interpretive difference arose at the NUSEC's annual council meeting on 5 March 1927. The union had been engaged in three years of active campaigning against restrictive legislation issues, and a resolution on the topic was tabled. It reflected a development from the union's original theory to a consideration of the most effective ways in which to implement such theory. The initial resolution read:

> That legislation for the protection of the workers should be based, not upon sex, but on the nature of the occupation... and to consider and decide according to the merits of each case whether to work for the extension of the regulation to both sexes or to oppose it for both sexes.[47]

This was not enough for Eleanor Rathbone, who proposed an amendment which embodied a flavour of the new feminism. She told the membership that working for 'pure equality' was 'an arid, barren, and obsessing idea'[48] and suggested considering:

>   a) Whether the proposed regulation will promote the well-being of the community and of the workers affected.
>   b) Whether the workers affected desire the regulation, and are promoting it through their organisations.
>   c) Whether the policy of securing equality through extension or through opposition is more likely to meet with a rapid and permanent success.[49]

These three clauses changed the NUSEC's position from a purist to an interpretive stance, introducing considerations likely to compromise its doctrine of equality. The amendment was carried by one vote, when Chrystal Macmillan moved that the resolution should stand as far as the word 'occupation' in line three. This fell by four votes, and the original resolution with its amendment was then carried.

The opposition stated their belief that any proposal had to be considered in the light of whether or not it promoted the objective of equality. However, the majority of those present felt that there were additional factors other than that of equality which needed to be addressed. A second resolution, complementary to the spirit of the first 'refused to declare that those reforms on the immediate programme which concern family allowances, information on methods of birth control... are an inferior brand of equality'. The new feminism was thus enshrined in the union's programme.[50]

This policy change cost the Union the resignation of eleven long-serving members of the executive, who expressed their opposition to the abandonment of the equalitarian principle of the primacy of equality, although they remained as ordinary members to work from within for a return to the NUSEC's original policy. A press statement correcting a journalistic error that the rift had been caused by disagreements over the equal franchise campaign demonstrated the conviction of the equalitarian stance that their acquiescence 'would have been a betrayal of the women's movement for which we have been working, some of us for more than 30 years'.[51] The open letter made it clear that this was a fundamental philosophical divide on priorities. Political rights, equal pay, the equal moral standard and discrimination against married women were the dissenters' prime objectives. Just as the SPG had demanded years before, they asked if the union's objective was equal citizenship or social reform. They reminded the executive that it was largely the pursuit of this principle of equality which 'has for so long united those whose opinions on other matters social and political are utterly diverse'.[52]

This group of women now became involved with the recently formed Open Door Council (ODC), which had its first annual meeting at the beginning of April 1927. The ODC largely concerned itself with the position of industrial women. Adopting the equalitarian stance of the SPG, the ODC concentrated on removing legislative restrictions from industrial women's work. As part of its education campaign, the ODC undertook a mass distribution of literature among Labour Party women's sections and trade unions. But despite this, the ODC was to be in conflict for several years to come with industrial women's views, as represented by the SJCIWO. By 1927 the SJCIWO and the ODC were engaged in a propaganda feud, countering one another's arguments in rival pamphlets. One of the ODC's main claims was that restrictive legislation denied women adult status.[53] The reality perceived by the SJCIWO was that by adopting their equalitarian stance, middle class feminists were actually assisting employers in their exploitation of working class women.

Yet despite such disagreements, there was also ground for solidarity. It was the subject of maternity that brought the SJCIWO and Eleanor Rathbone together in agreement on protective legislation. International Women's Labour Conference resolutions on maternity leave had been adopted by the Labour Women's Conference of 1920, but it was not until the mid-1920s that Rathbone ridiculed the 'me too' feminists who 'because no men have babies in the sense that women have them, (they) would reject every provision which applies exclusively to the pre- and post-confinement period'.[54] This was exactly where Rathbone's perception of 'special needs' was strongest, and the necessity for such measures as family allowances could be seen to be of greatest value. It was also the point at which the welfare feminists' ideas and the SJCIWO's concern for the welfare of its membership harmonised.

Conclusion

It was not surprising that such polarisation should exacerbate the divide along class and gender lines which indicated a lack of awareness on the part of some middle class feminists who were too obsessed with ideological purity. They failed to appreciate the grim reality of many working class women's lives and the urgent necessity of release from industrial oppression. Vera Brittain saw that 'one is concerned with the immediate practical advantages of a class, and the other with the completed future triumph of a sex'.[55] The failure of the equalitarians was assuming that all women were equal in their oppression, using the term 'women' without reference to class.

While recognising the differences in the position of industrial and professional workers, the SJCIWO believed that this did not disqualify them from a shared commitment to the same ideals as other women's organisations. Indeed it was because of its commitment to those same ideals that it was engaged in this struggle on behalf of working class women:

> It is because we believe in the emancipation of women, economic, social, and political, that we stand for the protection

of industrial women workers against the ruthless exploitation which has marred their history in industry.[56]

The development of these factions did not mark a deterioration in the women's movement: it signalled that the network was marked by a spirit of growth and development. No doubt the frustration engendered by the persistent opposition of the Government contributed to the feeling that a sense of priorities and resolve must be kept firm. Wrestling with such theoretical and ideological considerations demonstrated that there was nothing moribund about the organisations, although there was disappointment at some of the divisiveness when 'The crying need of the moment is co-operation'.[57] There were mitigating factors to explain such rivalry, as well as a sense of inevitability at its occurrence, considering that women were fighting on all fronts – social, economic and political. In the face of this sustained assault, disagreements as to tactical and campaign priorities are hardly surprising. The commitment of women, whether party or non-party, who had given their lives to the Cause was bound to induce a certain volatility. The statement of the resigning NUSEC members who refused to betray principles sustained over 30 years could be echoed by many in the movement who felt there was a lot to lose.

There had always been alliances and affiliations, but the widening of the movement's objectives induced· a need to re-examine and adjust policy to accommodate new ideas. For several years after the war the movement had been engulfed by the weight of practical considerations of survival; the subsequent period of readjustment was an attempt to refocus objectives in a changing political landscape. Such considerations cannot excuse the many destructive exchanges engendered by this conflict,[58] but it also assisted and extended understanding of the intricacies of the issues.

Finally, it is important to remember that the debate surrounding new and old feminism only represents part of the movement's campaigns. At a time when harsh words were being exchanged on this issue, the same organisations were co-operating on the final battle for franchise equality, which amply demonstrates the movement's unanimity of purpose and action.

Notes on Chapter 8

1   *The Woman's Leader*, 2 January 1925, front page
2   Gates, G. E. (ed.), *The Woman's Year Book 1923-24* (London, 1924, Women Publishers Ltd for the NUSEC), pp 38-39
3   Fawcett, Millicent, *What the Vote has Done* (London, 1927, NUSEC) contains a complete list of legislation from 1918.
4   Stocks, Mary, *Eleanor Rathbone* (London, 1950, Victor Gollancz), p 77
5   Ibid., p 84
6   *Equal Pay and the Family: A Proposal for the National Endowment of Motherhood*, Family Endowment Committee Report (London, 1918), p 10
7   Ibid., p 12
8   Rathbone, Eleanor F. & Stocks, Mary D., *Why Women's Societies Should Work for Family Endowment* (London, undated, FEC), p 1
9   *The Vote*, 12 June 1925, p 189
10   *The Woman's Leader*, 6 February 1925, p 12
11   NUSEC, Annual Report, 1926, p 13
12   *The Woman's Leader*, 21 October 1927, p 296. Labour and Liberal movements, WCAs and WCG were all represented.
13   Labour Party, Women's Conference Report: Report on Work in Women's Interests at Home and Abroad, May 1925-April 1927, p 42; Labour Party, Report by the Chief Woman Officer, May 1927-May 1928, pp 18 & 30
14   Stocks, Mary, *Eleanor Rathbone* (London, 1950, Victor Gollancz), p 77
15   Ibid., p 117
16   Ibid., p 116
17   *The Woman's Leader*, 31 December 1926, front page
18   *The Woman's Leader*, 11 February 1927, p 3
19   Ibid., p 4
20   Stocks, Mary, *The Case for Family Endowment* (London, 1927, Labour Publishing Company), p 38
21   Strachey, Ray (Ed.), *Our Freedom and its Results by Five Women* (London, 1936, Hogarth Press), p 58
22   *The Woman's Leader*, 11 February 1927, p 4
23   Ibid.
24   *Time & Tide*, 5 November 1926, p 998
25   Brittain, Vera & Holtby, Winifred, *Testament of a*

Generation: The Journalism of Vera Brittain & Winifred Holtby (London, 1985, Virago), p 48

26 Ibid., pp 98-99
27 *The Woman's Leader*, 2 October 1925, p 383
28 Russell, Dora, *The Tamarisk Tree: Volume 1: My Quest for Life and Love* (London, 1977, Virago), p 171
29 *The Woman's Leader*, 2 October 1925, p 283
30 NUSEC, Annual Report, 1926, p 66
31 Nurse Daniels, a health visitor for Edmonton Urban Council was sacked in December 1922 for giving women the address of a Marie Stopes clinic. The decision was endorsed by the Minister of Health. Liddington, Jill, *The Life and Times of a Respectable Rebel* (London, 1984, Virago), p 324
32 *Time & Tide*, 12 March 1926, p 243
33 *The Woman's Leader*, 21 April 1926, front page
34 *The Woman's Leader*, 30 April 1926, pp 114-115
35 *The Labour Woman*, 1 March 1924, p 46
36 Russell, Dora, *The Tamarisk Tree: Volume 1: My Quest for Life and Love* (London, 1977, Virago), p 171
37 *The Labour Woman*, 1 March 1924, p 34
38 Ibid.
39 Labour Party, Women's Conference Report, 1927, p 40. See also *The Labour Woman*, 1 July 1925, p 123
40 SJCIWO, Report, January-October 1924, p 4. Mrs F.N. Harrison Bell, (LP), Dr Ethel Bentham (LP/NUSEC), Mrs Eleanor Hood (WCG), Mrs C.D. Rackham (LP/NUSEC), Mrs Lowe (NFWW).
41 *The Vote*, 28 March 1924, p 101
42 SJCIWO, Report, January-November 1925, p 4
43 Ibid. It is interesting to note that a similar pronouncement on 'individual conscience' was made in 1990 by the Labour Party on voting in a Commons abortion debate.
44 *The Labour Woman*, 1 January 1925, p 2
45 *The Labour Woman*, 1 August 1924, p 124
46 *The Woman's Leader*, 30 April 1926, p 114
47 NUSEC, Annual Report, 1927, p 4
48 *Time & Tide*, 11 March 1927, p 229
49 NUSEC, Annual Report, 1927, pp 4-5
50 Ibid., p 7
51 Statement to the press by the eleven resigning officers and members of the NUSEC executive committee, 6 March 1927, Lady Astor Collection

52   Ibid., p 3
53   *Restrictive Legislation and the Industrial Women Worker: A Reply*, ODC pamphlet, 1928, p 2
54   Stocks, Mary, *Eleanor Rathbone* (London, 1950, Victor Gollancz), p 60
55   Brittain, Vera & Holtby, Winifred, *Testament of a Generation: The Journalism of Vera Brittain & Winifred Holtby* (London, 1985, Virago), p 110
56   *Protective Legislation and Women Workers*, SJCIWO pamphlet, October 1927, p 8
57   Manuscript of a BBC Radio talk, Hon. Mrs Franklin, NCW President, 12 October 1926, BBC Written Sound Archive, p 1
58   During 1926 and 1927, the correspondence column of *Time & Tide* carried letters which grew increasingly vituperative as NUSEC and SPG members defended their respective positions.

Chapter 9

The Franchise Extension Campaign

⸺►❧◄⸺

It was said if the vote were given to young women they
would invariably vote for the best looking candidate.
'Looking around this House,' said the Society's only woman
MP, amid a burst of laughter, 'I cannot see that there is any
need for honourable members to be worried'.[1]

As the women's movement's activities during the 1920s slowly continued to permeate all sectors of public life, the resultant groupings
and affiliations between organisations formed a multi-layered
network which operated along parallel and interconnecting lines.
Not surprisingly, considering the diversity of its campaigns, there
were factional interests and ideological rifts. But however contentious the differences, the strength of the network's bond lay in
the movement's common concerns. The analysis, solutions and
strategies might differ but issues such as equal pay, the equal moral
standard and the rights of married women comprised a common
agenda. Most dominant of all these shared concerns was the
campaign for the franchise extension.

The solidarity engendered by so many years of collective action
on this campaign was not to be undermined, despite the hardships
and vicissitudes of the post-war world. This unity of purpose
derived from the movement's awareness that:

The status of all women is lowered so long as the fact of being a woman entails the coming under different franchise laws to the fact of being a man... The fact that women are not fully enfranchised and that they are not considered fit to sit and legislate in one of our Houses of Parliament affects all women in all their comings and goings, affects the likelihood of their being elected to the House of Commons, affects the likelihood of their being elected to any seat on any local authority, affects their value in the labour market and in the home.[2]

The Forgotten Women

The Representation of the People Act of February 1918 enfranchised six million women and added 5 million to the local government electorate. Qualification meant that:

... the Parliamentary franchise is given to women of thirty or more who themselves have, or whose husbands have, a local government qualification; while the local government franchise is given to women of twenty-one or more who themselves have such qualification, and to women of thirty or more whose husbands have such qualification, where both reside together in qualifying premises.[3]

Women over thirty could qualify in nine ways: five in their own right and four as married women. Married or single women over thirty could qualify in their own right by virtue of their occupation of qualifying premises in the following five ways: through ownership or tenancy, as a lodger, by service (where her employment included accommodation) or as a university graduate (to vote for university members only). The emphasis, in some cases, of the supply or ownership of furniture for qualification led to a popular taunt by the women in the movement that as far as women were concerned the vote had been reduced to the price of a husband or a van load of furniture! The women's organisations were quick to point out the heavy irony which seemed to have escaped the Government's notice that the 3 million disenfranchised women under thirty were largely those whom the Government had lavishly praised for their contribution to the war effort. As such, this omission cast doubt on the claim that giving the vote to women had been in grateful recognition of their wartime service.

But there were also approximately 2 million women over thirty who failed to qualify. They fell into the following categories: professional and business women with business premises or unfurnished rooms, shop assistants and domestic workers who 'lived in', and daughters living at home. The right extended to male businessmen to vote in two constituencies if their domestic residence and their business premises were in two different counties, did not apply to women. Also the interpretation of 'joint occupation' meant that three single men sharing a house had a vote each, whereas in the case of three single women 'joint occupation' only entitled two of them to a vote.[4] Further categories which debarred these women from voting were:

> ... the daughter or sister who lived in the mother's or brother's house; the British wife of an alien cannot vote, but the British husband of an alien woman can do so; a widow who gives up her home and lives with her son cannot vote; the newly-made widow automatically came off the register.[5]

Such restrictions were parliament's way of ensuring that the male electorate was not 'swamped' by women voters: the prevalent fear being that if all women had the vote at twenty-one, they would outnumber the men by over 2 million and institute some kind of female rule. Anti-suffrage terms such as 'Petticoat Government' and the even older 'Monstrous Regiment', were frequently employed in such parliamentary discussions. The other justification for the limitation was that 'girls'[6] of twenty-one were not regarded as being responsible enough for the exacting task of citizenship. It was hoped, in some quarters, that by making marriage one of the methods of entitlement, control of the women's vote would be achieved via their more stable partners. In this way erratic female behaviour might be minimised at the ballot box. It was also possible that linking marriage and the vote was an inducement to women to return to their domestic role after the war. There was also a feeling among the movement that the delicacy which surrounded women revealing their age would mean that many women would not want to admit to being thirty and would not, therefore, register to vote.[7]

The movement's recognition of the interdependent nature of women's struggle activated all parts of the movement to work together for those women under thirty who had been denied the vote. In effect, this predominantly affected working class women and the Women's Freedom League (WFL) acknowledged that:

Women in the industrial world are more heavily handicapped than professional women by want of political power. The very great majority of women in industry are under 30 years of age and voteless.[8]

Ellen Wilkinson, the Labour MP, emphasised this point at a WFL meeting, when she said that it was a class under thirty who was powerless. But she also admitted that professional women over thirty also suffered, disenfranchised as they were through many technicalities. Wilkinson was aware that if the lobbying which she planned to carry out in the Commons was to have any chance of success, she needed to be able to call upon the support of the whole of the women's movement.[9] Throughout the years of the divisive debate between industrial and suffrage women on protective legislation, Ellen Wilkinson, Margaret Bondfield and other Labour women continued to work with the suffrage societies and the co-ordinating body of the Equal Political Rights Campaign Committee (EPRCC) on a vigorous franchise campaign.

Running parallel to the protective legislation controversy, Labour women were to be found attending meetings and demonstrations organised by the National Union of Societies for Equal Citizenship (NUSEC), the WFL, the Saint Joan Social and Political Alliance (SJSPA) and the Six Point Group (SPG). As Dr Ethel Bentham, Labour Party member and executive member of the Standing Joint Committee of Industrial Women's Organisations (SJCIWO) emphasised at an EPRCC meeting organised by the SPG in December 1926, chaired by Lady Rhondda, 'This was a question above party politics'.[10] Nor was it a struggle confined only to those women recognised as committed feminists. When Margaret Bondfield become an MP, *The Daily Herald* ventured that she could hardly be recognised as 'a feminist of the deepest dye',[11] whilst *Time & Tide* lamented that 'If only Margaret Bondfield were a feminist how unreservedly one could rejoice over her return to Parliament. Perhaps she will learn wisdom.'[12] She confounded such opinions by joining the NUSEC's equal franchise demonstration in March 1923 and speaking in favour of the resolution demanding equal franchise. She also wrote to *The Woman's Leader* at the end of the same year to 'urge all suffrage women to rekindle their enthusiasm for the last effort to remove the present franchise anomalies and to win for women at 21 and over the full rights of citizenship on the residential qualification'.[13]

The Sex Disqualification (Removal) Bill

The campaign to secure the franchise extension began with the inclusion of the demand for equal franchise as the chief priority on all the women's organisations' agendas. The National Union of Women's Suffrage Societies (NUWSS) issued leaflets with the imperative to 'Get busy now and urge your MP to see that the Government's pledge is kept...'[14] The WFL also reminded the Government of the movement's pre-war record, promising that 'Our new power, we have been urged to use, is a power to be reckoned with; no longer can women be pushed on one side as negligible'.[15] This was a reminder to Lloyd George of a speech he had given on the eve of the 1918 general election to a woman-only audience:

> You must demand equality, equality having regard to all physical conditions... You will never get any of these things if women do not vote. All those questions depend largely for their right solution upon the 6 million women exercising their votes.[16]

The WFL argued that it was now time for the 5 million disenfranchised women to expect the 'right solution' to be delivered by Lloyd George's Government.

The first post-war rebuff came when there was no mention of any such projected reforms in the 1919 King's speech. The Liberal and Labour parties had made similar manifesto promises of action in the women's Cause, and in April 1919 there was a welcome surprise for the movement when the Labour Party redeemed its manifesto commitment and introduced the Emancipation Bill. The bill intended to enfranchise all women aged between twenty-one and thirty, confer eligibility on women to sit in the Lords, open all professional and judicial posts to women and enable women MPs to hold ministerial office.[17] In its May edition, *The Labour Woman* charted the Bill's stumbling progress:

> Its second reading was not obtained without opposition and the full list of members who went into the Opposition

Lobby shows how strong is the prejudice which remains amongst the older parties. Practically all these members... were Coalition Unionists.[18]

The Government's intention to amend the franchise clause of the Bill at the committee stage was defeated in June and the women's societies were working full tilt at lobbying and propaganda work to ensure the passing of the entire Emancipation Bill. On 30 June 1919 women took to the streets again in a colourful 'women under thirty' procession in London. This was followed by a meeting jointly organised by the SJCIWO and the NUSEC, held just before the third reading of the bill was passed on 4 July.[19]

Success seemed assured as the Bill, now in its final stages, went to the House of Lords. But on 22 July 1919 the Government intervened to subvert this radical package of reforms by introducing its own Sex Disqualification (Removal) Bill which took precedence over the Emancipation Bill. The new 'skeleton' Bill, as the WFL termed it, would allow entry to the legal profession and the office of magistrate but it did not extend the franchise, nor did it allow access to the senior civil service. *The Labour Woman* contested vigorously that:

If this was the meaning of the Government's pledge, then Mr Lloyd George's speech to the women electors should never have been delivered... Has any Government ever more carelessly thrown down the challenge to those who have sought by constitutional action the rights which all admit to be justly theirs? Is it any wonder that the old militancy stirs again?[20]

As well as duping women, the NUSEC believed that this new Sex Disqualification (Removal) Bill had placed the Government in the unconstitutional position of defying the wishes of the Commons and, as a consequence, it should resign.[21]

But the women's societies were placed in a difficult position, for as with the restrictions placed on the 1918 suffrage legislation the NUSEC realised that again they were being forced to accept 'that half a loaf was better than no bread' and ought to 'try and improve the bill as it stood'.[22]

The NUSEC's amendments were put forward by its supporters in the House such as Lord Robert Cecil (Independent Conservative), Major Hills (Conservative Unionist) and Sir Samuel Hoare (Conservative). The amendments dealt with the extension of the franchise, the right of women to sit in the Lords, entry to the civil service on the same terms as men and the right of the wives of those eligible to be jurors to become jurors themselves.[23]

On 11 August 1919 a deputation from 14 women's societies, which included the British Federation of University Women (BFUW), the Federation of Women Civil Servants (FWCS), the Association of Women Clerks and Secretaries (AWCS – the organisation altered its initials to AWKS and adopted the bird of the same name as its emblem), the National Council of Women (NCW), the Women's Local Government Society (WLGS) and the London Society for Women's Suffrage (LSWS)[24] was seen by Bonar Law and the Lord Chancellor. The deputation specifically protested at a clause which related to the qualified entry of women into the civil service and the exclusion from certain branches of the service altogether. Three days later the second reading of this new Bill was passed in the Commons. On the following day Lloyd George conducted what the WFL called a piece of 'political trickery' which astonished everyone: the Government deliberately sabotaged its own Bill.

Ray Strachey surmised that it was evident from the strength of feeling in the House on the women's side that the four amendments to the bill would be carried transforming the Sex Disqualification (Removal) Bill into a duplicate of the original Emancipation Bill. If this was allowed to happen it would negate the purpose of the Government's own bill.[25] This was a bill which had been intended to delay the franchise extension by attempting to buy off the women's groups by bartering the franchise for a handful of less threatening reforms. With the House supporting the women's amendments, Government defeat was in the air. In order to prevent discussion of the Bill on the afternoon of Friday 5 August the Government's only recourse was to filibustering tactics. Firstly, it interrupted proceedings three times by introducing business new to the House, then as the afternoon wore on, the benches became packed with Government members and the unaccustomed attendance of the Prime Minister. After passing the second reading of the Land Settlement Bill, the Home Secretary moved that the House take the Lords' amendments to the Welsh Church Bill, amendments which members had not even seen, as they had originally been tabled for the following Monday. Although Lord Robert Cecil protested strongly at the postponement of the women's bill, the Government won the division and with parliament rising shortly afterwards until October, the women's hopes were dashed yet again.[26]

The Government's manipulation of events once more drew the resentment of the women's societies. The WFL were furious, and not just with the Government's tactics, but with the failure of the movement's supposed supporters in the House to be present to vote for the women:

Not more than 34 of our supporters took the trouble to be present. If this is the measure of the House of Commons' courtesy towards the women of the country and of its consideration of women's interests, can women reasonably be expected to have much respect for the present House of Commons? We ask, where were our supporters?[27]

Ray Strachey, in an interview with *The Times*, did not hide her disgust at the Government's 'chicanery', calling it 'a final discreditable betrayal'.[28]

In the new autumn session of 1919, the amended Sex Disqualification (Removal) Bill was put before the House again. In the interim the women's organisations had been working hard to ensure support for the amended bill. However, it was the original, unamended bill which passed through all its stages with little difficulty. Although the Government had had a few anxious moments during the bill's passage, it had manipulated the women into the position of accepting 'half a loaf'. It was a sound indicator of how thin the women's power base still was. It was clear from the WFL's analysis that MPs who had supported the women's election questionnaires failed to manifest that backing by attending the relevant debates. The movement was in one accord as to Lloyd George's and Bonar Law's failure to honour their election pledge, and the WFL declared that:

Women have no use for political claptrap and shiftless expediency, but what they demand from the Government of their country are honesty, plain-dealing and genuine statesmanship.[29]

This enduring optimism about the possibility of honesty within the political process might be regarded as more of a handicap to the women's struggle than an enviable moral position. There is an apparent contradiction between their awareness of individual politicians' lack of integrity and their ability to sustain an almost naive belief in the possibility of honest dealing.

Was the women's trust in the democratic process misplaced or was it all they had to work with?[30] They were to a large extent at the mercy of an establishment able to diminish the threat of a minority by embracing it within its institutions and denying it sufficient power to exercise autonomy. Once 'inside' the system, the power granted and the rights accorded were subject to control. In such a way minorities find themselves accepted, but with their actual power circumscribed.[31] Cicely Hamilton (WWSL) believed it was significant that women had gained formal entry to politics during wartime when 'the much-demanded vote had declined in value – since representative institutions and all they stand for had practically ceased to exist'. The national priorities relating to war and women's preoccupation with basic survival had overshadowed this achievement, diminishing its significance even for the activists.[32] The precise timing for ceding a right to a minority may also have more to do with how it reflects on those in power and accommodates their needs, rather than in their belief in justice and equality for the claimant. Evelyn Sharp, ex-WSPU member and founder member of the US, believed this to be the case in 1918 when, rather than acknowledging women's right to citizenship, the Government demonstrated 'that the art of politics consists in the provision of ladders to enable politicians to climb down from untenable positions'.[33] In this case, the 'untenable position' concerned the Government's treatment of women prisoners, which reflected its alarm at the increasing efficacy of the militants' campaign.[34]

The Franchise Extension Campaign

The battle for the franchise extension recommenced in February 1920 when a Representation of the People Bill was introduced again by a Labour MP. Thomas Grundy's bill aimed to lower the voting age for women from 30 to 21 and to reduce the franchise qualification for both sexes to residence only. Having passed its second reading with a large majority when it was referred to a standing committee, government members suggested there was insufficient time left in the current session to continue with the bill. But protests by the women's organisations and the Labour Party ensured the continuance of the standing committee. While leaving the House free to consider the bill, the Government did not give any assurances as to the allotment of time for its consideration.

The Government justified its opposition by returning to its perennial excuse that if the bill succeeded in becoming law, constitutional procedure would force the Government to call an election, which they were not prepared to do.[35]

In an effort to save the bill the NUSEC called the Government's bluff by suggesting an amendment which would postpone the legislation's coming into effect until the announcement of the next general election. The amendment was accepted and passed, but not even this imaginative solution was sufficient to salvage the bill and ensure the total political emancipation for women which the Government seemed determined to deny.[36] The WFL exploded, 'Was there ever such a Government of Wasters – both of the time and money of this nation?'[37] and was disgusted by the Government's explanation that it felt that the country wasn't ready for more sweeping constitutional change. Having mounted another propaganda campaign which succeeded in gaining so much support in the House, together with the passing of an enabling amendment, it was a bitter blow to be defeated by what the movement recognised as 'sheer trickery'.[38] Ignorant of parliamentary procedure and desiring to speed the bill's passage before time ran out, the Labour members steering the bill were manipulated by the chairman of the committee into proposing an 'obscurely worded resolution' which resulted in the committee rejecting the bill.[39] Although Nancy Astor was an MP by this time, and vociferous as she was, one woman in the House could do little.

Despite this disappointment the struggle continued. The WFL, in co-operation with eight major societies including the NUSEC, the Women's Engineering Society (WES), the Catholic Women's Suffrage Society (CWSS) and the National Union of Women Teachers (NUWT) organised a Votes for Women Under Thirty meeting in October 1920. Chaired by Charlotte Despard (WFL), the meeting was addressed by Dorothy Evans (SPG), Ray Strachey (LSWS) and Caroline Haslett (WES).[40] The meeting launched a petition to be sent to the Prime Minister. The AWKS urged its members to participate, emphasising that the Government's campaign against women earning their own living was reinforced by the fact that the majority of such women could not vote. They lacked the right to economic self-determination and held no constitutional power with which to resist the increasingly desperate employment situation forced on them by the Government.[41] They felt they were being denied the opportunity to serve their country in peace and that a wealth of talent was being wasted during this crucial period of reconstruction. In terms of solidarity, none of them could claim full enfranchisement until all women were enfranchised. Encouraged by the progress of the two previous bills, women's organisations believed that full enfranchisement was within their grasp, if not in the next few months, then certainly in time for the next election. It was crucial to sustain the pressure, to convince the public and parliament that young women craved their role as citizens. An opportunity for representatives of women under thirty to engage with MPs eventually took place when a deputation was received in March 1921 at a meeting chaired by Nancy Astor. Groups as diverse as the Women Shop Assistants' Union and the University Section of the WFL argued the inconsistency of the age of consent being set at sixteen whilst the vote was denied at twenty-one. They enforced their argument by referring to the case of the 28 countries that had enfranchised women since the beginning of the war, with Britain being alone in setting discriminatory terms.[42]

Meanwhile, after a conference on equal franchise, the NUSEC decided to concentrate on promoting the equal franchise message at by-elections 'on the old lines'. An election sub-committee was appointed, chaired by Evelyn Deakin, and in 1921 they worked on 12 by-elections utilising their pre-war campaigning tactics of open-air meetings, literature stalls, public meetings, leaflet distribution, press statements, questioning candidates and mounting deputations. The Louth by-election in October 1921 delivered the most satisfying result when Margaret Wintringham, standing as a Liberal, became the second woman MP. The NUSEC had sent one of its flying columns of 25 women workers to assist in the campaign, and the locally established Women Citizens' Associations (WCAs) came into their own, supported by women such as Ray Strachey and Eleanor Rathbone, who spoke at mass meetings on Mrs Wintringham's behalf.[43] After so many years of promoting their message through male candidates, there was the 'joy' of working for a woman candidate and 'the rapture of meeting in the women voters intelligent, well-informed citizens'.[44]

The Equal Franchise Special Committee, initiated the previous year, continued in 1921 chaired by Chrystal Macmillan, with co-opted members from the FWCS, the AWKS, the CWSS and the WFL. Two petitions had been launched, both urging the Government to introduce and pass a bill in the next session, but the Prime Minister refused to accept either petitions.[45] Asked in February 1922 if he intended to introduce such legislation into the

House, Lloyd George replied that it would not be wise to do so when the question had already been settled in the last parliament.[46] This interpretation provides an interesting insight into Lloyd George's later claims to have been on the women's side.

Although the Labour Party was the only party which had the franchise extension explicitly included in its manifesto, Strachey wrote to her husband in February 1922 that she was:

> ... now in the thick of the group of discontented Conservatives of whom Lord Robert Cecil is the chief. They are really indistinguishable from Liberals, and I expect there will be some kind of fusion in the end.[47]

Cecil tested parliament's feelings on the matter when he introduced a private member's bill under the ten minute rule to extend the franchise to women on the same terms as men. Working closely with Strachey, he asked the NUSEC if they would frame the bill. The resolution was carried by a majority of 208 to 60, and the WFL published the names of the members who had voted against it. The NUSEC concluded that this result indicated a favourable change of heart towards the women's position.[48] The Government claimed that such constitutional reform necessitated an election and as an election was expected, the women's organisations concentrated on pressurising the Government into extending the franchise before the 1922 election. It was a ploy that elicited no response.

Although four years of campaigning had not so far achieved legislative success, it had moved the issue forward on many fronts. The movement had heightened the awareness of sitting MPs, candidates and the electorate, fulfilling its educative role. It had extended its organisational framework with an expansion of the networks of new and established groups, both professional and industrial, party and non-party, and the NUSEC's equal franchise special committee (EFSC) had doubled its number of co-opted societies operating on a cross-party basis.[49] The framing of bills for eminent MPs such as Lord Robert Cecil was also a measure of the NUSEC's political credibility and growing influence. All these factors indicated a measure of progress for the political hopes of the movement.

The 1922 election underlined women's representational inequality, with only two women returned to parliament, and 1923 brought the start of a vigorous campaign which was to gather momentum during the middle years of the decade. The Government policy of procrastination and containment made it seem likely that the strategy of introducing a private member's franchise bill, boosted by lobbying, attempted deputations and publicity could have continued for many more years with no successful outcome. At the end of April 1923 this programme of campaigning events had repeated itself when the NUSEC and other organisations urged the Prime Minister, Bonar Law, to make a commitment to equal franchise. Yet again, it was omitted from the King's speech, leaving Foot's private member's bill, which was then given insufficient time to proceed, the only recourse open. The SPG now astutely observed the futility of using the private member's bill strategy, which was being subverted by the Government not only to obstruct the movement's claims but was retarding the movement's progress by absorbing the women's energies in a diversionary way. The SPG contended that what women should be doing was 'making themselves apparent, and if need be so unpleasant, to the powers that be that they decide to give them what they ask'.[50] This indication of the necessity of returning to militant methods also implied a criticism of the NUSEC's seemingly endless patient perseverance with parliament, very different from the SPG's more urgent style born out of its largely militant, ex-Women's Social and Political Union (WSPU) membership. These bills did have other functions, not least of which was their publicity value, but in the context of this campaign the SPG's observation concerning the self-perpetuating nature of such measures was valid: the movement was playing into the Government's hands. As long as the Government omitted the franchise extension from its parliamentary programme and the women's movement responded by pursuing a private member's bill the Government could happily ignore its 1918 election promise. The SPG believed that the only successful method was to exert sufficient force to ensure the introduction of a government bill. Traditionally, the strategy was to hope that publicity and pressure from within the House from those MPs who supported the women's claims would persuade the Government to adopt a private member's bill.

Despite the repetition of this well-known formula, 1923 seemed to mark a turning-point when several factors combined as a preparation for the final assault. A demonstration, planned for the previous autumn but postponed because of the 1922 election campaign, finally took place on 7 March at the Central Hall, Westminster. Organised by the NUSEC, it was attended by representatives from over 50 groups, with the two MPs Nancy Astor and Margaret Wintringham as speakers, along with Eleanor Rathbone, the NUSEC President, Margaret Bondfield speaking on behalf of Labour women and Helen Fraser, the former WSPU Scottish organiser and 1922 parliamentary candidate, presenting the international perspective.[51] Fraser revealed a prime piece of government hypocrisy when she informed the meeting that in contrast to British women, women in all countries of the British Empire now had equal enfranchisement. She was followed by Margaret Bondfield, who emphasised the importance of not allowing parliament to perpetuate the delusion that British women were quite reconciled to the notion of this inequality. Rathbone employed the unifying function of the NUSEC to emphasise that 'full enfranchisement for women' was now the chief priority for all women's societies, and 'all were thoroughly united on the point'.[52]

Ten days later, the NUSEC utilised the advent of its annual council meeting to mount a public, visible representation of its refusal to keep silent and accept the Government's 'half a loaf'. The council meeting provided the impetus for another rally attended by both women's and men's organisations. It was important to demonstrate to the Government and the country that the demand for full enfranchisement was widely recognised and supported by many men as women's constitutional right. This was an occasion at which 'the familiar banners of pre-war days, adapted to modern use, side by side with the banners of sister organisations of women were proudly displayed to symbolise the strength and continuity of the movement'.[53]

The success of eight women candidates in 1923's December election and the first Labour Government gave the women's movement high hopes that 1924 would bring the fulfilment of its franchise claims. The Labour Party had promoted equal franchise for men and women as party policy for several past elections and Florence Underwood, Secretary of the WFL, expressed the anticipation of many when she ventured that their opportunity to gain equal enfranchisement with men was higher than it had ever been.[54] Labour women were confident that their party would fulfil its past promises, as was the NUSEC, whose close working relationship with the Labour Party since pre-war days gave it confidence in such an outcome. Such expectations also seemed in line with Labour's policy of using its own women's sections to capture and secure women's allegiance to the party. What could be more effective for increasing its membership and share of the women's vote than being the party to extend the franchise?

In the early months of 1924, barely two weeks after Labour were asked to form a government, the WFL began to exert pressure on Labour in the first of three major rallies of the year. The first, on 6 February, opportunely doubled as a celebration of the sixth anniversary of the 1918 act, with two Labour MPs, Susan Lawrence and Dorothy Jewson, as the main speakers. Lawrence, a staunch Labour Party activist now placed herself firmly in the suffrage camp declaring that the franchise extension 'was a self-evident proposition'.[55] Dorothy Jewson, MP for Norwich and a WFL member, referred to her WSPU past and spoke of the plight of industrial women and the need for economic recognition. Emphasising the significance of the extension for working women there were also speakers from the National Women's Liberal Federation (NWLF), the NUWT, the WES and the Shop Assistants' Union (SAU). The rally concluded in time-honoured fashion by passing a resolution calling on the Government to pass an equal franchise law.[56]

Although the principle of equal franchise had been Labour Party policy since its early days and there was an expectation of a positive outcome, the women's movement still prepared to put into action its usual strategies of lobbying MPs and writing to the press, as well as holding meetings, demonstrations and rallies to keep the issue in the forefront of public attention. However, only nine days after their initial rally the WFL began to have serious misgivings about the Labour Government's evident lack of enthusiasm for equal enfranchisement.[57] This intimation was the result of correspondence between the WFL, Prime Minister Ramsay MacDonald and several of his ministers about the Government's intentions, which yielded nothing but formal acknowledgements.

By 29 February the time-honoured private member's bill, proposed by Labour MP W.M. Adamson and seconded by Dorothy Jewson, making her maiden speech, had passed its second reading. During her speech, she referred to the disappointment which the Prime Minister's recent comments had caused when he declared that the Government did not have the time to consider franchise extension.[58] This second reading also dealt with several items which complicated the passage of the bill. Suffrage societies had always been alert to the necessity of keeping proposed franchise bills as simple as possible, confining them to the women's franchise in order to limit the grounds for opposition. The Duchess of Atholl had been chosen to introduce the classic delaying tactic, the Tories' amendment that an all-party conference should be held, as with the previous franchise legislation, to discuss the full implications of the issue. But Atholl, a leading anti-suffragist before the war, also made great play of the wider electoral implications of Adamson's Bill. These included franchise extension for men (there were still approximately 313,000 disenfranchised men) and the local government franchise.[59] Sir William Bull, Conservative, also insisted that there had been an undertaking by leading women's societies in 1918 not only to accept the Speaker's conference measure but also to agree to no further political agitation for a ten-year period. He rather audaciously suggested that it was the women's undertaking which consequently bound the House from further action within this that period.[60]

Most significantly, this was the first debate in which the alarming suggestion of an age limit of twenty-five for women was put forward as being the most practical. The speech by Sir Martin Conway, Conservative, proposing this new limit floridly illustrated the Victorian legacy of paternalistic chivalry which compounded the women's struggle:

> A woman between twenty-one and twenty-five years of age arrives at her flowering time... I suggest that the young woman of that age ought to be paying attention to other matters than voting. She ought to have her eye upon... the prospects of family, of man's devotion... I must say that the older I get, the more wonderfully, the more beautiful, and the more admirable to me is that glorious flowering time of the young woman between the ages of 21 and 25.[61]

One wonders how much of the 'glorious flowering time' of young women in sweated industries Sir Martin had witnessed. This suggestion of an age limit other than that of twenty-one introduced a further obstacle to the women's campaign. Determined to block the passage of the bill, the Duchess of Atholl overplayed her hand and managed to rouse the House and women's groups to indignation with her objection to the fact that under the proposed bill even women tinkers would be entitled to the vote![62] Whilst counteracting the Duchess's objection to tinkers, Mr Rhys Davies, Under-Secretary of State for the Home Office, explained that while in favour of the women's claims, as a minority Government they might not actually be able to prioritise equal franchise.[63] Nancy

Astor explained that women were not asking for a revolution but for their rights, and unable to suffer fools of any party she responded to the bill's opponents by maintaining that they 'represented nobody except people who were living in the Middle Ages'.[64] The Bill was passed by 288 to 72.

When Adamson's Bill had gone to the committee stage it was imperative that the women's movement sustained the pressure on Labour to demand that they gave the bill sufficient time during the parliamentary session for it to pass through its requisite stages. Once again, the WFL organised a public meeting insisting that either the Government give the bill adequate time or introduce its own bill. The movement's apprehension concerning the effect of the bill's additional proposals was validated when a list of amendments was proposed by Conservative members opposing either the contentious clauses or the entire bill.[65] However, singling out clauses for amendment was another common opposition ploy to utilise parliamentary time and strand a bill. It also provided the bill's framers with additional preoccupations for future attempts where time, energy and resources could be monopolised in trying to resolve such objections.

The bill passed its final committee stage on 19 June 1924 before parliamentary time expired. The non-party societies harried the Government into making some kind of commitment to the bill and by the end of July the Prime Minister assured Margaret Wintringham that the Government would adopt the bill and proceed with it later in that session.[66] But the session came to an end, as did the Labour Government, without the bill making further progress. It was a matter of considerable shock and intense disappointment to the movement that the Labour Government had failed them. Indeed, the abruptness of the Government's fall left the WFL with a mass meeting planned to press the Government into pushing through the final stages of the franchise bill the day after parliament was dissolved. The meeting went ahead on 10 October 1924 and was the largest to date, with representatives of nearly 24 women's organisations and trade unions in attendance. Organisations included many old stalwarts such as the Actresses' Franchise League (AFL), the Fabian Society Women's Group (FSWG), the Women's Auxiliary Service (WAS), the Union of Jewish Women (UJW) and the League of the Church Militant (LCM).[67]

There had been a large degree of all-party support for this bill and the majority of the work had been accomplished. It would have been a relatively simple matter in June for the Government to have adopted the bill and put it through its remaining stages. The advantage to Labour's reputation would have been great, as would the gains at the ballot box. As the women's societies were always pointing out, a very large proportion of the women employed in industry were under thirty. These were women who were in unions or were members of the women's section of the Labour Party, and whose votes would have been assured, whereas, as the WFL regularly warned in 1924, failure by Labour to grant equal franchise could result in a loss of support.

In consideration of these circumstances it may seem difficult to understand why MacDonald failed the women. But it was not just the suffrage movement that Labour disappointed. Their brief spell in office achieved little for anyone: 'Labour was unready. It was a minority Government, in office, but not in power, shackled to the Liberals and pursuing a policy of moderation'.[68] The composition of the cabinet was of moderate men who were largely from upper and middle class backgrounds. Traditional left-wingers and trade unionists were few in number; as Mannie Shinwell observed, 'MacDonald... had no intention of practising Socialism in a country where five out of every seven voters were anti-Socialist'.[69] Labour had no experience of government and the Conservatives were ready at every turn to ensure, as their pact with the Liberals intended, that Labour's period in office failed. Even with regard to the franchise issue, the Conservatives manipulated the situation to advantage:

> When in May it (the bill) finally went upstairs progress was greatly retarded by obstruction on the part of some Conservative Members, who although not willing actually to oppose the principle of equality in citizenship directly, found plenty of opportunities for oblique attack.[70]

However, the movement's despondency at Labour's failure and the Tories' adroitness did not manifest itself in any lack of energy with which to pursue its mission during the election campaign which followed.

Notes on Chapter 9

1   *Daily Sketch*, Saturday 21 February 1925, p 3. The MP was Ellen Wilkinson.
2   *Time & Tide*, 'Equal political rights', 29 January 1926, quoted in Spender, Dale, *Time & Tide Waits For No Man* (London, 1984, Pandora Press), p 167
3   Macmillan, Chrystal, *And Shall I Have a Parliamentary Vote?* (London, 1918, NUSEC), p 1
4   *Votes for Women Left Out*, NUWSS pamphlet (London, 1918)
5   *The Vote*, 4 April 1924, p 106
6   'Girls', not women is the word used by the establishment in this debate.
7   Monica O'Connor, under-thirty member of the SJSPA, speaking at the July 1926 suffrage demonstration, *The Daily Herald*, 5 July 1926, p 5
8   *The Vote*, 21 January 1927, p 20
9   *The Vote*, 22 January 1926, p 29
10 *The Vote*, 10 December 1926, p 390
11 *The Daily Herald*, 11 January 1924, p 4
12 *Time & Tide*, 30 July 1926, p 701
13 *The Woman's Leader*, 21 December 1923, p 379
14 NUWSS pamphlet, *Votes for Women Left Out* (London, 1918)
15 *The Vote*, 3 January 1919, p 35
16 *The Vote*, 13 December 1918, pp 12-13
17 *The Labour Woman*, February 1919, p 10
18 *The Labour Woman*, May 1919, p 46
19 NUSEC, Annual Report, 1919, p 30
20 *The Labour Woman*, August 1919, p 94
21 *International Woman Suffrage News*, September 1919, p 171
22 NUSEC, Annual Report, 1919, p 31
23 ibid.
24 FWCS Association Notes, July-September 1919, p 228. The other societies involved were the Association of Hospital Matrons, the Civil Service Alliance, the Association of Senior Women Officers, the Civil Service Typists' Association, the Association of Temporary Clerks in Government Offices, the National Union of Clerks and the Women Sanitary Inspectors and Health Visitors Association.

25 *International Woman Suffrage News*, 1919, p 172

26 *The Vote*, 22 August 1919, p 300

27 *The Vote*, 22 August 1919, front page

28 Smith Papers, Oxford, Folder 2, 1919, p 12

29 *The Vote*, 22 August 1919, front page

30 In an interview with Ray Strachey's daughter, Barbara, in Oxford on 12 June 1989, she expressed the opinion that they had no other option than to continue with their struggle within the system, there was no other avenue open to them.

31 An example of this reduction of power occurred in 1927 at the University of Oxford. Alarmed at the rapid increase in women students in residence at the women's colleges which entitled them to the election of a woman to its ranks, the Hebdominal Council succeeded in limiting the number of women students by statute thereby reducing women's access to the power of the Council. See Brittain, Vera, *Women at Oxford* (London, 1960, George G. Harrap), pp 161-172

32 Hamilton, Cicely, 'The new group' quoted in Spender, Dale, *Time & Tide Waits For No Man* (London, 1984, Pandora Press), p 172

33 Sharp, Evelyn, *Unfinished Adventure* (London, 1933, John Lane), pp 155-156

34 A memorandum, from the Home Secretary, marked 'secret' was circulated to members of the cabinet dated 25 January 1913. It contained advice from the Commissioner of Police to the Home Secretary for cabinet members that 'In view of possible developments in connection with the Woman Suffrage question' he felt that it was unsafe for them to walk to and from the House. John Johnson Collection, Pamphlets Female Suffrage

35 NUSEC, Annual Report, 1920, p 20

36 NUSEC, Annual Report, 1920, p 5; *International Woman Suffrage News*, May-June 1920, p 140; *The Vote*, 5 March 1920, p 524

37 *The Vote*, 5 March 1920, p 524

38 *International Woman Suffrage News*, August 1920, p 177

39 Ibid.

40 *The Vote*, 8 October 1920, p 221. The other groups participating were the AWCS, the FWCS, the WIL and the NFWW.

41 *The Woman Clerk*, November 1920, p 1

42 *The Vote*, 18 March 1921, p 407

43 NUSEC, Annual Report, 1921, pp 5-8
44 LSWS, Annual Report, 1921, pp 6-7
45 Idid., pp 9-10
46 *International Woman Suffrage News*, March 1922, p 85
47 Smith Papers, Oxford, 18 February 1922, p 1
48 NUSEC, Annual Report, 1922, p 14
49 Compare NUSEC, Annual Report, 1921, p 9 with NUSEC, Annual Report, 1922, p 13
50 *Time & Tide*, 2 March 1923, pp 242-243
51 *The Vote*, 16 March 1923, p 85
52 Ibid.
53 NUSEC, Annual Report, 1923, p 8
54 *Time & Tide*, 5 February 1924, p 149
55 *The Vote*, 15 February 1925, p 50
56 *The Vote*, 15 February 1924, front page
57 Ibid., p 54
58 *The Labour Woman*, 1 April 1924, p 52
59 Parliamentary Debates, House of Commons, 25 February-14 March 1924, Vol. 170, February 29, col 866
60 Ibid., cols 897-899
61 Parliamentary Debates, House of Commons, 25 February-14 March 1924, Vol. 170, February 29, cols 918-919
62 *The Labour Woman*, 1 April 1924, p 52
63 Ibid., p 53
64 Parliamentary Debates, House of Commons, 25 February-14 March 1924, Vol. 170, February 29, col 937
65 *The Woman's Leader*, 23 May 1924, front page
66 *The Vote*, 17 October 1924, p 332
67 *The Vote*, 3 October 1924, front page; 17 October 1924, p 330
68 Mowat, Charles Loch, *Britain Between the Wars 1918-1940* (London, 1955, Methuen), p 174
69 Shinwell, Emmanuel, *The Labour Story* (London, 1963, Macdonald), p 118
70 *The Woman's Leader*, 2 January 1925, front page

Chapter 10
Victory

The Unionist Party is in favour of equal political rights for men and women, and desires that the question of the extension of the franchise should, if possible, be settled by agreement. With this in view, they would, if returned to power, propose that the matter be referred to a Conference of all political Parties on the lines of the Ullswater Committee.[1]

In the run-up to the 1924 general election, in customary fashion, non-party women activists were pressing the leaders of political parties for statements as to their intentions on the equal franchise issue. The Conservative leader, Stanley Baldwin, responded with the above 'pledge', published in the newspapers. Baldwin's declaration might be interpreted as an attempt to trade on the women's disillusion with the Labour Party's failure by holding out the hope of a Conservative Government franchise bill as a means of encouraging existing women voters to support the Conservatives. The 1924 election did, indeed, result in a Conservative landslide, and with its parliamentary power renewed, unsurprisingly, Baldwin's electoral promise to women evaporated, noticeable by its absence from the party's programme for the next parliamentary session.[2]

The women's movement was not so easily dismissed. Seeking to convert any vouchsafed offer to advantage, the movement was consistently to parade Baldwin's commitment, using it as a lever to strengthen its franchise claims. Within weeks of the new session, in February 1925, William Whiteley's (Labour) Representation of the People Bill kept the issue alive. It was seconded by Ellen Wilkinson,[3] indicating the emergence of a new convention of women MPs seconding franchise bills. This served several useful propaganda purposes for the movement by publicising women's new political presence and active involvement, confirming women's allegiance to the measure to the Government of the day, while also providing the public with evidence of one of the women's movement successes. On 20 February, the Home Secretary, Sir William Joynson-Hicks, rejected the bill on grounds once used by Lloyd George: namely that the Government could not pass a new franchise bill at such an early stage in the parliamentary session as it would necessitate an election which would interrupt important legislation already in hand. In mitigation, Joynson-Hicks played into the women's hands by referring the House to Baldwin's electoral pledge and reinforcing the sincerity of his promise.[4] Baldwin's promised conference now became a moveable feast: guaranteed for 1925, it was postponed until 1926.

The National Union of Societies for Equal Citizenship (NUSEC), habitually both cautious and optimistic, was on this occasion less than convinced on several fronts. These were the lack of a firm commitment for a conference in 1926, fear that the Conservative's proposals would be unacceptable to the other parties and, finally, the absence of discussion regarding the vexed question of raising the voting age for men.[5] The issue of raising the age limit was coming to be regarded by the NUSEC and other societies as more than just another delaying tactic. Some Unionists guaranteed alarming Labour MPs with the implication that as part of the franchise package the age limit should also be raised for men. Labour would not even consider a franchise bill for women which threatened to disenfranchise some men, thus reducing Labour Party support. The conference idea was also interpreted by the women's movement as a particularly devious means of procrastination, as it stalled the implementation of the franchise extension, but without the Conservatives actually denying their belief in it as such. This diminished the grounds on which the women's movement could attack the Tories' duplicity, and persuaded the Women's Freedom League (WFL) that 'the suggested Conference is not only unnecessary but mischievous'.[6] The confidence of the Conservatives in the longevity of their Government, which had guaranteed the conference for the following year, was also not shared by the women's groups, which felt that recent events did not augur well for political stability.

The Nature of the Opposition

The characterisation by some historians of the opposition to the women's movement as a backlash against feminism during the 1920s presupposes a widespread degree of acceptance of feminist ideals during the pre-war years.[7] It would be difficult to make such a case. The post-war intolerance of and resistance to women's claims for equal rights was more complex than such a reversal of fortunes would imply. This antipathy to women moving from the private to the public arena had been an ongoing feature of the war years.

Such antagonism appears partially to be a response to the psychological and emotional repercussions of a devastating war. As the decade progressed there was a need to ascribe blame and identify a scapegoat for economic and social upheaval. The residual Victorian desire for middle class women to lead lives of domestic seclusion, underpinned by the legal and political principle of coverture,[8] was mixed with post-war resentment and incomprehension of the demands of 'the modern woman'. Confusion at the disintegration of the social order and the refusal of working class girls to fall back into the penury and oppression of domestic service after their increased financial and social wartime independence induced not only derision, but vindictiveness.

Male fears of female political supremacy were further endorsed by the numerical imbalance of the sexes. Although nearly one million before the war, the number of 'surplus' women in the 1920s stood at almost double that figure, and the social consequences of such a disparity gave rise to great concern.[9]

The term 'surplus women', indicated how widely single women were regarded as being a problem for a society where women's primary function was as housewife and mother. There had been an 'imbalance' in the numbers of women in relation to men since the middle of the nineteenth century in Britain, as revealed in the 1851 census. Now, after the war, the need to regenerate a lost generation and put men back to work to stimulate the economy was considered of primary importance to the survival of Britain and its Empire. A solution to the 'problem' of unmarried, militant women had been put forward before the war by Sir Almoth Wright in 1913, when he suggested shipping them off to the colonies to find husbands.[10] This same idea was revived in 1920 with the foundation of the Society for the Overseas Settlement of British Women, which provided a service for settling women abroad in such places as South Africa and Australia.[11] However, the pragmatism of using 'surplus' single women to provide good colonial wives to contribute to the stabilisation of the Empire was by no means new.

Single women now inhabited three broad categories: those women who wanted to marry, but whom the war had deprived of suitable husbands; those who in the face of the marriage bar in most professions chose their career in preference to marriage; and those women whose relationships were with other women, or who had decided to be celibate. Increasingly, after the war single women became a target for hostility, scorn and derision. Magazines and newspapers were full of articles establishing marriage as the pinnacle of fulfilment for women and thereby alternately ridiculing or patronising the single woman:

> ... the type of unmarried woman who talks as though man was her enemy, man who has schemed through the ages to keep women in subjection... All women are not spinsters from choice. To put it bluntly many of them 'never had the chance'. There are tens of thousands of such women... Sometimes it strikes me there has grown into the countenances of these spinsters a look of resentment... because they have never known the warm love of a man.[12]

But there were more choices open for women in the 1920s which made marriage less attractive. Many middle class women, being among the first female generation of their family to have a career, married late and with certain reservations. 'The career was a competitor. The question was, do I like this person well enough to give up work, or to do it less, or whatever.'[13] Vera Brittain and Winifred Holtby's writings and diaries contain much discussion about the advisability of marriage for the professional woman. There were other considerations for working class women in the light of the marriage bar, ways of subverting the system to avoid losing a job after marriage when 'If you wanted to keep your job, you kept your big mouth shut, there was nothing else to do'.[14] Stealth and secrecy must also have played a part for those women who wanted to sustain professional careers but saw no reason why they should forfeit long-standing relationships.

But other women forced to adopt subterfuge and secrecy were those who endured the greatest calumny, women who loved other women. What Vera Brittain (SPG) called 'the repressive spirit of this era, arising from the moral exhaustion produced by the War'[15] directed its worst hostility towards 'the invert'. The hostility which lesbians faced encompassed all single women because, 'Like lesbians, they are all women who are not subject to men's social and sexual power through a personal relationship'.[16]

In the period directly following the war the issue of lesbianism emerged into the public arena to some extent through a series of scandals involving libel cases and novels on the theme.[17] Feminists had always been popularly characterised as man-haters. In the distressed post-war world which sought to re-establish the order and security associated with the family, women who consorted together were bound to be viewed as a threat to the re-establishment of such a moral order. How far did those libel cases where women challenged male opinion by taking them to court influence parliament's attempt in 1921 to criminalise lesbianism as a sexual practice in the new Criminal Law Amendment Act? This would have meant that sexual acts between women would be classed as 'misdemeanours' and would be punishable by two years' hard labour. The motion was supported by references to the recent decline in female morality. Jeffrey Weeks suggests the other relevant factor was the post-war backlash against feminism, which was thought to be 'masculising' women and threatening the natural function of child-birth.[18] This played on establishment insecurity about a consequent decline in the nation and the empire if women refused to have children.

Beliefs that lesbianism promoted debauchery and was both a result of, and contributed to, insanity among women ensured that the motion was passed by the Commons. However, the House of Lords felt that such a measure would only publicise a practice that most decent women were ignorant of. Falling back on the conviction that women were weak and morally dubious creatures, introducing them to 'this noxious and horrible suspicion' would be a 'very great mischief'.[19] The motion fell and was not pursued by the Commons. But it was not only men who were vocal in their condemnation of lesbianism. Marie Stopes, whose work was heralded and promoted by many feminists and their organisations, denounced lesbian practices in her published work and in correspondence with clients and colleagues.

Despite the virulence of public condemnation, there were women in the movement and sympathisers of the women's rights campaign who did not disguise their sexual preference, albeit they were safeguarded by the privileged circumstances of their social position.[20] Many of the most prominent feminists working within the suffrage and labour organisations were single, living with other women.[21] At a time of increased pressure on women to conform to the heterosexual model, choosing to remain single was choosing to make a socially challenging statement.

There were numerous newspaper and magazine articles about 'the modern woman' which exuded prejudice against young women, who categorised by the pejorative term 'flappers'. This term was more generally used for all women under thirty, who were characterised as feckless and immoral. It was not just reserved for the handful of rich, Eton-cropped women who later came, erroneously, to personify the popular image of the period. Very often, such articles would be signed, anonymously, by 'A Mere Male'. One such magazine article, 'What Does the Girl of Today Want?' was far from atypical in its derogatory and aggressive tone, containing not only verbal, but also threats of physical abuse:

> Are her brains fitted for the vote, which is so soon to be conferred upon her?... She is an idiot, our girl of 1924... why not let her have her own way, as you let kittens and puppies have their own way, until she, as they say, commits some domestic activity so ghastly that even the kindest-hearted house-owner must have recourse to the chain in the backyard and the stick behind the hat-stand... that chain and that stick are still the prerogatives of us mere males, whom your Modern Girl affects to treat so lightly. In ultimate issues, we – and not she – possess the greater physical strength and the greater mental capacity.[22]

Ellen Wilkinson, feminist and Labour MP, kept an article written in a similar style in her cuttings collection, whose headline proclaimed that 'Woman Has Failed! Why She is an Outsider in Public Life' by a Truthful Man. The Truthful Man's analysis was that by 1925 there was still only a handful of women in public affairs, that women would not vote for women, women did not possess the necessary skills and temperament for such success and that the only 'affairs' they were interested in concerned love. He concluded that:

> After ten years of enfranchisement, there are only four women in Parliament, not one of whom succeeds in raising herself above the dead level of mediocrity.[23]

The mediocre women to whom he referred were Nancy Astor, Ellen Wilkinson, Mrs Hilton Phillipson and the Duchess of Atholl. The resistance to the presence of women members in the Commons was picked up in the press, where they were far from taken seriously. Both Nancy Astor and Ellen Wilkinson complained vehemently about the trivialisation of their role through endless press reports which concentrated on their physical appearance.

With such attitudes in the press and similar opinions expressed in parliament by Unionist 'die-hards' like Lord Hugh Cecil, that the House had lost much of its dignity since women had been allowed in,[24] it was hardly surprising that the opinion in circulation was that 'flappers' were not responsible enough to have the vote. More indicative of the male fear of loss of power was the prejudice expressed by Lt-Col. Archer Shee during the 1923 debate in the Commons on Isaac Foot's Franchise Bill. Shee argued that to have more women voting than men was tantamount to handing over electoral power to women, which would 'make an election a joke'.[25] He also maintained that it was well known that at least 4.5 of the 5 million disenfranchised women had absolutely no interest in the vote and did not want the inconvenience of it. These were all regular arguments in the House throughout the 1920s. The reality was that while many politicians paid lip-service to the concept of women's equality, they had no intention of giving it practical expression, especially where the balance of power might be concerned.

The Final Phase

Faced with what began to look like interminable delay, the NUSEC instructed its extensive network of Women Citizens' Associations (WCAs) and other affiliated societies to galvanise its forces and mount a more integrated and concentrated phase of the franchise campaign during the winter of 1925. Using part of a £1000 gift from Millicent Fawcett to launch this attack, a concerted struggle began which dominated the next two-and-a-half years. The strength and unity of the women's struggle was fired by their abiding conviction in the rightness of their Cause. Their sense of loyalty to the struggle, to the women pioneers of the nineteenth century, to their movement and to one another had deepened over the years. They were determined to achieve the ultimate prize of equal franchise in order to claim 'equality between men and women for which women have laboured, suffered and even died'.[26] Women paid the full rate of income tax, they were employed in large numbers as teachers and civil servants, they were represented, to some extent, in most other professions and made a significant contribution to the industrial production of the country. They could become MPs at 21, they were JPs and councillors, and yet they were denied the right to vote at 21.

In this final phase, the re-emergence of the concept of militancy, albeit reserved for discussion only, was revived as a potential threat, though never as an actual weapon. Dorothy Jewson, the Labour MP and ex-suffragette, believed that 'The militant spirit was still needed to solve the many problems that remained'.[27] The Six Point Group (SPG), whose membership was largely composed of ex-Women's Social and Political Union (WSPU) women, favoured direct action, and insisted that suffrage societies ought to be more 'unpleasant' if they were to succeed in pressurising the Government into extending the franchise. The renewed energy and determination of the movement was noted by the press. *The Daily Sketch*, for instance, observed in February 1925 that the amount of activity was reminiscent of the early suffrage days, although 'without, however, the old danger'.[28] A year later the WFL was recording that equal franchise had yet again been 'betrayed', as the Unionists had made no mention of the issue in its parliamentary programme and had even abandoned its promise of a conference. This prolonged Tory obstruction prompted the WFL to hint strongly at the possibility of a militant challenge, warning that, as in the past, it would have no hesitation in fighting a Government 'which refused to do justice to women'.[29]

With the absence of any intended government franchise activity, 1926 was dominated by the movement's work on a spring and summer offensive combining the maximum number of deputations to MPs, meetings and demonstrations on a regional and national level. Turning once more to the old strategy of mounting a massive public display of discontent, its activities were to culminate in a mass procession and rally on 3 July in London. Originated by the

Six Point Group (SPG), an Equal Political Rights Demonstration Committee (EPRDC) co-ordinated the event and the high percentage of previous WSPU members reflected the militant spirit of the enterprise. Lady Rhondda was the EPRDC's Chairman, Ethel E. Froud (General Secretary, NUWT) was Vice-Chairman, the Honorary Secretary was Daisy D. Solomon (WFL), Dr Elizabeth Knight (WFL Treasurer) was in charge of press and publicity and Miss Margaret Digby was the committee's organising secretary. The NUSEC launched the 1926 propaganda campaign with a demonstration on 26 February at the Central Hall, Westminster, timed to coincide with its annual council meeting. In this way, representatives from all its regional branches and affiliated societies were present to gain renewed motivation from speeches by the movement's heavy brigade of Millicent Fawcett, Eleanor Rathbone, Maude Royden and Ellen Wilkinson and take that inspiration back to their members.[30]

Parliamentary activity was sustained in March with Wedgewood Benn's Private Franchise Bill, backed by one of the women's suffrage stalwarts, Frederick Pethick-Lawrence, and Ellen Wilkinson, but it failed to proceed beyond its first reading. Prior to the bill's introduction, Wilkinson had asked Baldwin when the Government would introduce its own bill, but Baldwin had 'no comment' to make. By the end of March, not having grasped the opportunity of adopting Wedgwood Benn's Bill, Baldwin still refused to be drawn, although the Home Secretary disclosed in the Commons that a conference would supposedly be set up in 1927.[31]

Meanwhile, the public profile of this offensive was maintained with WFL Sunday morning meetings in Hyde Park and a major rally organised by the Saint Joan Social and Political Alliance (SJSPA), represented by a symbolic 30 organisations, addressed by Millicent Fawcett, Ellen Wilkinson, and Monica O'Connor of the Alliance's 'Under Thirty Section'.[32] At a celebratory dinner to mark Mrs Pankhurst's return to London after a seven year absence,[33] she was also present to speak to a press meeting held in June at Lady Rhondda's Chelsea home. The press was invited to meet representatives of the 40 women's groups supporting the July demonstration in a move to ensure maximum coverage of the event and explain the women's franchise concerns.[34] Sustaining the momentum, days later, the Actresses' Franchise League (AFL) held an 'at home' at the popular suffrage venue, the Criterion Restaurant where Ellen Wilkinson proposed a resolution for equal enfranchisement and peeresses' right to sit in the Lords.[35] The latter resolution was timed to support Lord Astor's Parliament (Qualification of Peeresses) Bill, which was heavily defeated, much to the delight of many peers.

The debate provided a further illustration of the level of extant prejudice against women in parliament, with Lord Newton and Lord Birkenhead, Secretary for India, making speeches which 'savoured more of the pothouse than of Parliament'.[36] Newton's rationale for denying this right to peeresses ranged from stating that women were 'much more unchristian-like in their characteristics than men' to contesting that women MPs had not improved the Commons in any way, were inferior to male MPs and would be of no use in the Lords. Their one possible function might be as an attraction to ensure the attendance of younger peers, but Newton thought chorus girls would probably be better, because they were more attractive! Birkenhead supplemented this catalogue of abuse by assuring that 'There is no one of those ladies who would be nominated by any competent tribunal to sit in this or any other legislative assembly.' He elaborated on his perception of the only proper function for a peeress, which was to be 'fecund' and provide the Lords with its future members, although he doubted that any of the peeresses in question qualified even on those terms.[37] Inured though they were to ridicule, the women's societies were enraged by such insults.[38]

This affront from the Lords was compounded by another parliamentary rebuff from Baldwin, when he refused to receive the NUSEC's deputation, convened with the intention of discussing the terms of the proposed government conference for the following year.[39] The rationale for the July procession and demonstration, which formed the crescendo to the year's franchise extension campaign, was thus reinforced. It was imperative that the movement's claim for the franchise extension was expressed and endorsed through a public display of intent. The event had been publicised for months with traditional poster parades and the more modern use of fleets of decorated cars for advertising. Now came a last rallying call:

Which side are you on? Dependence or independence? Independence is certainly the happiest side. Watch the women who are marching to-morrow to demand political independence. All have broken the chains of dependence in some measure, all have tasted in some measure the peace of independence.[40]

211

The National Union of Women Teachers (NUWT) hesitantly proclaimed it 'The Last Procession?' and articulated the movement's overwhelming desire for this event to presage victory. *The Woman Teacher* noted that an evening paper's headline read, 'Suffragettes Out Again', for despite being smaller, the procession certainly lacked none of the style and dramatic impact of former occasions. There were other positive features which marked this demonstration out from those of the pre-war period, as *Time & Tide* noted:

> ... the business-like injunction to 'line-up on the Embankment' is a reminder of how much has already been wrested from the clutches of reluctant prejudice... less than twenty years ago a women's procession for political ends and propaganda was looked on as a daring novelty...[41]

Women had come from all over the country and abroad to join the procession, which had been orchestrated to produce the maximum effect as 3,500 women marched to Hyde Park.[42] Cohorts of women drawn up by occupation, 'including women journalists who walked in a procession as a professional group for the first time',[43] to emphasise the scale of the contribution women were now making to society, and to stand as a reproof to a legislative assembly which refused to recognise all women's right to citizenship. The procession was headed by young women in various 'under thirties' groups, such as the Guild of Girl Citizens (GGC), followed by political and suffrage societies from Britain and America. Parliamentary candidates came next behind a red and black banner of Big Ben, with this section completed by women mayors and magistrates. Veteran suffragettes wearing their prison badges were part of the NUSEC's 'old gang' contingent, with Millicent Fawcett, Maude Royden and Margaret Ashton among them. Mrs Pankhurst with her old colleague, Flora (General) Drummond, Charlotte Despard and Dr Annie Besant also walked the entire route and with a flourish, as Mrs Elliott-Lynn, the pioneer aviator and Women's Engineering Society (WES) member, flew her plane over the marchers in salute. Decorated motorcades, bands, banners and pennants made an impressive sight:

> One after another, each with its distinctive colours, the contingents swept across the park; green, white and gold; blue and silver; green and rose; blue, white and silver; red, white

and green; purple, green and white; red; green and gold. In one section the members wore pink dresses with wreathes of green leaves, or green dresses trimmed with roses; in another section, a group of 'Under-Thirties' very appropriately wore bright green dresses, the colour symbolical of spring and hope; and a further group wore academic robes, but there were no traces of the solemnity and gloom usually associated with this garb.[44]

The procession was a reminder of the underlying unity of the extraordinary network which the women's movement had created in less than 60 years. The differences of party and non-party, industrial working class and professional middle class; welfare and equalitarian; militant and constitutionalist were reconciled, or at least laid to one side. It was an important way for the marchers to demonstrate to parliament and to themselves that ideological difference did not destroy the bonds of co-operation. The 15 platforms in Hyde Park where the speeches were made also demonstrated the catholic nature of the movement and the mixed allegiances, as speakers from a cross-section of organisations spoke from 'rival' platforms. The speeches covered every aspect of the campaign, culminating in the passing of resolutions for equal enfranchisement on the same terms as men and seats for peeresses in their own right in the Lords.[45]

Although the event was a major publicity success and reasserted the movement's strength of purpose, there was some sense of bitterness:

And yet, upon reflection, was it good? Good, indeed, to know the old faith living and the old power there, but not good to be obliged to re-sharpen the old weapons. It was not good to think that eight long years had elapsed since the barrier had been pushed grudgingly a little aside and still the gateway to political and economic equality had not been pushed freely wide open in the name of justice.[46]

The SPG reflected that the proceedings could only be regarded as a success if the women's movement concentrated all its efforts on an effective follow-up. In line with its equalitarian belief in the primacy of the franchise struggle, the SPG affirmed that if the movement continued to 'spread itself thin' by working on non-feminist issues then equality would remain but a distant hope.[47]

In the weeks which followed, the EPRDC decided to extend its life-span in order to co-ordinate the concentrated campaign for the franchise and continue as the Equal Political Rights Campaign Committee (EPRCC). Emmeline Pethick-Lawrence had said in her speech that the demonstration marked a fresh stage in campaigning which was to begin in the autumn, and the EPRCC confirmed that the necessary organisational framework would be in place by then.[48] A new group to join the struggle was the Young Suffragists (YS) whose inception was inspired at a WEC dinner in July and whose president was Barbara Wootton, the economist and Principal of Morley College.[49] Further organisational development came with the formation of special junior sections of established organisations like the junior council of the London and National Society for Women's Service (LNSWS), initiated in September 1926. Such groups aimed to politicise the under thirties, fight for the franchise and combat public criticism of 'flappers'.[50]

By autumn 1926, the time limit for entering a woman's vote on the electoral register in time for the next election had become a pressing factor for consideration. Frank Briant MP told a WFL meeting at Caxton Hall on 22 October that there were only six to nine months left in which parliamentary action could be taken in time to enable women to cast their vote. The EPRCC now initiated a network of local constituency meetings as a systematic regional method of raising awareness, increasing women's involvement and access to political information, sustaining women candidates and co-opting male support. These meetings were hosted by a variety of local women's groups with a view to attracting as many cross-party candidates as possible, as well as aiming to interview local MPs.

The movement had fulfilled its objective of making 1926 a year of intense propaganda activity. The NUSEC's affiliates; for example, had held over 200 meetings nationwide: public meetings, demonstrations, deputations, public lecture programmes and education classes had been arranged by groups both large and small.[51] The goal of achieving extensive publicity had succeeded with the press recording the power of the women's campaign from the *Glasgow Bulletin's*, 'Petticoat Rule? Great Sex Equality Campaign This Week. Suffragette Zeal' to the *Westminster Gazette's* observation that, 'Suffragettes of today may be more peaceable, but they are just as persistent'.[52] The movement felt that such widespread and diverse activity had also been strengthened by the large number of major women's movement conferences taking place in London and abroad during 1926, which had helped to focus attention on women's issues. Some of these consisted of the Women's International League for Peace and Freedom in Dublin, the International Woman Suffrage Alliance (IWSA) in Paris, the International Federation of University Women (IFUW) in Amsterdam and the Peacemakers' Pilgrimage, where women from all over Britain had journeyed to a London rally on 19 June to promote international law as a means of settling disputes and potential conflict. All such conferences had furnished additional vehicles for promotion of the franchise message.[53]

Despite all this effort, *The Woman's Leader* recorded at the end of 1926 that:

> We look back among our own columns and week after week paragraphs dealing with Equal Franchise with titles such as 'Hope Deferred', 'Dilly Dally', 'No Progress', etc... we have been faced the whole time with a policy of complete negation on the part of the Government with regard to their intentions.[54]

A large meeting held by the WFL before the King's Speech on 8 February 1927, supported by over 20 organisations, calling upon the Government to include equal franchise in its parliamentary programme was totally disregarded as Baldwin's pledge entered its third year without implementation.

Meanwhile the movement's campaign machine ground on relentlessly, and on 8 March the Prime Minister finally agreed to receive a deputation organised by the EPRCC and supported by 56 societies. Although only 24 women representatives were permitted to attend,[55] it was a significant event as this was the first time since 1918 that a prime minister had received such a deputation. Introduced by Nancy Astor, the main spokeswomen were Lady Rhondda as President of the EPRCC, Eleanor Rathbone from the NUSEC, Mrs Hood for the Standing Joint Committee of Industrial Women's Organisations (SJCIWO), Dr Elizabeth Knight representing the WFL, Nancy Parnell from the under thirty section of the SJSPA, the Hon. Mrs Franklin speaking on behalf of the NCW and Ethel Froud of the NUWT. Baldwin justified the neglect of the women's franchise claims throughout 1926 on the grounds that the general strike, rapidly followed by the miners' strike and the war in China had preoccupied Government time. However, he assured them that he would make a statement in the House before Easter.[56]

With so many years of disappointment and broken politicians' promises behind them, such an undertaking did not interfere with the pace of their campaign. Rather, they determined that they should escalate their programme to maintain pressure. With a Cabinet meeting taking place on 12 April, the NUSEC concentrated its efforts on a meticulous lobbying exercise which presented all members of the Government and parliament with the complete text of every Government promise on the women's franchise extension. The next day, Baldwin announced that the Government would introduce a bill to extend the franchise in the next parliamentary session, and most importantly, that the age limit would be twenty-one years of age, and not twenty-five, which Unionist 'Die-Hards' had been arguing for. Baldwin, ever cautious, covered himself with a disclaimer that only an unexpected catastrophe would prevent the bill from being passed. Familiar as they were with catastrophe, the movement determined to intensify its campaign to ensure that the bill was passed as soon as possible.[57]

The NUSEC now engaged organisers who were allocated the particular brief of canvassing the support of MPs for the proposed bill. They were particularly anxious to register the views of Conservative MPs and to monitor all those who had supported the Prime Minister's pledge. The established Tory pattern of promises and assurances, followed by inaction and procrastination, now took a new turn when on 20 May a Labour Party bill for the equalisation of the franchise, due for its second reading, had its parliamentary time appropriated for Government business. The WFL, in an editorial in *The Vote*, responded angrily, restating its belief in the vote as the key to 'real equality with men in any other sphere'.[58] Desperate for any indications of good faith, the movement took heart at a speech made by Baldwin on 27 May 1927 at a conference of Unionist women, when he made what were, in reality, rather vague remarks concerning democracy and women's enfranchisement.[59] The situation had become one of clutching at straws; as the WFL diagnosed, danger came from 'the delay of politicians outwardly friendly to this cause'. This observation was prompted by the latest obstacle to their goal. Baldwin having declared in April 1927 that franchise measures would be introduced in the next session, which was due to begin that autumn, rumours emerged in May implying that the parliamentary sessions were now to be re-arranged.[60] This meant the next session would commence in February 1928, which heightened the problem of the electoral registration time limit. In the face of such sustained obstruction, the women once again took to the streets on 16 July in a mass protest rally which pressed for a Government bill in time to include new women voters at the next election. The resolution to allow peeresses in the Lords was also included. This time the protest took the form of a huge demonstration in Trafalgar Square. Arranged by the EPRCC, the speakers from the supporting 42 organisations were heard from three speakers' platforms which surrounded the central plinth on which all the societies' banners were displayed.[61]

By the end of 1927, the EPRCC had strategically planned its 1928 opening meeting for 8 February, the day after the King's speech. Meanwhile, the programme of meetings and lobbying was sustained by a movement which did not intend to take any chances until the bill was on the statute book. Expectations at the opening of parliament on 7 February 1928 were dashed when the antici-pated statement again failed to materialise. However, during the debate later that evening, in response to an attack on the omissions in the Government's future agenda, Baldwin announced that the Franchise Bill would be introduced in that session, with the neces-sary clause to enable all women to participate in the next election. What effect incidents perpetrated during that day by suffragists had on Baldwin's evening speech are a matter of speculation. Seeking to bolster its lobbying efforts until success was assured, that morning Young Suffragist members had delivered a petition to the Prime Minister's house. Daringly, they followed this up with a break-in at Buckingham Palace in an attempt to present a letter to the King which had already been published in that morning's papers. Additionally, at the time of the opening parliamentary ceremony, there was an Equal Political Rights Campaign Committee demonstration in the form of a fleet of cars owned and driven by women, festooned with placards demanding votes for women. This flotilla drove down Whitehall and circled Parliament Square to the racket of whistles and car horns.[62]

At long last, the Government's Representation of the People (Equal Franchise) Bill was introduced in March 1928. Several Conservatives hung on to their illogical arguments as to why women should not have the vote, but the bill passed its second reading on 29 March with a majority of 377, only 10 members having voted against, although it is notable that as many as 218 members absented themselves from the House during this historic vote.[63] When the bill reached the committee stage, the Labour Party attempted to introduce an amendment which would abolish plural voting. As on past occasions, it was just such an issue that the suffrage societies had been concerned to avoid, fearing that the introduction of any complexities would lead to the bill's defeat. Margaret Bondfield argued that without this amendment some households might have as many as six possible votes between husband and wife. The Labour concern was that 'It is a duplication of a fancy franchise... to perpetuate existing anomalies and privileges for a very small section of the voters'.[64] Such voters were unlikely to be using those additional votes to support a Labour candidate! Although this amendment was lost, the bill received the royal assent on 2 July 1928 and enfranchised an additional 5,221,902 women. It had taken the women's movement 61 years to achieve equal enfranchisement with men.

Conclusion

Why did successive governments not have the political will to complete the enfranchisement of women before 1928? In response to such determined opposition and repeated postponements, why did the women's movement not return to its threatened militancy? Was it only as a result of the movement's tenacity and manipulation of every small advantage that the franchise extension was achieved in 1928 or was there an agreed ten-year waiting period which parliament was determined to enforce? If the latter was the case, then what was the rationale informing it and can the opposition that the women's movement faced to retard its political progress be viewed in the light of a male conspiracy to deny citizenship to all women? Could there have been other, more effective, tactics which the movement might have employed to have progressed its case more rapidly? What might such tactics have been? Did the women at any point in this ten-year struggle set the agenda, or were they always a reactive force? Did they make best use of the measure of power which the partial franchise and qualifications to stand for parliament gave them? How damaging was the continuance of the non-party stance by the suffrage societies and how effective was the contribution of the Labour and industrial women to securing the franchise extension? Finally, did the political containment of women all come down to numbers, to the fear of the unknown voting power of women, the threat of the 'petticoat avalanche' and potential loss of power?

In terms of credit, the NUSEC displayed its usual confidence in believing itself to have been primarily responsible for the 1928 success. It reflected on the differing opinions among women at the outset of the campaign, where some women felt equal enfranchisement would be delivered as part of an inevitable chronological progress and others thought it too soon to begin a fresh fight. The NUSEC believed its tactics of inexorable pressure had been the political lever it needed to press the claim home:

> If the National Union had yielded to either section in 1922, we should not have obtained from Mr Bonar Law... his declaration of personal belief in equal franchise, which is said to have considerably influenced the present Government... If we had not again pressed the question on all three Parties at the General Election of 1924, we should not have obtained from the present Prime Minister his now famous promise of 'equal political rights'.[65]

By contrast, the SPG had never put any faith in such pledges.[66] If it had been a larger organisation it might well have revived the militancy which it so frequently discussed. The movement's intelligence network must have been aware of just how intense the fear of pre-war suffrage militancy had been in parliament. Then why didn't the women's movement make use of the fear of the revival of militancy to progress the franchise extension more rapidly in the 1920s? Times and the women's movement had changed, and tactics needed to acknowledge and respond to those developments. Giving verbal expression to the possibility of militancy may also have been all the additional power the movement needed at this time. Militancy would certainly have split the movement again on an issue on which it was solidly united, and it could ill-afford such a schism if it was to mount a successful campaign.

As it was the first to recognise, the movement had progressed a long way since the war. Even with the limited franchise, women were in quite a different position from that of the pre-war militant years. They now had something to lose; they were inside the establishment, and militancy against the establishment would, strictly speaking, have been militancy against themselves. Yet being in a position where their power was limited also restricted their options; they had to play by the rules of the club of which they wanted to have full membership. Brian Harrison's description, 'prudent revolutionaries',[67] captures the movement's predicament most precisely.

No sooner had their key objective finally been accomplished than the many organisations which comprised the movement began the process of planning for the future, realigning their aims in the light of their full citizenship and potential parliamentary power. Similar to the review process of 1918, when the movement's agenda had been scrutinised with a view to future campaigning, the feeling endured that the movement was still very much only at the beginning of its journey towards equality. In the words of the WFL:

> To have won equal voting rights for women and men is a great victory, but it will be an infinitely greater achievement when we have succeeded in abolishing for ever the 'woman's sphere', 'woman's work', and a 'woman's wage', and have decided that the whole wide world and all its opportunities is just as much the sphere of women, as of men...[68]

This is an achievement yet to be realised.[69]

Notes on Chapter 10

1   NUSEC, Annual Report, 1924, p 9-10. Lord Ullswater was the Speaker who had chaired the committee which had decided on the terms of the 1918 Representation of the People Act when women over 30 gained the franchise.

2   *The Labour Woman*, 1 January 1925, p 5

3   *The Labour Woman*, 1 March 1925, p 40

4   *Equal Franchise 1918-1928*, NUSEC pamphlet (London, June 1927), p 5

5   NUSEC, Annual Report, 1925, p 6

6   WFL, Annual Report, April 1924-April 1925, p 3

7   See Beddoe, Deirdre, *Back to Home and Duty: Women Between the Wars 1918-1939* (London, 1989, Pandora) and Pugh, Martin, *Women and the Women's Movement in Britain 1914-1959* (London, 1992, Macmillan)

8   Coverture was the principle whereby a woman's political and legal existence were 'covered', that is represented by her husband, obviating the necessity for her to have an independent legal existence.

9   See Royden, Maude, 'The problem of the sexes in 1921' in *Time & Tide,* July 8 1921, p 642 for the perspective as to women's sexual concerns and rights as a result of this imbalance.

10   Hamilton, Cicely, *Marriage as a Trade* (London, 1981, The Women's Press), p 7

11   Society for the Overseas Settlement of British Women, Annual Reports, 1921-1930

12   Foster-Fraser, Sir John, 'The Spinster' in *Woman,* June/July 1926, pp 279 & 316. He was a special parliamentary correspondent.

13   Janet Carlton, born 1905, former editor of *The Listener,* interviewed 1989

14   Molly Musson, born 1904, Labour Party and WCG member, interviewed 1989

15   Brittain, Vera, *Halcyon or The Future of Monogamy* (London, 1929, Kegan Paul), p 17

16   Oram, Alison, 'Embittered, sexless or homosexual' in *Lesbian History Group, Not a Passing Phase: Reclaiming Lesbians in History 1840-1985* (London, 1989, The Women's Press), p 101

17   See Weeks, Jeffrey, *Coming Out: Homosexual Politics in Britain from the Nineteenth Century to the Present* (London, 1990, Quartet) for details of the legal cases of Maud Allen and Radclyffe Hall. Some novels of the period dealing with lesbianism were D.H. Lawrence, *The Rainbow* in 1915; A.T. Fitzroy, *Despised and Rejected* in 1918; Clemence Dane, *A Regiment of Women* in 1919; Rosamond Lehmann, *Dusty Answer,* early 1920s; Compton Mackenzie, *Extraordinary Women,* in 1928.

18   Weeks, Jeffrey, *Coming Out: Homosexual Politics in Britain from the Nineteenth Century to the Present* (London, 1990, Quartet) p 106

19   Ibid., p 107

20   Such women as Edith (Edy) Craig (WFL/AFL) who lived with Christabel Marshall (Christopher St John), who wrote for *Time & Tide* and *The Woman's Leader* and Clare (Tony) Atwood. Ethel Smyth (WSPU/SPG), the composer, was a friend of Edy and St John.

21   Alberti, Johanna, *Beyond Suffrage: Feminists in War and Peace 1914-1928* (London, 1989, Macmillan) pp 112-116. This gives details of women's friendships in the movement.

22 Frankau, Gilbert, 'What does the girl of today want?' in *Woman* (London, August 1924), pp 399-401. Frankau became the Governing Director of British National Newspapers; during the First World War he had fought at Loos, Ypres and the Somme and had been invalided from the service towards the end of the war.

23 *Newcastle Chronicle*, 22 December 1925, p 3

24 Nevinson, Henry W., 'Votes for Women' in *The New Leader* (London, March 7, 1924), p 8

25 Parliamentary Debates, House of Commons, 23 April-1 May 1923, Vol. 163, 25 April, cols 472-474

26 Hopkinson, Diana, *Family Inheritance: A Life of Eva Hubback* (London, 1954, Staples Press), p 92

27 *The Vote*, 20 February 1924, front page

28 *The Sketch*, 20 February 1925, p 3

29 *The Vote*, 5 February 1926, p 44

30 *The Woman's Leader*, 15 January 1926, front page

31 *The Woman Leader*, 26 March 1926, p 70

32 *The Vote*, 7 May 1926, p 147

33 *The Vote*, 12 March 1926, p 82

34 *The Woman Leader*, 25 June 1926, p 188

35 Ibid.

36 *The Vote*, 31 December 1926, p 413

37 Parliamentary Papers, House of Lords, 4 May-15 July 1926, Vol 64, June 24, cols 593-605

38 NUSEC, Annual Report, 1926, p 8

39 *The Vote*, 2 July 1926, p 204

40 *Time & Tide*, 2 July 1926, p 605

41 *Time & Tide*, 2 July 1926, p 593

42 Some of the organisations taking part were: AWCS, AFL, BCL, BFUW, CSSA, ESW, FWCS, GGC, IWSA, LCM, LDA, LSWS, NCW, NUSEC, NUT, NUWT, POWCA, SJSPA, SPG, SJCIWO, TOS, WCG, WEC, WES, WFL, WGEU, WGE, WILPF, WNLF, WSIHVA, WU.

43 *Time & Tide*, 9 July 1926, p 605

44 *The Woman Teacher*, 9 July 1926, p 305

45 WFL, Annual Report, April 1926-April 1927, p 9

46 *The Woman Teacher*, 9 July 1926, p 305

47 *Time & Tide*, 9 July 1926, p 605

48 *The Vote*, 23 July 1926, p 228

49 *The Woman's Leader*, 30 July 1926, p 240

50 LNSWS, Junior Council Report and List of Members, May

1927, p 2

51 NUSEC, Annual Report, 1926, pp 20-28. Large events had not been confined to London; in Edinburgh a mass meeting was attended by representatives from 18 organisations and addressed by two MPs and in Birkenhead women had held their own regional campaign conference.

52 *Glasgow Bulletin*, 22 February 1926, p 15; *Westminster Gazette*, 1 January 1926, Ellen Wilkinson newspaper cuttings, LP archive

53 *The Vote*, 31 December 1926, p 43. The women's movement continued to nurture the international aspects of its work which had been shown to be especially vital in the light of events during and after the war.

54 *The Woman's Leader*, 31 December 1926, front page

55 *The Vote*, 11 March 1927, front page

56 Ibid., p 74

57 NUSEC, Annual Report, 1927, p 9

58 *The Vote*, 20 May 1927, p 150

59 *The Woman's Leader*, 30 December 1927, p 374

60 *The Vote*, 3 June 1927, p 172

61 *The Woman Teacher*, 22 July 1927, front page & pp 318-321

62 *The Times*, 8 February 1928, p 9

63 *The Vote*, 6 April 1928, front page

64 *The Labour Magazine*, May 1928, Vol VII, No 1, p 37

65 NUSEC, Annual Report, 1928, p 7

66 *Time & Tide*, 8 April 1927, p 327

67 Harrison, Brian, *Prudent Revolutionaries: Portraits of British Feminists Between the Wars* (Oxford, 1987, Clarendon Press)

68 *The Vote*, 6 July 1928, p 212

69 See Law, Cheryl, 'The old faith living and the old power there: the movement to extend women's franchise' in *The Women's Suffrage Movement: New Feminist Perspectives* (Manchester, 1997 Manchester University Press) for a further discussion of the possible factors influencing the delay in the franchise extension for women.

Chapter 11
Conclusion

⸻⟫●⟪⸻

> For sixty-one years women have striven to win an equal
> political footing with men; it is only an equal footing they
> have gained, not equal political power.[1]

After attaining the equalisation of the franchise in July 1928 the
Women's Freedom League (WFL) was under no illusion about the
shortcomings which still attended its political position. This was
no time to rest. As both the WFL and the National Union of
Societies for Equal Citizenship (NUSEC) reminded the membership
in their 1928 annual reports, women still did not have economic
equality, indeed their employment position was deteriorating. The
rights of married women were still under attack, there was still
only a handful of women in the Commons and no entry for women
to the Lords, and the concept of the equal moral standard had
not become a reality. These were only a few illustrations that
inequalities were still too numerous and too significant to warrant
any cessation of the movement's work.

As in 1918, there was a parallel recognition of the need, after
this final franchise reform, for the movement's continuing evolution to cope with changing circumstances, while appreciating the
difficulties the movement might face. In July 1928, an article in
The Woman's Leader warned that:

Some of the white-heat of their (the leaders') ardour has gone, the need for headlong battling with circumstances has given place to the need for stabilisation everywhere... Inevitably, too, the people concerned have changed; the suffragist to whom the vote was all in all has given place to the woman who, intent on her own work, absorbed in a variety of interests, is, by the very fact of being a feminist, in honour bound to get on quietly with the work... Any movement worth the name must first and foremost possess the individual... To do that it needs a broader base than one group or generation can give. Especially is this important in the case of the women's movement... to see it as the sum of countless aspirations and viewpoints.[2]

This shows, above all, an awareness of the many subtle factors which define a movement and the necessity for awareness of relocations in time and circumstance which sustain the movement's momentum and coherence, with the goal which inspired its genesis yet to be fully attained.

The interpretation of this period has been based on appreciating the 1920s as a phase of the women's movement, a development and progression arising out of and fuelled by all that had preceded it, rather than a diminished remnant, a period which determined the adoption of altered strategies and reassessed objectives in the light of the First World War. With this altered perspective, Harrison's understanding that it is necessary to 'prevent the First World War from artificially separating Edwardian from interwar feminism'[3] is an expedient indicator of the dangers of false periodisation.

Turning to the findings of this research, the contention has been made and demonstrated that sustaining suffrage and women's rights agitation throughout the First World War were essential to the evolution of the movement. Without such wartime activity, there would have been insufficient pressure available to take advantage of the constitutional loophole whereby women's suffrage amendments were forced on to the legislative agenda in 1916. To use Mrs Fawcett's analogy of the progress of the movement:

Sometimes the pace was fairly rapid; sometimes it was very slow, but it was constant and always in one direction. I have compared it to a glacier; but, like a glacier, it was ceaseless and irresistible... it always moved in the direction of the removal of the statutory and social disabilities of women.[4]

Rather than losing its impetus, despite the exhaustion of the war years, the movement gained new vigour from its franchise success, and went on to entrench its position by constructing an extended network. Utilising the accumulated skill of the previous 50 years, the need was to consolidate its gains, extend its sphere of operation, effect further legislative change and fight the continued pressure to restrict women's lives.

Movements continue to operate successfully when the revolutionary impetus which prompted their foundation is still fuelled by unredressed injustice. They are organic entities which must respond to changes in the society in which they aspire to participate. In order to succeed, the nature of the women's movement was bound to transform to deal with the post-war world. Martin Luther King maintained that 'The riot is the language of the unheard'.[5] The women's movement had had its riots and it had been heard. The post-war objective was to move on to more sophisticated strategies which progressed its cause within the institutions to which it had now gained access, to enable it to take the next step towards complete emancipation.

Far from the proliferation of organisations duplicating effort and diluting effectiveness, this network was essential to cope with the enormity of the task in hand which concerned itself with every aspect of women's lives. Women were responding to and recognising the truth of the maxim of industrial and political groups, that strength lies in organisation and co-operation. Pugh has dismissed the period, stating that 'No historian, of either sex, has felt moved to characterise the inter-war decades as the "Age of Women"'.[6] On the contrary, we might want to contend that the decade 1918-1928 was the movement's most democratic so far, especially when considering the huge number of women who 'surged into the Labour Party and the Co-operative Movement as if they had been waiting for the doors to open',[7] together with the success of the non-party Women Citizens' Associations (WCAs) which blanketed the country.

In the case of judgements such as Pugh's, we need to ask whose value-system and perspective are determining the process of assessing the period for a characterisation of 'achievement'? It is not only a question of evidence, for 'If historians until now have not used women's own sources to reconstruct the past, it is only

because they have not looked for them'.[8] It is also an issue of
context and interpretation, of understanding that 'truth is mainly a
question of giving events their true proportion'.[9]

What was the size of the challenge the movement set itself and
what was the political and economic climate in which its struggle
was set? We have seen that the task was immense, yet not one facet
of the emancipation agenda was shirked. Women were seeking to
overturn centuries of political apartheid in a post-war atmosphere
of reaction where economic reconstruction was vying for attention
with an inflamed power struggle between the parties. The divided
Liberals were sinking fast, while the Conservatives were engaged in
an hysterical rearguard action to defeat the threat of 'Bolshevism',
represented for them by the vigorous growth of the Labour Party.
For the Tories, women's total political emancipation represented a
genuine fear of a further loss of power: the colour of the women's
movement, as far as the Tories were concerned, was red. They
evidently did not perceive the women's movement as being a
compliant and spent force. The panoply of tactics used against the
movement testify to that: disregard, rejection, mendacity, procrastination and enticement.

It has also been contended that the passion went out of the
movement in the post-war world, that acting within constitutional
confines they became cautious and lost their revolutionary potential.
Eleanor Rathbone answered similar criticisms:

> We knew when it was necessary to compromise. There is a
> school of reformers which despises compromise... we
> acquired by experience a certain flair which told us when a
> charge of dynamite would come in useful and when it was
> better to rely on the methods of a skilled engineer.[10]

Alternately, the question might be what would challenging the
system have consisted of, if not what women from 1918 to 1928
were engaged in?

In the face of sustained resistance, the women's movement
stood firm. It pushed its demands, lobbied politicians, strengthened
and educated its membership using its political campaign weaponry
for developing strategic electioneering tactics, while targeting its
message at press, public and politicians. Apart from the successes
detailed in the preceding chapters, mechanisms had been established for effecting reforms, and women themselves had changed
irrevocably. By 1925 there were 14,000 women enrolled on

diploma and degree course; half a million women clerical workers and approximately 1300 qualified women doctors;[11] the first women were allowed to sit for the administrative class of the civil service;[12] and by 1927 the struggle for women police had resulted in an increase to 142 women employed with the same powers as male officers.[13]

As to the existence of factions and opposing ideologies which have been interpreted as evidence of weakness and disunity, an examination of the course of the movement from its origins in 1867 demonstrates a history of such divisions over procedural matters, differing doctrines and ideological conflict. No movement or party working out ideas and beliefs on its journey from oppression to emancipation, while devising campaign policies to effect that transition in the face of continued opposition, could realistically hope to avoid conflict.[14] As Margaret Bondfield wrote of her particular sphere, 'The Labour Movement is like all human movements – full of little wars, wrestlings, disagreements and minor disputes...'[15] Any other expectation serves to devalue the scale of the undertaking in hand. Although excessive conflict which overshadows all else becomes destructive, debate is a necessary tool to determine weaknesses in convincing policy. All movements benefit from the stimulation which arises from combining radical and conservative elements to locate an effective middle ground.

The feminist movement was largely sustained by 'professional' women's rights workers, large numbers of whom worked through from the movement's earliest years to the 1920s and beyond. The belief that the majority of the experienced suffrage workers gave up the struggle in 1918 is quickly dispelled by the most cursory reading of suffrage periodicals and annual reports. On the contrary, it is the continuity of personnel which reveals the level of commitment of these activists who made the emancipation of women their life's work. Tenacity was one of their biggest assets.

Although the need for the movement to attract larger numbers of younger women in the 1920s and the consequent frustration at its lost attempts was lamented by some,[16] it was also recognised as being partially the result of the movement's success in enabling such women to enjoy a profession or other employment.[17] Its fight for feminism was, as E.C. Ewing claimed, to gain recognition in the world of employment. Janet Carlton, studying at Somerville, was tasting the fruits of the post-war successes: 'I think one felt that one had come in at a very enjoyable time for a woman and the big battle of the vote had been won, and entry into the professions, in a way it was up to us to make good'.[18] Only women who had been through the whole journey could ascertain how far they had come, and how far they still had to go. It was their inspiration that recruited numbers of women under thirty in the mid-1920s, when the final push for the franchise extension made its direct appeal.

A factor which underpins the belief in a waning of the movement during this period was the contention that the raw edge of feminism gave way to the more traditional pursuit of welfare goals relating to women and children. Implicit in this belief is the implication that such legislation presented less of a challenge and was more easily achieved, that the movement was no longer directly confronting the patriarchal system, but was engaged in reforming certain aspects of it. To dismiss the value of the welfare work pursued by all sections of the movement marks a failure to recognise the wretchedness of the poverty, dismal housing and lack of health care which burdened large numbers of women and children in particular. Conditions such as those described by Mrs C.S. Peel in her research on housing conditions dispel any doubt as to the significance of such work on a feminist agenda:

> In the bedroom the bugs were crawling over the walls and dropping on to the beds… Father, mother and two youngest children slept in this room. Three girls slept in the ground-floor room and the two boys in the kitchen.[19]

To get welfare problems addressed had always been a prime motivation for women gaining the vote. The concentration on such goals in the 1920s was no dereliction of the feminist credo but a fulfilment of its manifesto, as 'the inexorable advance of social welfare through state action'.[20]

The significance of a movement of resilient women during this period to sustain the women's Cause should not be underestimated. How far would women have progressed towards emancipation if these organisations had not resisted each and every attempt to retard the gains which had been won and to fight for yet more? By 1928, the fundamental importance of what had been achieved marked the movement's universal significance:

> For Liberty is in itself wider than the Liberty of any class which enjoys it; and each step towards freedom, whether it be political or social or moral, makes progress in all other directions easier and surer, and adds to the justice and the

civilisation of the world. We can therefore rejoice in our victory without alloy. We have won our cause, and by so doing we have helped forward an ideal even wider and greater and nobler than our own.[21]

Notes on Chapter 11

1   *The Vote*, 6 July 1928, p 212

2   *The Woman's Leader*, 13 July 1928, pp 187-189

3   Harrison, Brian, *Prudent Revolutionaries: Portraits of British Feminists Between the Wars* (Oxford, 1987, Clarendon Press), p 8

4   Fawcett, Mrs Henry, *Women and the Use of Their Vote*, undated, approximately 1918/1919, p 262

5   'Eyes on the Prize: The History of the Black Civil Rights Movement', BBC Television, September-October 1990

6   Pugh, Martin, *Women and the Women's Movement in Britain 1914-1959* (London, 1992, Macmillan), preface

7   Graves, Pamela M., *Labour Women: Women in British Working-Class Politics 1918-1939* (Cambridge, 1994, CUP), p 1

8   Riemer, Eleanor S., *European Women: A Documentary History 1789-1945* (New York, 1980, Schocken Books), p xiv

9   Power, Eileen, *A Bibliography for School Teachers of History* (London, 1921, Methuen), p 8. Eileen Power was a celebrated medievalist historian.

10   Stocks, Mary, *Eleanor Rathbone* (London, 1950, Victor Gollancz), p 113

11   Rhondda, Viscountess, Margaret Haig, Leisured Women (London, 1928, Hogarth Press), p 16

12   Meynell, Dame Alix, *Public Servant, Private Woman* (London, 1988, Victor Gollancz), pp 78-81

13   Fawcett, Millicent, *What the Vote Has Done* (London, 1927, NUSEC), p 4. On the copy of this pamphlet held by the Fawcett Library, under Fawcett's name, handwritten in brackets is, 'Most of it by E.M.H!' E.M.H were the initials of Eva Hubback, the NUSEC's parliamentary secretary, who seems not to have got the credit for her work in this publication.

14   There has certainly been plenty evidence of this with regard to the contemporary movement in Britain.

15   Bondfield, Margaret, *A Life's Work* (London, 1950, Hutchinson), p 271

16   At the same time there was also an appreciation of the number of young women who were still joining the movement. See *The Woman's Leader*, February 1920, p 7

17   *The Woman's Leader*, 13 July 1928, p 187

18   Interview with Janet Carlton, 1989, Assistant Editor of *The Listener* in 1930

19   Peel, Mrs C.S., *Life's Enchanted Cup: An Autobiography 1872-1933* (London, 1933, John Lane, Bodley Head), p 241

20   Mowat, Charles Loch, *Britain Between the Wars 1918-1940* (London, 1955, Methuen), p 284

21   *The Woman's Leader*, 13 July 1928, p 187

Appendix I

List of Organisations

This is a list of organisations which either appear in the text or are of related interest. The date for inauguration has been given in all cases where it could be traced. '*' marks organisational name changes.

AFL	Actresses' Franchise League	1908
AAMSS	Association of Assistant Mistresses in Secondary Schools	1884
ACSSA	Association of Civil Service Sorting Assistants	
AH	Association of Headmistresses	1874
AMCWC	Association of Maternity and Child Welfare Centres	1911
AMSH*	Association for Moral and Social Hygiene	1915
APOWC*	Association of Post Office Women Clerks	1901-13
ASWCML	Association of Senior Women Clerks in the Ministry of Labour	
ASW	Association of Service Women	1920
ATDS	Association of Teachers of Domestic Subjects	1896
ATCGO	Association of Temporary Clerks in Government Offices	
AUWT	Association of University Women Teachers	
AWASPCPO	Association of Women Assistant Superintendents and Principal Clerks of the Post Office	
AWCS/AWKS	Association of Women Clerks and Secretaries (Because of its initials, this group took the bird, the Awk, as its emblem, and thereby changed the C to a K).	1903
AWL	Association of Women Launderers	1921
AWP	Association of Women Pharmacists	1905
AWST	Association of Women Science Teachers	1912

BWSS*	Belfast Women's Suffrage Society	
BAWC	British-American Women's Crusade	
BCL	British Commonwealth League	1925
BDWSU*	British Dominions Woman Suffrage Union	1914
BDWCU*	British Dominions Women Citizens' Union	1919
BFUW	British Federation of University Women	1907
BHA	British Housewives Association	1925
BLWS	British Legion Women's Section	1921
BWILPF	British Women's International League for Peace and Freedom	1915
CWL	Catholic Women's League	1906
CWSS*	Catholic Women's Suffrage Society	1911
CCWI	Central Council of the Women of Ireland	
CLWS	Church League for Women's Suffrage	1909
CSA	Civil Service Alliance	1916
CSSA	Civil Service Sorting Assistants	
CSTA	Civil Service Typists' Association	1912-13
CPW	Communist Party Women	
CUWFA	Conservative and Unionist Women's Franchise Association	1911
CWRA	Conservative Women's Reform Association	1908
CCWO	Consultative Committee of Women's Organisations	1921
CRWLN	Council for the Representation of Women in the League of Nations	1919
CWCS	Council of Women Civil Servants	1920
DWU	Domestic Workers' Union	
ELFS*	East London Federation of Suffragettes	1914
EAW/ESW	Electrical Association/Society for Women	1924
FSWB/FWG	Fabian Society Women's Branch/ Fabian Women's Group	1908
FEC*	Family Endowment Committee	1917
FECl*	Family Endowment Council	1918
FES*	Family Endowment Society	1924
FWCS	Federation of Women Civil Servants	1913
FWGC	Federation of Working Girls' Clubs	
FCSU	Forward Cymric Suffrage Union	1912

FCLWS	Free Church League for Women's Suffrage	1910
FCWC	Free Church Women's Council	
GGC	Guild of Girl Citizens	
IWSPU*	Independent Women's Social and Political Union	1916
IWCLGA*	Irish Women's Citizens' and Local Government Association	1918
IWFL	Irish Women's Franchise League	1908
IWSLGA*	Irish Women's Suffrage and Local Government Association	1876
IRL	Irishwomen's Reform League	
ISF	Irishwomen's Suffrage Federation	
IAWSEC	International Alliance of Women for Suffrage and Equal Citizenship	1926
ICWG	International Co-operative Women's Guild	1921
ICW	International Council of Women	1888
IFUW	International Federation of University Women	1919
IWSA	International Woman Suffrage Alliance	1904
LPWS*	Labour Party Women's Sections	1918
LCM	League of the Church Militant	1919
LDA	Liverpool Dressmakers' Association	
LNSWS*	London and National Society for Women's Service	1926
LCCWTU	London County Council Women Teachers' Union	
LSWS*	London Society for Women's Service	1919
LSWS*	London Society for Women's Suffrage	1907
MMLWS	Manchester Men's League for Women's Suffrage	
MWF	Medical Women's Federation	1916
MWIA	Medical Women's International Association	
MU	Mothers' Union	1876
NAPIM	National Association for the Prevention of Infant Mortality	
NCUMC	National Council for the Unmarried Mother and her Child	1918
NCGC	National Council of Girls' Clubs	1926
NCW	National Council of Women	1895

NFWT*	National Federation of Women Teachers	1906
NFWW*	National Federation of Women Workers	1906-20
NFWI	National Federation of Women's Institutes	1915
NIPWSS	National Industrial and Professional Women's Suffrage Society	1905
NOGC	National Organisation of Girls' Clubs	1911
NUC	National Union of Clerks	
NUSEC*	National Union of Societies for Equal Citizenship	1919
NUWT*	National Union of Women Teachers	1920
NUWW*	National Union of Women Workers	1895
NUWSS*	National Union of Women's Suffrage Societies	1897
NWCA	National Women Citizens' Association	1918
NLMPU	North London Men's Political Union	
NMFWS	Northern Men's Federation of Women's Suffrage	1913
ODC	Open Door Council	1926
ODI	Open Door International	1926
POWCA	Post Office Women's Clerk Association	
PL	Primrose League	1883
RWG	Railway Women's Guild	
SCLWS	Scottish Churches League for Women's Suffrage	
SCWG	Scottish Co-operative Women's Guild	1892
SCWCA	Scottish Council of Women Citizens' Associations	1919
SCWT	Scottish Council for Women's Trades	
SAU	Shop Assistants' Union	
SPG	Six Point Group	1921
SSS	Sligo Suffrage Society	
SCBCRP	Society for Constructive Birth Control and Racial Progress (usually known as CBC)	1921
SOSBW	Society for Overseas Settlement of British Women	1920-62
SPBCC*	Society for the Provision of Birth Control Clinics	1924
SWWJ	Society of Women Writers and Journalists	1894
SJSPA*	St Joan Social and Political Alliance	1923

SJCIWO	Standing Joint Committee of Industrial Women's Organisations	1916
SC	Suffragette Crusaders	
SF	Suffragette Fellowship	1926
SWSPU*	Suffragettes of the Women's Social and Political Union	1916
TOS	Theosophical Order of Service	
UJW	Union of Jewish Women	1902
UPOWWS	Union of Post Office Workers Women's Section	1919
US	United Suffragists	1914-18
WPHOA	Women Public Health Officers Association	1896
WSISS	Women Sanitary Inspectors Suffrage Society	
WSIHVA	Women Sanitary Inspectors and Health Visitors' Association	1896
WTFU	Women Teachers' Franchise Union	
WAS	Women's Auxiliary Service	1914
WCG	Women's Co-operative Guild	1883
WEC	Women's Election Committee	1920
WES	Women's Engineering Society	1919
WFGA	Women's Farm and Garden Association	1899
WFL*	Women's Freedom League	1907
WGEU	Women's Group of the Ethical Union	
WGE	Women's Guild of Empire	
WHVCF	Women's Housing and Village Council Federation	
WIC	Women's Industrial Council	1894
WIL*	Women's Industrial League	1918
WLL	Women's Labour League	1906-18
WLF*	Women's Liberal Federation	1886
WLGS	Women's Local Government Society	1888-1925
WNLA*	Women's National Liberal Association	1892
WNLF*	Women's National Liberal Federation	1919
WP*	Women's Party	1918
WPH	Women's Pioneer Housing	1920
WPL	Women's Political League	1918
WPS	Women's Printing Society	1897
WSPU*	Women's Social and Political Union	1903
WTRL	Women's Tax Resistance League	

WTUL*	Women's Trade Union League	1874-1922
WUO	Women's Unionist Organisation	1918
WWG*	Women Workers' Group (of the TUC)	1921
WWSL	Women Writers' Suffrage League	1908
WBCG	Workers' Birth Control Group	1924
WSF*	Workers' Suffrage Federation	1916
WU	Workers' Union	
YWCA	Young Women's Christian Association	1855
YS	Young Suffragists	1926

Organisational Changes Indicated by an Asterisk – *

AMSH	The British branch of the International Abolitionist Federation, founded by Josephine Butler in 1875; successor to the Ladies' National Association for the Abolition of State Regulation of Vice and for the Promotion of Social Purity, founded by J.B. in 1870.
APOWC	Became part of the Federation of Civil Service Clerks in 1913, which was later FWCS.
BDWSU	Became the BDWCU in April 1919.
BWSS	Became the WPL in February 1918.
CWSS	Became the SJSPA in October 1923.
ELFS	Became the WSF in March 1916; then in June 1920 the WSF was renamed the Communist Party (British Section of the Third International).
EAW	Originally known as the Women's Electrical Association, WEA. This caused confusion with the Workers' Education Association, so the name was changed.
FEC	Begun in October 1917, became the FECl after the autumn of 1918 and then the FES in 1924.
IWSPU	This and the SWSPU were breakaway factions of the WSPU.
IWSLGA	Became the IWCULGA in November 1918.
LPWS	Came into existence in June 1918 from the WLL, as a result of the LP's new constitution.
LSWS	Became the LSW Service in February 1919; became the LNSWS February 1926; 1953 the LNSWS renamed the Fawcett Society.

NFWT	Became the NUWT at its Bath Conference 1920.
NFWW	Became the Women Workers' Section of the National Union of General Workers in 1920.
NUWSS	Became the NUSEC in March 1919.
NUWW	Its governing body was the NCW; in October 1918 it merged with the NCW and ceased to exist as a separate entity.
SPBCC	Originated in 1921 as the Walworth Women's Advisory Clinic.
WFL	Broke away from the WSPU in September 1907.
WLF	Split in their ranks in 1892 over suffrage with the formation of the WNLA who were not interested in the suffrage question. WLF and the WNLA merged in April 1919 to form the WNLF.
WP	Formed from the WSPU in November 1917.
WTUL	Became the Women Workers' Group operating through the Women's Department of the General Council of the TUC.

Some of the Organisations Still in Operation

BFUW	British Federation of University Women
BLWS	British Legion Women's Section
FS	Fawcett Society, LNSWS' successor (see above)
HVA	Health Visitors' Association (WSI&HVA)
JBS	Josephine Butler Society
MU	Mothers' Union
NCW	National Council of Women
NFWI	National Federation of Women's Institutes
UJW	Union of Jewish Women
WCG	Now the Co-operative Women's Guild
WES	Women's Engineering Society
WILPF	Women's International League for Peace and Freedom
WPH	Women's Pioneer Housing
YWCA	Young Women's Christian Association

Appendix II

Political Affiliations – Biographical Sketches

These biographical sketches represent indications of the major political work and membership affiliations of key women mentioned in the text prior to and during the period under discussion.

Mrs Margery Corbett Ashby (Corbett), BA, 1882-1981, pacifist and suffrage worker; Independent Liberal parliamentary candidate; member of deputation to the League of Nations Commission in 1919; Vice-Chairman of NUSEC; Executive Committee Women's Liberal Federation; Honorary Secretary/President IWSA; member of AMSH.

Nancy Witcher Astor, Viscountess (Langhorne), 1879-1964, politician; first woman MP, Unionist for Plymouth, 1919; MP until 1944; temperance advocate; tireless supporter of women's organisations, eg in 1926 alone President, VP or member of AMSH, Association of Women House Property Managers, CCWO, Council for the Representation of Women on the League of Nations, EAW, IWSA, NCUMC, NUSEC, WES, WSIHVA, SPG.

Margaret Grace Bondfield, 1873-1953, politician; elected as Labour MP Northampton 1923; first woman Cabinet Minister 1929; trade unionist; joint founder WLL in 1906; Chair SJCIWO; 1923 first woman Chair TUC; peace movement activist; worked with NUSEC.

Nina Boyle, 1866-1943, WSPU member, arrested three times; member WFL; 1920 founder Women's Election Committee; member IAWSEC, CCWO; founder of women police patrols.

Mrs Charlotte Despard (French), 1844-1939, pacifist, suffrage and social activist; Labour parliamentary candidate; founder and President WFL after leaving WSPU; member WILPF; Revolutionary Irish Republican supporter.

Dame Millicent Garrett Fawcett (Garrett), DBE, 1847-1929, leader and one of the founders of the suffrage movement; President NUWSS, resigned in 1919 but acted in various offices of NUSEC; member IWSA.

Margaret Haig Thomas, Viscountess Rhondda, 1888-1958, industrialist; WSPU member, arrested and imprisoned; founded SPG and WIL; owner of *Time & Tide*; member EAW, WPH, WSIHVA, SWWJ, NWCA, WIL, CWCS, CCWO.

Dame Caroline Haslett, DBE, 1895-1957, engineer; WSPU member; Hon. Sec. WES; editor *Woman Engineer*; founder EAW; executive committee member SPG.

Dorothy Jewson, BA, 1884-1964, Labour MP Norwich; WSPU member; trade unionist; Chief of the Organising Dept NUWW; pacifist; ILP delegate on SJCIWO; birth control advocate, President WBCG.

Arabella Susan Lawrence, BA, 1871-1947, Labour MP North East Ham; trade unionist; WTUL worker; NFWW organiser; representative of the Women's Section NUGW; Vice-Chair SJCIWO; VP NUSEC.

Mrs Emmeline Pethick-Lawrence (Pethick), 1867-1943, member WSPU, imprisoned; edited *Votes for Women*; left WSPU and joined US; Honorary Treasurer WILPF; Labour candidate; WFL President.

Dame Christabel Harriette Pankhurst, 1880-1958, lawyer; co-founder with her mother of the WSPU; 1918 Coalition candidate, Smethwick, defeated by only 775 votes; founded the Women's Party with her mother.

Mrs Emmeline Pankhurst (Goulden), 1858-1928, social reformer and suffragette leader; founded the WSPU in 1903; spent much of the 1920s in America; returned in 1925; involved in franchise extension campaign 1926.

Sylvia Estelle Pankhurst, 1882-1960, artist; WSPU worker until expelled early 1914; founded the ELFS 1914; passionate socialist; ELFS became the WSF in 1916 and in 1920 renamed the British Section of the Third International; pacifist, member WILPF.

Dr Marion Phillips, BA, DSc, 1881-1932, trade unionist, Labour Party Chief Women's Officer; briefly secretary NUWSS; WTUL and WLL worker; Secretary SJCIWO; organiser of Labour

Women's Sections; editor of *Labour Woman*; 1929 Labour MP Sunderland.

Eleanor Rathbone, BA, 1872-1946, social economist; first woman councillor in Liverpool, 1909; NUWSS executive member; IWSA delegate; President NUSEC 1919-1929; 1929 Independent MP for Combined English Universities.

Agnes Maude Royden, DD, CH, 1876-1956, preacher; President LCM; first woman to preach in cathedrals in Geneva and Glasgow; VP NUSEC and AMSH; pacifist, member IWSA.

Mrs Ray Strachey (Rachel Conn Costelloe), BSc, 1887-1940, engineer and builder; Parliamentary Secretary NUWSS; Chairman Employment Committee LSWS; President Society of Women Welders; member NCW; active League of Nations; founded Women Builders Group; political secretary to Nancy Astor; Independent parliamentary candidate; writer.

Mrs Helena Maria Lucy Swanwick (Sickert), MA, CH, 1864-1939, writer and journalist; member NUWSS; active pacifist WILPF and League of Nations.

Gertrude Mary Tuckwell, CH, 1861-1951, social reformer and trade unionist; President WTUL; President NFWW; first JP for county of London; President WSIHVA; member SJCIWO.

Ellen Cicely Wilkinson, MA, 1891-1947, politician; NUWSS organiser; trade union organiser; Labour MP Middlesborough East; indefatigable speaker on suffrage platforms for NUSEC, AFL, WES, IWSA; VP EAW.

Mrs Margaret Wintringham (Longbottom), 1879-1955, teacher; Liberal MP Louth; President WNLF; VP SPG; member NUSEC, WSIHVA; temperance supporter; championed economic cause of the housewife and working women.

Bibliography

Secondary Sources

Adlard, Eleanor (ed.) (1949), *Edy: Recollections of Edith Craig* (London, Frederick Muller)

AJR (ed.) (1913), *The Suffrage Annual and Women's Who's Who* (London, Stanley Paul & Co.)

Allen, Mary S. (1925), *The Pioneer Policewoman* (London, Chatto & Windus)

Anderson, Adelaide (1922), *Women in the Factory* (London, John Murray)

Anthony, Sylvia (1932), *Women's Place in Industry and Home* (London, Routledge & Sons Ltd)

Banks, Olive (1990), *The Biographical Dictionary of British Feminists Volume II: A Supplement, 1900-1945* (New York, New York University Press)

Banks, Olive (1986), *Becoming a Feminist: The Social Origins of 'First Wave' Feminism* (Brighton, Wheatsheaf Books)

Barrow, Margaret (1985), *Women 1870-1928: A Select Guide to Printed and Archival Sources in the the UK* (New York, Mansell)

Beard, Mary Ritter (1946), *Woman as a Force in History* (London, Macmillan)

Beddoe, Deirdre (1989), *Back to Home and Duty: Women between the Wars 1918-1939* (London, Pandora)

Beddoe, Deirdre (1983), *Discovering Women's History* (London, Pandora)

Bell, Anne Olivier (ed.) (1981-1983), *The Diaries of Virginia Woolf* (Middlesex, Penguin)

Beloff, Max (1984), *Wars and Welfare: Britain 1914-1945* (London, Edward Arnold)

Bellamy, J., & Saville, J. (1972), *The Dictionary of Labour Biography, Vols I-VIII* (London, Macmillan)

Bird, Stephen (1982), *Guide to the Labour Party Archives* (London Labour Party)

Bishop, A. (ed) (1986), *Chronicles of Friendship: Vera Brittain's Diary of the Thirties 1932-39* (London, Victor Gollancz)

Black, Clementina, (ed.) (1983), *Married Women's Work* (London, Virago)

Blainey, J. (1928), *The Woman Worker and Restrictive Legislation* (London, Arrowsmith)

Brittain, Vera (1968), *Radclyffe Hall: A Case of Obscenity?* (London, Femina Books)

Bull, L.M.& G.E. (1909), *Women Workers Directory* (London, John Bale & Sons)

Bussey, Gertrude & TIMS, Margaret (1980), *Pioneers for Peace: WILPF 1915-1965* (London, WILPF British Section)

Butler, David & Gareth (1986), *British Political Facts 1900-1985* (London, Macmillan)

Byles, Joan Montgomery (1985), 'Women's experience of world war one: suffragists, pacifists and poets', in *Women's Studies International Forum, 8/5* (Oxford, Pergamon Press, Oxford) pp 473-487

Caldecott, Leonie (1984), *Women of Our Century* (London, Ariel Books)

Castle, Barbara (1987), *Sylvia and Christabel Pankhurst* (Middlesex, Penguin)

Challoner, Phyllis C. & Laughton, Vera (1928), *Towards Citizenship: A Handbook of Women's Emancipation* (London, P.S.King & Son Ltd)

Clegg, Hugh Armstrong (1985), *A History of the British Trade Unions Since 1889, Vol II, 1911-1933* (Oxford, Clarendon)

Clinton, Alan (1984), 'Women and the UPW' in *Post Office Workers: A Trade Union and Social History* (London, Allen & Unwin) pp 425-435

Cole, G.D.H. (1937), *A Short History of the British Working Class Movement 1789-1937* (London, Allen & Unwin)

Cole, G.D.H. & Cole, M.I. (1937), *The Condition of Britain* (London, Gollancz)

Cole, G.D.H. & Postgate, R. (1938), *The Common People 1746-1946* (London, Methuen)

Cole, Margaret (1949), *Growing Up into Revolution* (London, Longmans)

Courtney, Janet (1934), *The Women of My Time* (London, Lovat Dickson)

Doughan, David (1980), *Lobbying for Liberation: British Feminism 1918-68* (London, City of London Polytechnic)

Doughan, David & Sanchez, Denise (1987), *Feminist Periodicals 1855-1984: An Annotated Critical Bibliography of British, Irish, Commonwealth and International Titles* (Brighton, Harvester Press)

Eyles, Leonora (1926), *Women's Problems of Today* (London, Labour Publishing Co.)

Forster, Margaret (1984), *Significant Sisters: The Grassroots of Active Feminism 1839-1939* (Middlesex, Penguin)

Fulford, Roger (1958), *Votes for Women* (London, Faber & Faber)

Gaffin, Jean & Thoms, David (1983), *Caring and Sharing: The Centenary History of the Co-operative Women's Guild*, (Manchester, Co-operative Union)

Garner, Les (1984), *Stepping Stones to Women's Liberty: Feminist Ideas in the Women's Suffrage Movement 1900-1918* (London, Heinemann Educational Books)

Hall, Ruth (1977), *Marie Stopes – A Biography* (London, Andre Deutsch)

Hamilton, Mary Agnes (1944), *Remembering My Good Friends*, Jonathon Cape, London.

Hamilton, Cicely (1935), *Life Errant*, (London, J.M. Dent)

Hannam, June (1990), *Isabella Ford* (Oxford, Basil Blackwell)

Holdsworth, Angela (1988), *Out of the Doll's House* (London, BBC Books)

Holledge, Julie (1981), *Innocent Flowers: Women in the Edwardian Theatre* (London, Virago)

Holton, Sandra Stanley (1986), *Feminism and Democracy: Women's Suffrage and Reform Politics in Britain* (Cambridge, CUP)

Hume, Leslie Parker (1982), *The National Union of Women's Suffrage Societies, 1897-1914* (NY & London, Garland Publishing)

Jeffreys, Sheila (1985), *The Spinster and her Enemies: Feminism and Sexuality 1880-1930* (London, Pandora)

Jenkins, Inez (1953), *The History of the Women's Institute Movement of England and Wales* (Oxford, OUP)

Labour Party (1924 & 1927), *The Labour Who's Who* (London, Labour Publishing Co.)

Lewenhak, Sheila (1980), *Women and Work* (Glasgow, Fontana)

Lewis, Jane (1984), *Women in England 1870-1950: Sexual Divisions and Social Change* (Brighton, Wheatsheaf Books)

Liddington, Jill & Norris, Jill (1984), *One Hand Tied Behind Us: The Rise of the Women's Suffrage Movement* (London, Virago)

Liddle, Peter H. (1988), *Voices of War: Front Line and Home Front 1914-1918* (London, Leo Cooper Ltd)

Lyman, Richard W. (1957), *The First Labour Government, 1924* (New York, Russell & Russell)

Mappen, Ellen (1985), *Helping Women at Work: The Women's Industrial Council 1889-1914* (London, Hutchinson)

Marwick, Arthur (1977), *Women at War 1914-18* (London, Fontana)

Messenger, Rosalind (1967), *The Doors of Opportunity: A Biography of Dame Caroline Haslett* (London, Femina Books)

Middleton, Lucy (ed.) (1977), *Women in the Labour Movement* (London, Croom Helm)

Mitchison, Naomi (1979), *You May Well Ask: A Memoir 1920-40* (London, Victor Gollancz)

Mitton, G.E. (1916), *The Englishwoman's Year Book* (London, A. & C. Black Ltd)

Montefiore, Dora (1927), *From a Victorian to a Modern* (London, Archer)

McFeely, Mary Drake (1988), *Lady Inspectors: The Campaign for a Better Workplace 1893-1921* (Oxford, Basil Blackwell)

Oxford, Margot (ed.) (1938), *Myself When Young by Famous Women of Today* (London, Frederick Muller)

Pankhurst, Christabel (1987), *Unshackled: The Story of How We Won the Vote* (London, Century Hutchinson)

Pankhurst, Emmeline (1979), *My Own Story* (London, Virago)

Pankhurst, Sylvia (1977), *The Suffragette Movement* (London, Virago)

Pankhurst, Sylvia (1987), *The Home Front: A Mirror to Life in England During the First World War* (London, The Cresset Library)

Pethick-Lawrence, Frederick (1942), *Fate Has Been Kind* (London, Hutchinson)

Phillips, Melanie (1980), *The Divided House: Women at Westminster* (London, Sidgwick & Jackson)

Rhondda, Viscountess, Margaret Haig (1937), *Notes on the Way* (London, Macmillan & Co.)

Richardson, Mary R. (1953), *Laugh a Defiance* (London, Weidenfeld & Nicholson)

Rover, Constance (1967), *Women's Suffrage and Party Politics in Britain 1866-1914* (London, Routledge & Kegan Paul)

Rowbothom, Sheila (1989), *The Past Before Us* (London, Pandora)

Rowlands, Robyn (ed.) (1984), *Women Who Do and Women Who Don't Join the Women's Movement* (London, Routledge & Kegan Paul)

Rubinstein, David (1980), *Before the Suffragettes: Women's Emancipation in the 1890s* (Brighton, Harvester Press)

Soldon, Norbert C. (1978), *Women in British Trade Unions 1874-1976* (Dublin, Gill & Macmillan)

Sondheimer, J.H. (1957), *History of the British Federation of University Women* (London, BFUW)

Smith, Harold L. (ed.) (1990), *British Feminism in the Twentieth Century* (Cheltenham, Edward Elgar)

Spender, Dale (1983), *There's Always Been a Women's Movement this Century* (London, Pandora)

Stocks, Mary (1921), *The Meaning of Family Endowment* (London, Labour Publishing Company)

Stocks, Mary (1927), *The Case for Family Endowment*, (London, Labour Publishing Company)

Stocks, Mary (1970), *My Commonplace Book* (London, Peter Davies)

Stocks, Mary (1973), *Still More Commonplace* (London, Peter Davies)

Stott, Mary (1985), *Before I Go: Reflections on My Life and Times* (London, Virago)

Strachey, Ray (1931), *Millicent Garrett Fawcett*, (London, John Murray)

Strachey, Ray (1937), *Careers and Openings for Women: A Survey of Women's Employment and a Guide for those Seeking Work* (London, Faber & Faber)

Thane, Pat (1990), 'The women of the British Labour Party and feminism 1906-45' in Harold L. Smith (ed.), *British Feminism in the Twentieth Century* (Cheltenham, Edward Elgar)

Troubridge, Lady Una (1961), *The Life and Death of Radclyffe Hall* (London, Hammond Hammond)

Tuckwell, Gertrude et al (1908), *Women in Industry from Seven Points of View* (London, Duckworth)

Whittick, Arnold (1979), *Woman into Citizen* (London, Frederick Muller)

Primary Sources
Individuals

Maud Arncliffe-Sennett: February 14 1907-1936 in 28 volumes of ephemera and documents relating to the suffrage movement; British Library, c.121.g.1

Viscountess Nancy Astor: 1800 files, covering all aspects of her life. University of Reading Archive:

MS 1416/1/1: 822-828: Societies IV: Women's Associations 1922-29

MS 1416/1/1: 829-833: Societies V: membership or office accepted 1925-29.

Clivedon Visitors' Books: June 1914-July 1938

Conservative Women's Organisations: Bodleian Library, Oxford. Women's Parliamentary Committee 1920-27: ARE/7/11/1; ARE/9/11/1

John Johnson Collection of Printed Ephemera: JJ/SJC/11.86: 7 boxes of women's suffrage material, plus a postcard collection: Room 132, New Library, Bodleian Library, Oxford

J.S. Middleton: Labour Party Archive, National Museum of Labour History, Manchester; these papers are to be found in Women's Rights' Folder; Women's Industrial Organisations' Folder in Box 7; Women's Suffrage Folder in Box 8

Smith Papers: private collection, Barbara Strachey, Oxford; it contains a draft biography of Ray Strachey by her mother, Mary Costelloe/Berenson. The folders also contain letters and ephemera

Philippa Strachey: Box 61, Fawcett Library

Evelyn Sharp: Bodleian Library, Oxford. MSS ENG. MISC. c.278 Letters to; d.277 Letters from; d.669 Notebook; d.670 Scrapbook

Gertrude Tuckwell: The TUC Library Collections, University of North London: consists of newspaper cuttings and a draft autobiography

Ellen Wilkinson: Labour Party Archive; set of personal scrapbooks of newspaper cuttings: Book 1: April 1924-April 1925; Book 2: February 1925-May 1926; Book 3: May 1926-December 1927; Book 4: January 1928-August 1930

Organisations
Annual Reports and/or Miscellaneous Papers of:
1 *Political – Party and Non-Party:*

Catholic Women's Suffrage Society/St Joan Social & Political Alliance: Fawcett Library and Labour Party

Consultative Committee of Women's Organisations: Fawcett Library and Lady Astor Collection

Fabian Women's Group: The TUC Library Collections, University of North London

Labour Party: Labour Party Archive, National Museum of Labour History

London Society for Women's Suffrage, LSWS, LNSWS: Fawcett Library and Lady Astor Collection

National Council of Women: Fawcett Library and Lady Astor Collection

National Union of Women's Suffrage Societies/NUSEC: Fawcett Library and Lady Astor Collection

National Women's Citizens' Associations: Fawcett Library and The TUC Library Collections, University of North London

Open Door Council: Lady Astor Collection and Labour Party

Six Point Group: The TUC Library Collections, University of North London, Labour Party Archive, Manchester, Lady Astor Collection and Fawcett Library

Women's Election Committee: Lady Astor Collection.

Women's Freedom League: Fawcett Library and Labour Party

Women's Social and Political Union/Women's Party: Fawcett Library and London Museum Archive

Women's Unionist Organisation: Lady Astor Collection

East London Federation of Suffragettes/Workers' Suffrage Federation: Fawcett Library

2 Industrial:

National Federation of Women Workers: The TUC Library Collections, University of North London

National Union General Workers: The TUC Library Collections, University of North London

National Union of Railway Women's Guild: The TUC Library Collections, University of North London and Fawcett Library

Standing Joint Committee of Industrial Women's Organisations: Labour Party and The TUC Library Collections, University of North London

Women's Co-operative Guild: The TUC Library Collections, University of North London

Women's Labour League: The TUC Library Collections, University of North London and Labour Party

Women Workers' Group of TUC: The TUC Library Collections, University of North London

3 Professional:

Association of Women Civil Servants: The TUC Library
   Collections, University of North London and Fawcett Library
Council of Women Civil Servants: Fawcett Library
Electrical Association for Women: Lady Astor Collection
Federation of Women Civil Servants: The TUC Library
   Collections, University of North London
Society for Overseas Settlement of British Women: Bodleian
   Library and Lady Astor Collection
National Federation of Women Teachers/NUWT: Fawcett Library
Women Engineering Society: WES Archive, Imperial College
Women Sanitary Inspectors & Health Visitors' Association: HVA
   Archive, Wellcome Institute

4 Welfare/Voluntary:

Association for Moral & Social Hygiene: The TUC Library
   Collections, University of North London
British Housewives Association: Lady Astor Collection
Family Edowment Committee/Council: Fawcett Library
National Council for the Unmarried Mother and her Child: Lady
   Astor Collection
Society for Constructive Birth Control: Lady Astor Collection
Women's Pioneer Housing: WPH Archive, London
Young Women's Christian Association: Lady Astor Collection

Newspapers and Periodicals

Association News, FWCS
Britannia, WP
The Catholic Citizen, CWSS/SJSPA
The Common Cause, NUWSS
The Daily Herald
Home & Politics, WUO
International Woman Suffrage News (Jus Sufragii), IWSA
The Labour Woman, WLL; LPWS
The Times
Time & Tide, SPG
The Vote, WFL

Votes For Women, WSPU; US
Woman
The Woman Clerk, AWCS
The Woman Engineer, WES
The Woman Teacher, NFWT/NUWT
The Woman's Dreadnought, ELFS
The Woman's Industrial News, WIC
The Woman's Leader, NUSEC

Other Collections

BBC Written Sound Archive: Caversham, Reading
Suffragette Fellowship: Museum of London Archive

Interviews

Dr Ina Beasley, b. 1898
Miss Margaret Broadley, b. 1903
Mrs Janet Carlton (Adam-Smith), b. 1905
Miss Lettuce Cooper, b. 1897-1995
Mrs Rebecca Evans, b. 1898-1988
Miss Hart, b. 1895
Mrs Annie Huggett, b. 1892
Mrs Victoria Lidiard, b. 1889-1995
Mrs Naomi Mitchison, b. 1897
Mrs Mollie Musson, b. 1904-1990
Mrs Mary Stott, b. 1907
Mrs Barbara Halpern (Strachey), b. 1912

Index